100 Years of

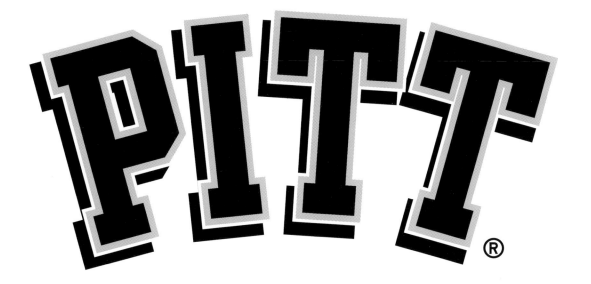

PITT®

BASKETBALL

SAM SCIULLO JR.

www.SportsPublishingLLC.com

ISBN: 1-59670-081-5

Publishers: Peter L. Bannon and Joseph J. Bannon Sr.
Senior managing editor: Susan M. Moyer
Acquisitions editor: Scott Musgrave
Developmental editor: Travis W. Moran
Art director: K. Jeffrey Higgerson
Dust jacket design: Kenneth J. O'Brien
Interior layout: Kathryn R. Holleman
Imaging: Kathryn R. Holleman, Dustin Hubbart
Photo editor: Erin Linden-Levy
Media and promotions managers: Letha Caudill (regional),
    Randy Fouts (national), Maurey Williamson (print)

Printed in the United States of America

Sports Publishing L.L.C.
804 North Neil Street
Champaign, IL 61820

Phone: 1-877-424-2665
Fax: 217-363-2073
www.SportsPublishingLLC.com

CONTENTS

ACKNOWLEDGMENTS IV

THE 2004–2005 SEASON 1

ORIGINS: 1905–1922 13

THE DOC CARLSON ERA: 1922–1953 19

THE FORGOTTEN YEARS: 1953–1968 33

THE RIDL REVIVAL: 1968–1975 47

SETBACKS, RESURGENCE, AND RESIGNATION: 1975–1980 61

TRANSITIONS: 1980–1986 75

BIG EAST CHAMPS ... AND BEYOND: 1986–1994 89

UNFULFILLED PROMISE(s): 1994–1999 109

RENAISSANCE: 1999–2004 121

PITT RECORDS 143

ACKNOWLEDGMENTS

The author expresses his thanks and appreciation to the following people for sharing their thoughts, stories, and memories:

Curtis Aiken, Orlando Antigua, Bernie Artman, Dean Billick, Marc Boehm, Jaron Brown, Kirk Bruce, Bob Caldwell, Carroll "Beano" Cook, Joe David, Jamie Dixon, Jarrett Durham, Joe Fenwick, Brian Generalovich, Darrell Gissendanner, Frank Gustine, Jr., Dick Groat, Larry Harris, Don Hennon, Bill Hillgrove, Ben Howland, Oval Jaynes, Jeff Kamis, Terry Knight, Carl Krauser, Jerome Lane, Ed Lawry, Jason Maile, Jason Matthews, Sean Miller, Mark Nordenberg, Julius Pegues, Ed Raymond, Tom Richards, Betty Ridl, Dave Roman, Tony Salesi, Ed Scheuermann, Kent Scott, Bob Smizik, Jim Spanarkel, Pete Strickland, John Swacus, Chevon Troutman, Dwayne Wallace, Reggie Warford and Mickey Zernich.

Special thanks to E. J. Borghetti, Burt Lauten, Brad Cuprik, Greg Hotchkiss, and Celeste Welsh of the Pitt Athletics Media Relations Office—as well as Dave Saba (Duquesne University), Joe Swan and John Antonik (West Virginia University), and Heather Ryan of the *Pittsburgh Post-Gazette* also were helpful in gathering photographs. Thanks also to Miriam Meislik from the University of Pittsburgh Archives Service Center. A good friend, Chris Weber, provided special help and assistance with much of the legwork. My sister, Maria, offered computer expertise when it was needed—and a special thanks to Travis W. Moran of Sports Publishing L.L.C.

A tip of the hat to the photographers whose images appear within these pages. They include Will Babin of IMAGE POINT PITTSBURGH, Harry Bloomberg, Sean Brady, Mike Drazdzinski, George Gojkovich, Michael E. Haritan, Joe Kapelewski, William McBride, Chaz Palla, Bruce Schwartzman, and Keith Srakocic.

THE 2004–2005 SEASON

"WE HAD A GOOD YEAR. WE WANTED TO DO BETTER. WE HAD A LOT OF GOOD WINS, AND WE LOST TO SOME GOOD TEAMS. WE IMPROVED IN A LOT OF AREAS. THE LAST TWO GAMES, OBVIOUSLY, DIDN'T GO THE WAY WE WANTED. I THOUGHT WE WERE PLAYING OUR BEST BASKETBALL GOING INTO THOSE LAST TWO GAMES."

—Jamie Dixon
March 30, 2005

From his office inside the Petersen Events Center on a late March afternoon in Pittsburgh, Jamie Dixon looked back at the 2004-2005 season. His second Pitt team had gone 20-9, and had made a school-record fourth consecutive trip to the NCAA tournament. Still, the relative success of the season was something Pitt fans and the local media continued to debate.

"This [2004-2005] year's team, when compared to last year's 31 wins, we didn't meet those standards when you compare it to the 31 wins," Dixon said. "It's the youngest we've been in recent years, and it looks like we'll be significantly younger next year [in 2005-2006]. That's not necessarily the formula you're looking for, but that's how things go."

Pitt's basketball teams had win totals of 29, 28, and 31 in the three seasons leading up to 2004-2005. A strong nucleus, composed of center Chris Taft, power forward Chevon Troutman, and point guard Carl Krauser was backed by two seniors—wings Yuri Demetris and Mark McCarroll, who had

significant experience. However, there were two major losses from the year before—second guard Julius Page and do-it-all Jaron Brown. In its college basketball preview magazine, *The Sporting News* included this ominous forecast from an anonymous Big East coach:

"They [Pitt] lost two of their best defenders [Page and Brown]," he noted. "Who's going to play on the wings? . . . Unless they find somebody to score from the wings, they have a problem."

Although he tried many combinations, Dixon was unable to find consistent replacements for the two departed seniors—particularly Brown.

"Those guys had started 290-some games," Dixon said. "Coming into this season, we were coming in with players who had started about 90 games in their careers. Before that, we lost 250 starts [from the 2002-2003 team] with Donatas [Zavackas], Brandin [Knight], and Ontario [Lett]. When you put those things together, you see the effect. We had a stretch here where we were replacing some good

players. We didn't have a guy in our program who was ready—this year—to play that role that we needed."

Dixon refuses to admit, however, that his second season was anything but a success.

"You always know how things can change, but I thought we made good progress," he said. "We put ourselves in a good position. We finished at 10-6 in the conference, with how strong the conference is, and how our schedule was set up. We had definitely shown growth and improvement."

Following a pattern established several years before, the nonconference portion of Pitt's early-season schedule included many home games against teams from low- to mid-major conferences. The Panthers' only road game was a trip to Penn State on December 11. Carl Krauser scored 28 points to lead the Panthers to an 84-71 win against the three-point-happy Nittany Lions. Penn State made 11 of 22 three-point attempts to give the crowd hope for an upset. Richmond and South Carolina provided tough challenges for the Panthers in late December, but Pitt was 10-0 heading into its January 2 meeting with Bucknell—the final nonconference game on the schedule.

Playing before the second smallest crowd (8,351) of the season at the Petersen Events Center, Pitt turned the ball over 15 times in the first half and found itself trailing the Bisons 42-33 by halftime. The Panthers finally forged ahead in the second half on a three-pointer by Krauser. Leading 65-64, Krauser seemed gone for a breakaway lay-up, but Bucknell's Abe Badmus blocked the attempt from behind. The Bisons converted several crucial free throws after that, and Pitt—ranked No. 10 at the time—had lost for only the second time in its new facility. The upset triggered a fine season for Bucknell, which won the Patriot League tournament, then upset Kansas in an NCAA tournament first-round game. Dixon wasn't surprised by either of Bucknell's big wins.

"Obviously, Bucknell was a good team," he said after the season. "I told people that Bucknell was a good team. We were good early, but we had questions early. We were replacing two guys who had started for four years with two guys who hadn't started."

Three nights after the loss to Bucknell, Georgetown came to Pittsburgh for the start of Big East play. The Hoyas were coached by John Thompson II (the son of the former Hoyas coach), who had been hired away from Princeton, and he brought the Tigers' deliberate offensive style with him. The Hoyas built an early 19-point lead on 75 percent (nine-of-12) three-point shooting. Pitt managed to close the margin to 39-34 at halftime and appeared to have the game won when three-pointers by Krauser and Antonio Graves made the score 59-53 with 5:03 remaining.

The Hoyas, however, rallied to tie the score at 64 on a Darrel Owens lay-up with 1:28 left. Pitt misfired on a pair of shots before the Hoyas' Brandon Bowman made a driving lay-up with eight seconds left to put Georgetown ahead 66-64. Following a Pitt turnover, Ashanti Cook made a free throw in the final second to make the final score Georgetown 67, Pitt 64. Pitt had not lost two straight since dropping back-to-back games to Notre Dame and Miami during the 2001-2002 season.

"There are a lot of good teams and players out there but, in the final analysis, anybody can beat anybody on a given night," Dixon observed after the season. "There are good players in every program at every level. The three-point shot has had a lot to do with it. Georgetown was significantly improved. Four of our losses were to Villanova and West Virginia, both NCAA [tournament] teams. As we look back at it now, we didn't lose to any poor teams."

Two of Pitt's younger players gave the team a much-needed boost in Pitt's next game, a must-win road match-up with Rutgers. Ronald Ramon, a six-foot-one guard from the Bronx, made five of nine three-point attempts and scored 21 points—including a trey with eight seconds remaining in regulation to give Pitt a seemingly safe 58-55 lead. Rutgers' Ricky Shields then made a three-pointer of his own to send the game into overtime—where Pitt sophomore Antonio Graves scored on a drive with 41 seconds remaining. He later made a free throw to produce the 66-63 final score—Pitt's seventh straight win against Rutgers. Chevon Troutman, who scored 10 points and collected 13 rebounds, became the

CHEVON TROUTMAN ENGINEERED A LATE COMEBACK TO DEFEAT SETON HALL. *Photo by Joe Kapelewski/CIDDE*

32nd player in Pitt history to reach 1,000 career points.

Troutman, a six-foot-seven senior from Williamsport, Pennsylvania, became Pitt's cornerstone throughout the 2004-2005 season.

"He [Troutman] played a significantly different role for us this season," said Dixon. "He was a guy who was always kind of in the background, especially on the offensive end. This year we needed him to be a scorer every night for us, and a consistent threat, and he did a great job. While he had played and started a lot of games before this season, his role had changed significantly."

One of Troutman's signature performances came seven days later when Seton Hall visited the Petersen Events Center. Trailing 58-51 with 5:12 remaining, Troutman converted three three-point plays and scored 10 of the Panthers' final 14 points as Pitt rallied to defeat the Pirates, 67-63. Pitt had led by 14 points in the second half, but Seton Hall enjoyed a 23-3 run during an eight-minute stretch to seize the lead. The 67-63 win—the 100th victory for Pitt's seniors—gave the Panthers a modest two-game winning streak heading into a game against St. John's at Madison Square Garden. Before that date, however, Dixon announced that one of the seniors, Yuri Demetris—who had started all 14 games to that

COACH JAMIE DIXON URGES HIS TEAM ON FROM THE SIDELINE. *Photo by Joe Kapelewski/CIDDE*

point—had been suspended from the team following his arrest for charges stemming from an off-campus incident.

"Losing Yuri was a piece of adversity that was probably understated by everybody," commented former Pitt coach Ben Howland after the 2004-2005 season. Howland, who had just completed his second season at UCLA by taking the Bruins to the NCAA tournament, watched his former team as best he could from the West Coast. "It's important having somebody on the wing who can pass and make plays."

The Panthers were unable to make some plays in the closing moments against St. John's and suffered a 65-62 upset loss to the Red Storm. Carl Krauser scored 22 points to lead Pitt, which dropped to 12-3 overall and 2-2 in the Big East. Later that night, the players and coaches met for more than three hours in the Harlem Room of the Hilton Hotel. A nationally televised game at Connecticut loomed four nights later.

All roads didn't lead to Gampel Pavilion in Storrs on January 22, but it seemed that way. A major snowstorm had blanketed much of the Northeast, and motorists in New England were urged to stay indoors. UConn officials asked their season-ticket holders to turn in their tickets so that more students—already on campus—could attend the game, which was telecast on ESPN. The rowdy crowd was ready for the first Pitt-Connecticut matchup of the 2004-2005 season. It became even rowdier when the Huskies opened a 43-26 lead late in the first half. Pitt trimmed the deficit to 43-32 at intermission, but the Panthers' prospects appeared bleak. Then Chevon Troutman took the Panthers on his broad shoulders and almost singlehandedly led them to one of their sweetest wins in school history.

Troutman scored 25 of his game-high 29 points in the second half to ignite a 44-point second half for the Panthers, who won 76-66. Pitt still had trailed by 12 points (53-41) with 15:06 remaining, but outscored UConn 15-1 over the next seven minutes. Krauser scored 15 points, including 10 of 11 free throws. Sophomore Levon Kendall came off the bench and made two important blocks. The Panthers held the Huskies without a basket during one nine-minute stretch of the second half.

"I just wanted to go out there and show them [UConn] that I could be physical," Troutman explained. "That's what our team needed."

Dixon was elated with his team's performance.

"The guys just did an unbelievable job getting it done," he said. "I really don't know what to start with. We had a number of guys step up in so many ways. Chevy just wouldn't be denied. This is obviously a hostile environment. It's a tough place to play. Their record here speaks for itself."

"They [Pitt] executed their offense, took their time, took the shots they wanted," said Huskies coach Jim Calhoun afterward. "We did not take the shots we wanted. I'd probably have to go back quite a way, even with some of the Pittsburgh games that we've had, to think of a more disappointing loss. Give Pitt credit. They played good defense. I don't think their defense changed, frankly. They persevered and did a good job. Congratulations to them."

The Panthers had a week off to savor their comeback victory before Syracuse visited Pittsburgh on January 29. It was déjà vu all over again for Dixon and his players. The Orange befuddled the Panthers with their zone defense in the early going, racing to a 17-point lead (22-5) at the start of the game, Pitt's second 17-point deficit in as many games. This time, Pitt shaved the halftime margin to five points, 34-29, and then blitzed Syracuse in the second half for a 76-69 victory to the delight of the capacity crowd of 12,508.

"We adjusted and did some things better against the zone," Dixon told the press. "The big thing was rebounding. We wanted to hurt them on the boards."

Levon Kendall, in his first career start, scored nine points and grabbed five rebounds. Troutman added 18 points and nine rebounds for the Panthers, who won the battle on the boards, 39-28. Freshman guard Keith Benjamin scored 10 points in 21 minutes.

"Levon [Kendall] was tremendous defensively, and around the ball," said Dixon, who ordered the Panthers into a zone defense of their own in the second half, a circumstance that bothered the Orange.

"Our failure to attack their zone defense was really the problem," said Syracuse coach Jim Boeheim. "The problem in this game was strictly our offense.

CHEVON

In an era when most of Pitt's basketball stars came from outside state lines, Chevon Troutman was an anomaly—a native Pennsylvanian who carried the 2004-05 Panthers to several key victories.

Interestingly, Duquesne—not Pitt—was the first area school Troutman was considering during his senior year at Williamsport High School, but our fans are grateful the six-foot-seven, 250-pound Troutman chose Pitt instead.

"I wanted to stay in Pennsylvania," said Troutman. "I knew that most of the good basketball players who were from the state were leaving the state to go to college. I just felt that if I stayed in Pennsylvania that I could help out the program that I went to."

Troutman was a five-year man at Pitt, and with the departures of Brandin Knight, Ontario Lett, Donatas Zavackas, Julius Page, and Jaron Brown, he knew he had to step forward as a leader during his senior year.

"I knew I had to follow those guys, but when it was my time to do well, I did," he explained. "I didn't want to put everything on my shoulders and try to do too much. I just let things come to me. I didn't force things."

Troutman came up big—especially at crunch time—in many games for the 2004-05 Panthers. He converted three three-point plays in the last six minutes in a 67-63 home win against Seton Hall on January 15. He scored a game-high 29 points to help Pitt rally from a 17-point deficit to defeat Connecticut 75-66 on January 22. He made only two baskets, but finished with 20 points, converting several key free throws down the stretch to lift the Panthers to an important 68-64 win at Syracuse on February 14.

Jaron Brown—one of the program's most valuable performers from 2000-2004—wasn't at all surprised by Troutman's emergence as a senior.

"I always knew what kind of player Chevon could be, from being around him at practice," said Brown. "He's a dominating player—since I was a freshman. It was just a matter of him getting a chance to play regularly to show what he could do."

"I might go unnoticed sometimes, but I still think I'm one of the best in the country," Troutman told reporters after Pitt's win at Connecticut.

Big East coaches took notice of Troutman during his senior year, naming him first-team All-Conference at the end of the regular season. He also became the 32nd player in school history to reach 1,000 career points during the

Courtesy of University of Pittsburgh/CIDDE

Panthers' overtime road win at Rutgers on January 8.

One of the more popular Pitt players of his era, Troutman—one of eight children—attracted crowds wherever he went, becoming a magnet for fans of all ages.

"I come from a big family, so I know what it's like when a younger sibling wants an autograph," he said. "It makes their day when they see you on TV. It's like you're somebody they want to grow up and be like. They watch you and think, 'That could be me in a few years.'"

We can't win with those two guys [Hakim Warrick and Gerry McNamara] only."

Warrick and McNamara played 40 minutes each and scored 25 and 26 points respectively. Carl Krauser played the entire game for Pitt, and later he was asked about Pitt's dramatic resurgence in the game.

"We just tell each other to stick together," he said. "We tried to limit McNamara's outside shot and contain Warrick inside."

The win, which improved Pitt's overall record to 14-3, left Dixon elated…yet cautious.

"I don't know if we want to keep following that game plan," he responded, when asked about the second straight comeback effort. "It wasn't a panic situation. It's a great sign for us. We had some young guys [Kendall and Benjamin] who hadn't been out there in that situation."

Energized by the back-to-back wins against two of the Big East's elite programs, the Panthers had little difficulty with Providence two nights later at the Petersen Events Center. Chris Taft scored a career-high 25 points to go with 15 rebounds, while Krauser contributed 19 points and nine assists. Pitt

CHRIS TAFT HAD AN INCONSISTENT SECOND—AND FINAL—
SEASON WITH PITT. HE ENTERED THE NBA DRAFT.

Photo by Image Point Pittsburgh

work. Starting in place of the ill D'or Fischer, Pittsnogle dropped a career-high 27 points—including eight in overtime—to lead WVU to an 83-78 victory. Pitt had won five straight in the series. The Mountaineers made 13 of a school-record 40 three-point shot attempts during the contest. Troutman led Pitt with 25 points, including a tip-in with three seconds left to send the game past regulation.

Returning home, the Panthers avenged an earlier loss to St. John's with a hard-fought 55-44 win on February 8.

"We knew it would be this type of game," Dixon explained.

Ronald Ramon, who had missed the West Virginia game because of a shoulder injury (and would be affected by it the rest of the season) returned to action against St. John's. Troutman led Pitt with 19 points, and Carl Krauser became the 33rd player in school history to reach 1,000 career points.

"I don't think we're playing our best basketball," Dixon told the media. Notre Dame was due in Pittsburgh four days later.

Relying, much as West Virginia had, on three-point baskets, Notre Dame scored 14 of its 23 baskets from beyond the arc. Yet, Krauser's driving lay-up with nine seconds remaining gave the Panthers an important 68-66 win against the Irish. Krauser had several teeth dislodged when he collided with a Notre Dame player during the second half, and missed several minutes as a result. With the score tied at 65-65, though, he took command of the situation.

"I knew what I had to do," he explained. "I had to hit that shot. I was in pain, but it didn't matter, because my teammates needed me."

Krauser hadn't been Pitt's first option on the play.

"We wanted to look inside to Chevy [Troutman] first," said Krauser.

But Troutman set a screen for Krauser, enabling the point guard to drive toward the basket for the winning shot.

Pitt received contributions from its younger players. Ramon played 31 minutes and scored 13

cruised past the Friars, 86-66. The Panthers never trailed during the game.

Riding a three-game winning streak, the Panthers traveled to Morgantown to play West Virginia, a team that had lost six of its previous seven games. Pitt led by seven at halftime and increased the lead to 34-23 to start the second half before the Mountaineers found their three-point stroke. Kevin Pittsnogle—a six-foot-11 forward from Martinsburg, West Virginia, whom the Pitt coaches had recruited three years earlier—went to

NEW YORK CITY BUDDIES CARL KRAUSER (LEFT) AND CHRIS TAFT. *Photo by Image Point Pittsburgh*

points. Seven-foot center Aaron Gray added nine points and five rebounds while playing in crunch time in place of Taft, who played only 17 minutes.

"We wanted to be real physical with them," said Gray, who was a big part of Pitt's 38-31 rebounding edge.

The Panthers had precious time for celebrating. The team flew to Syracuse the next day for a Valentine's Day ESPN Big Monday rematch with Syracuse. Pitt maintained a slight lead throughout most of the first half, and held a 29-28 edge at half-time. As the Orange came back and grabbed a 58-50 lead with 6:58 to play, Carl Krauser took over again.

Pitt held the Orange without a field goal for four minutes, and Krauser hit a pair of three-pointers during a 10-2 run that tied the game at 60. A free throw by Chris Taft gave the Panthers a 61-60 lead, and then Krauser made a clutch three-pointer to extend the lead to 64-60. Gerry McNamara misfired on several trey attempts in the game's final minutes, and Chevon Troutman made nine straight free throws in the second half to clinch the 68-64 victory. Troutman made only two baskets overall, but scored 20 points and grabbed 10 rebounds. Taft, following his disappearance against Notre Dame two days earlier, contributed 14 points and 10 rebounds. It was Pitt's third win in its last four games at the Carrier Dome, a fact not lost on Pitt's coach.

"We don't want to take winning up here for granted," said Jamie Dixon. "We did a lot of things well at the end. I thought the whole game we were getting good shots."

Troutman—tired of all the questions about the team's inconsistency—was blunt in his assessment.

"People think that because we have a couple of tough losses that we aren't any good anymore," he said. "But we've been good for a long time."

The Panthers' euphoria was short-lived. Pitt followed the win at Syracuse by losing its next three games, the first three-game losing streak the program had endured since the 2000-2001 season—Ben Howland's second year as head coach. Pitt ran into an aggressive, hot-shooting Villanova Wildcats team at Villanova on February 20. The Panthers led for much of the first half, but the Wildcats' overall performance—12 of 23 from beyond the three-point arc—was a familiar scenario for Pitt's woes. The Panthers could get no closer than three points late in the game, and Villanova won—80-72.

West Virginia completed its first regular-season sweep of Pitt since 1997-98 when it rallied from a 14-point second-half deficit to stun the Panthers 70-66 on February 23 at Petersen Events Center. Once again, torrid outside shooting—which Pitt seemed powerless to defend—spelled defeat. The Mountaineers made 72 percent of their shots, and six of eight three-pointers, in the second half alone. Kevin Pittsnogle, who scored only two points in the first half, scored 20 points in the final nine minutes to spark WVU's comeback. Pitt missed its last nine shots in the game.

Chris Taft, who had seven offensive rebounds in the first half—and 10 total rebounds for the game—was on the bench during the game's final minutes as Dixon tried different combinations to try to slow Pittsnogle's three-point attack. Pitt had 39 rebounds to West Virginia's 22, but couldn't score—or stop West Virginia—down the stretch.

Saturday, February 26, 2005, was Senior Day at Pitt. Troutman and Mark McCarroll were making their final home appearances, and suddenly the Panthers appeared to be in a fight for their NCAA tournament lives. Connecticut, looking to avenge its loss to Pitt at home five weeks earlier, had emerged as the Big East's hottest team and chased Boston College for the league's regular-season title.

It was a disappointing farewell for the seniors, who were honored during a brief ceremony fol-

lowing the 73-64 loss to the Huskies. Unlike Pitt's other losses, where the Panthers were victimized by torrid outside shooting, UConn—playing without its top outside threat, Rashad Anderson—utilized one of the nation's top front lines to negate Pitt's inside strength. Forwards Charlie Villanueva and Rudy Gay combined for 31 points and 18 rebounds, while freshman guard Marcus Williams made all three of UConn's three-pointers.

Chevon Troutman's 15 first-half points boosted the Panthers to a 37-31 halftime lead, but the Huskies scored 10 of the second half's first 12 points to take a 41-39 lead. Pitt came back to take its final lead, 63-62, with 4:02 to play, but failed to hit

FRESHMAN RONALD RAMON MADE A SIGNIFICANT CONTRIBUTION IN HIS FIRST SEASON.
Courtesy of University of Pittsburgh/CIDDE

another basket. The Panthers also hurt their own cause by converting just 14 of 29 free-throw attempts in the contest.

With the Panthers' record now at 18-7 (8-6 in the Big East), there was legitimate concern about Pitt's chances of returning to the NCAA Tournament. UConn coach Jim Calhoun was convinced otherwise.

"People of Pittsburgh, I'm not telling you how to think. But I just think that they [Pitt] are a really good basketball team. They will go to the NCAA tournament, in my opinion, without question. You look around the country, and our league is such a brutal, brutal league. You can lose to anyone. When you have a Troutman and a Krauser on your team, you have a chance to win any basketball game that you play. Competing against them is the way the game should be played."

Road games against Boston College and Notre Dame were the last two regular-season games on Pitt's schedule. The Eagles, 23-2 overall and undefeated at home, welcomed the Panthers to Conte Forum on February 28, but the Panthers scored their third major road victory in the conference by overwhelming the Eagles, 72-50. It was Pitt's sixth straight win against the Eagles since losing to BC in the championship game of the 2001 Big East tournament.

John DeGroat, a junior-college transfer forward whose playing time and effectiveness had been limited by injury, stepped up and had his most productive game in a Pitt uniform. DeGroat scored 10 points and gathered seven rebounds in 16 minutes of play. Antonio Graves helped key an 11-0 run early in the second half to give the Panthers a 45-32 lead with 14 minutes left to play. Pitt outscored the Eagles 44-25 in the second half, and had 49 rebounds to BC's 27. Five Pitt players, led by Graves (13) and Chris Taft (12) scored in double figures. BC coach Al Skinner said the lopsided result was easy to explain.

"We were dominated," he told the media gathering. "It's just that plain and simple. They dominated us."

Craig Smith, BC's star forward, was bitter about what had just happened on the Eagles' home court.

"They [Pitt] lost three in a row, then they came into our house and bullied us," Smith noted. "They basically beat us at our own game. They sent a message to other teams to be physical with us. We have to make sure that doesn't happen again."

Chris Taft understood what was at stake for the Panthers.

"We discussed that this [game] was basically do or die for us right now," he said. "We did what we had to do to win this game."

Five days later in South Bend, Indiana—before boarding the team bus for the Joyce Center—assistant coach Barry Rohrssen approached Chris Taft and told him how important he was to his team's chances that day. Taft got the message.

"I was yelling for the ball like crazy," he said after the game, a satisfying 85-77 victory that spoiled the Senior Day festivities at Notre Dame. Shooting guard Chris Quinn, who had hurt Pitt with his three-point shooting in the earlier game in Pittsburgh, was limited by an ankle sprain this time. That didn't stop Colin Falls from making eight of 14 three-point attempts for 28 points, but this Pitt win was strictly an inside job. The Panthers were dominant in the paint, scoring 56 points underneath. Taft had 26 points and 11 rebounds.

"When Chris [Taft] decides to step up and play good, he's unstoppable," said Carl Krauser, who had 15 points and a game-high 11 assists.

"They [Pitt] were big-time men today," a disappointed Chris Thomas told the press. "We couldn't match that. We just didn't have any kind of fight at all."

"They're men; they're men; they're men," Notre Dame coach Mike Brey emphasized. "They're a tough bunch—have been—especially when they go on the road."

"It was a great win for us against a very good team, and I believe an NCAA tournament team," said Jamie Dixon. "We battled through some things early, especially Colin Falls hitting shots from all over the place."

"We played very well at BC and at Notre Dame," said Dixon. "We had improved and gotten to that point."

At 20-7, the Panthers no longer feared being left out of March Madness. They shifted their attention

to the upcoming Big East tournament. The win at Notre Dame had clinched the No. 5 seed—and a bye in the tournament's first round. Pitt would get another crack at Villanova, a team that had exploited the Panthers' defense back in February. The Panthers would be attempting to make their fourth consecutive appearance in the Big East title game at Madison Square Garden. Reaching New York, however, turned out to be something of a chore. The Panthers' original flight to Newark Airport was unable to land due to a snowstorm, so the Panthers flew back to Pittsburgh, where they took a flight to Philadelphia, then went to New York by bus. The Panthers—along with West Virginia and Notre Dame—were unable to attend the Big East's annual awards banquet the night before the opening round of the tournament.

On March 10, both Pitt and Villanova came out frigid in the first half. Pitt made only five of 25 shots before halftime. Villanova was nine of 30, but four of those were three-pointers. The Wildcats held a 31-19 lead at intermission, and the Panthers were unable to mount a serious threat. Villanova won 67-58. There would be no fourth consecutive appearance in the finals. Not since 2000 had Pitt been defeated in its first round of the conference tournament.

Having to wait three days to find out whom—and where—they would be playing in the NCAAs, the Panthers were surprised to learn that they were a No. 9 seed. They would be traveling to Boise, Idaho to meet the No. 8-seeded Pacific Tigers.

There were more travel problems—this time with the team's charter plane to Idaho. While stopping to refuel in Sioux Falls, South Dakota, a faulty

JAMIE DIXON (RIGHT) AND KEITH BENJAMIN REVIEW TAPE DURING AN EXTENDED DELAY AT THE AIRPORT IN SIOUX FALLS, SOUTH DAKOTA EN ROUTE TO THE NCAAS IN BOISE, IDAHO. *Photo by Mike Drazdzinski/CIDDE*

oil gauge was discovered that required a replacement. That meant an extended wait in the airport for the official travel party of 85. The Pitt group arrived in Boise well after midnight, having missed its scheduled practice for earlier that day.

Carl Krauser talked about the Panthers' up-and-down season on the eve of the Pitt-Pacific game:

"At the beginning of the season, we definitely didn't think it was going to be this tough of a road," he said. "We thought we were going to be undefeated for a while, and we thought that we were going to go into the Big East tournament and win that. Obviously, we didn't play our best basketball. We were just trying to get to the next game."

The Panthers fell into a 6-0 hole against Pacific, and soon it was apparent that advancing past the first round was not in the cards. The Panthers trailed 45-30 at halftime, their largest halftime deficit of the season. Krauser tried to bring Pitt back in the second half, scoring 25 of his 27 points after the break, but it wasn't enough. Pitt's season ended with a disappointing 79-71 loss. There would not be a fourth straight trip to the Sweet 16.

"I don't know whether to cry or punch somebody," said Chris Taft. "It's crazy."

"It really hurts," said Krauser. "We kind of took a step back this season. It's one and done. I never had this feeling here at Pitt."

Chevon Troutman, who had just played his final game for Pitt, was analytical about the loss.

"A lot of the shots I usually make weren't falling," he said. "I may have been rushing them a little bit."

Seniors Troutman and McCarroll were leaving Pitt after being part of 108 victories, the most during any four-year span at Pitt. Looking ahead, Dixon was pleased with certain aspects of the season, including the play of young guards Ramon and Graves.

"Ronald got significant minutes, and Antonio as well," Dixon said. "Twenty-seven, twenty-eight minutes . . . those are a lot for young guys. They got better defensively as the year went on. They shot the ball well and gave us good floor presence."

DeGroat, who has an even greater opportunity to make an impact in 2005-2006, also caught Dixon's eye.

"He improved as the year went on," he said. "He had injuries that slowed his progress. He wasn't coming into a situation where a team was trying to be at .500. He was coming to a team that was going to play in the NCAA tournament. That was its goal. There are even greater needs."

Dixon understands the concerns of fans and supporters who look at the 2004-2005 team's 20-9 record as something of a setback, but prefers to look at the big picture concerning the performance of the program.

"There were a few teams this season, including us, who had been to the Sweet 16 three years in a row who didn't make it this time around," he said. "It shows where we've been—at a level where not too many programs had been."

The competition becomes even tougher with Cincinnati, Louisville, Marquette, DePaul, and South Florida joining the Big East. Dixon is confident about his ability to meet the challenge. He recognizes that the 2004-2005 season was a learning process for the players and for Pitt's coaches.

"You're always looking to learn new things, and improve as you go along," Dixon said. "It's the same for anybody in coaching."

ORIGINS: 1905–1922

"THO' COLLEGE DAYS HAVE THEIR DELIGHTS, THEY CAN'T COMPARE WITH COLLEGE NIGHTS."

—From the 1907 *Owl*,
Western University of Pennsylvania Yearbook

Pitt was playing basketball before it officially became the University of Pittsburgh in 1908. Originally known as the Western University of Pennsylvania, its intercollegiate athletics program dated as far back as 1869 (baseball). Major League Baseball originated in this country that same year.

Looking to keep themselves fit, an informal squad of male WUP students played their first intercollegiate basketball game on February 20, 1904 in Morgantown, West Virginia against West Virginia University. WVU won—15-12. The game was played at the campus armory. West Virginia's student newspaper, *The Daily Athenaeum*, saw it this way:

"On last Saturday evening, a basketball team, representing the Western University of Pennsylvania, came to Morgantown to teach our boys the game and incidentally to take our scalps. Even though this was our first game with a visiting team, we did not propose to let it appear so by our playing."

WUP's starting lineup that night consisted of Rosenbloom, Gormley, White, Edwards, and Mason.

"Rosenbloom, for the visitors, showed that he thoroughly understood and was master of the game," wrote *The Athenaeum*.

Two weeks later, the WUP contingent paid a return visit to Morgantown—where they lost again, 40-9.

WUP's first organized basketball team, sanctioned by the athletics department, was conceived during the fall months of 1905. Benjamin F. Printz, who also coached the school's track and field team, was at the helm for the university's opening game—a 34-14 loss to Wooster in early January 1906. The "Wups," as Pittsburgh newspapers called them, picked up their first victory by defeating Geneva College, 24-18, on January 19, 1906. WUP ended that inaugural season with a 2-9 record, including a 30-4 loss to Penn State in early March.

According to the 1907 *Owl*, WUP's starters for much of that first season were Jim McCormick and Bill McCandless in the backcourt, Wally Gill at center, and Nellie Marsh and Bob Whyte in the frontcourt. The unit included several "Big Men on Campus."

PITT

FROM PITTSBURGH TO PALO ALTO

Everybody knows that Walt Harris left Pitt to become head football coach at Stanford following the 2004 season, but are you aware that legendary Panthers coach Glenn Scobey "Pop" Warner also migrated to Palo Alto to coach the Cardinal in 1924? Did you know that, around that same time, a Pitt basketball coach left Pittsburgh to become head football coach at Stanford?

The strange series of events began early in 1922, when Stanford officials approached Warner with an offer to become its next football coach. Warner—who was under contract to Pitt through the 1923 season—wanted to accept the new opportunity, but didn't want to break his contract with Pitt. In a highly unusual scenario, Warner agreed to take the Stanford job, but only after coaching the Panthers in both the 1922 and 1923 seasons. He proposed to send immediately two of his Pitt assistants, Andy Kerr and Claude "Tiny" Thornhill, to Stanford, where they would install Warner's sophisticated offense and utilize it in 1922 and 1923. Kerr, who was also Pitt's track and field coach, also served for one season (1921-22) as Pitt's basketball coach. Thornhill had been a Pitt football letterman from 1913-16.

Kerr was Stanford's head football coach in 1922 and 1923, compiling an 11-7 record. He remained at Stanford as an assistant to Warner in 1924 and 1925 before coming back to Pennsylvania as Washington & Jefferson's new head coach in 1926. He later coached at Colgate for 18 seasons, where the football stadium bears his name.

Warner coached Stanford from 1924-32. He was replaced by Thornhill—the one-time Pitt football player. Thornhill coached Stanford from 1933-39, but he was replaced in 1940 by Clark Shaughnessy—who coached the Cardinal for two seasons. When Pitt officials were searching for a new football coach after the 1942 campaign, they hired Shaughnessy!

McCormick was editor-in-chief of the *Owl*. Gill, a star member of the track and field team, was described this way in his yearbook profile:

"Gill is a ladies man—he seeks the best—preachers' daughters. He can be distinguished blocks away by his ostrich-like stride."

WUP registered its first winning season with a 6-5 mark in its second year (1906-07), and was 10-6 under new coach Harry Hough in 1907-08, playing against schools primarily from the Pennsylvania-Ohio-West Virginia tri-state area. However, school officials suddenly decided to drop the sport, and there was no team in either 1908-09 or 1909-10.

"Although the game had been popular, it had not received adequate support, and had proved a financial drain upon the University," the *Owl* observed. "For the next two years, Pitt students sent petitions, in vain, to the Athletic Committee to have the sport reinstated."

Club basketball was popular around Pittsburgh during that time. Teams such as "Company G," "Business Men," "L.S. Levins," and "Perrysville Reserves" competed against "Southside," "Joliet," and "Ivanhoe Club of Wilkinsburg." Collegiate hockey received more coverage in the sports pages, but University of Pittsburgh basketball was back in business in 1910.

Coach Wohlparth Wegner welcomed approximately 30 prospects to fall tryouts at Duquesne Garden in late December. Pitt went 6-6 in its first season back—losing all six road games, but going undefeated at home—not that Pitt enjoyed any significant home-court advantage in those years.

The team played games and practiced on any available floor—including Duquesne Garden. Motor Square Garden in East Liberty was another facility, along with the Westinghouse Club in Wilkinsburg, or Washington Park. The Pittsburgh Athletic Association (PAA), which opened in 1911, also hosted some Pitt home games. Not until the 1912-13 season—when Trees Gym opened near the site where the Veterans Administration Hospital was later built—did the team have a permanent facility for its home games.

By then, Pitt had something else—a nickname. Suggested by undergraduate George Baird, "Panther" was officially adopted by the University of Pittsburgh Publicity Committee on November 16, 1909.

Pitt also appointed Charles S. Miller Director of Athletics in 1911—a position he held for many years. Miller's son, Harbaugh Miller, became a Pittsburgh attorney and longtime Pitt athletics supporter. Harbaugh, who died in 2000, held the distinction of having witnessed both the first (1925)

THE 1905-06 WESTERN UNIVERSITY OF PENNSYLVANIA BASKETBALL TEAM—THE SCHOOL'S FIRST.
Courtesy of University of Pittsburgh Archives

and last (1999) football games played at Pitt Stadium.

Stability came to Pitt's basketball program when former University of Pennsylvania All-American George Flint arrived as coach that same year. He had winning records in eight of his ten seasons. Flint had graduated from Penn in 1907, where he is said to have made a basket once while prone on his back. A Canadian by birth, his family moved to Pennsylvania during his early childhood. Before going off to college in Philadelphia, Flint played for a youth basketball team in 1903 organized by legendary Pittsburgh Pirates shortstop Honus Wagner.

Flint had to rebuild Pitt's program from scratch, and he compiled a record of 105-68 (.607) during his term. Some of his better players at Pitt were H.C. Carlson (who later carved his own unique and substantial niche at Pitt as "Doc" Carlson), Lloyd

Jordan, John "Speedo" Loughran, Andy Hastings and Norman Ochsenhirt.

Flint, who later practiced dentistry in the Pittsburgh area for 50 years, died in 1960. He was remembered by Carlson in a local obituary.

"He was a personable fellow, very efficient and capable," said Carlson. "Of course it was only a part-time job with little salary. We didn't start, though, until football [season] was over, and there wasn't the emphasis on the sport that there is today. Games were played before small crowds in old Trees Gymnasium."

Basketball was significantly different during Flint's day. Today's fans would have trouble recognizing the sport as it was played in the early 1900s. Consider a few of the early rules governing college basketball, as noted in the *NCAA Official Records Book*:

TREES GYM, LOCATED ON PITT'S UPPER CAMPUS, WAS THE SCHOOL'S PLAYING FACILITY FROM THE EARLY 1910S UNTIL PITT STADIUM WAS OPENED IN 1925. *Courtesy of University of Pittsburgh Archives*

• Upon leaving a game, a player could not re-enter. That was in effect until 1921.

• Traveling was a foul—rather than a violation—until 1922.

GEORGE FLINT STARRED AT PENN AND COACHED PITT FROM 1911-1921. HE WAS ALSO A DENTIST FOR MANY YEARS IN THE PITTSBURGH AREA.

Courtesy of University of Pittsburgh Archives

• Until 1924, a team could select a single player to shoot all its free throws.

• The ten-second violation for not advancing the ball past mid-court was instituted in 1933.

• A jump ball was done after every made basket before 1938.

• Goaltending was banned in 1945.

• Coaches weren't permitted to speak to players during the game until 1949—and then only during timeouts.

In that environment, Flint set the course for Pitt's basketball teams in the years before World War I. His 1912-13 team was 15-7. Upon returning from a successful road trip, there was a large gathering of fans and students waiting for the team at Union Station in Pittsburgh. A celebration was held in honor of the team the next day at Trees Stadium—then a large, grassy field located just below Trees Gym.

The following season, Pitt made an extended road trip north for games against Niagara, Colgate, Syracuse, St. Lawrence, and Rochester. The return home wasn't as cheerful as the previous year's trip had been. During the tour, team manager C.K. Murray contracted scarlet fever, and basketball team members were forced into quarantine for 10 days after arriving in Pittsburgh.

Following a losing season (7-8) in 1913-14, Flint's Panthers rebounded with a 13-5 season the following year. "Basketball honors were showered upon Mother Pitt by her stellar team this year, the

PITT ALSO PLAYED SOME EARLY HOME GAMES AT MOTOR SQUARE GARDEN IN ITS EARLY YEARS. THIS PHOTO WAS TAKEN IN 2002. *Courtesy of Image Point Pittsburgh*

quintet winning the State Collegiate title the first time in the history of this institution," wrote the *Owl*. Pitt earned the crown by defeating Swarthmore, 40-26, on March 13, 1915 at Cooper Battalion Hall in Philadelphia.

Pitt won at Penn State for the first time in school history with a 31-27 win in State College on February 25, 1916. The Panthers were 15-2 that year, sparked by the all-around play of captain Ben Lubic, an excellent free throw shooter whose teams were a combined 65-15.

On January 13, 1915, Pitt's Athletic Council implemented a "one-year residence rule," whereby "no student may represent the University of Pittsburgh in intercollegiate contests until he has been in residence in the University for one calendar year." The rule went into effect with the 1916-17 season, but something more significant cast a shadow of doubt across all of college sports. The Athletic Council held a special meeting on March 31, 1917—and war was declared April 6, 1917. Many colleges in the East suspended athletics immediately. Pitt officials waited to see what policy—if any—the government would set. President Woodrow Wilson and other officials publicly expressed their desire for the continuance of intercollegiate sports. Pitt would continue playing basketball, but there were some noticeable ramifications: "Pitt teams did

A TEAM CAPTAIN, BEN LUBIC LETTERED FROM 1914-1917 AND LATER BECAME HEAD COACH AT DUQUESNE UNIVERSITY.

Courtesy of University of Pittsburgh Archives

their part to keep expenses down," noted the *Owl*. "No training house was provided, and players lived in their homes. Crowds were down, generally speaking."

Schedules were reduced as well. Pitt played only 14 games in each of the next two seasons, 1917-18, and 1918-19. Carlson, who was a senior at Pitt in 1917-18, did not go out for basketball that year. Jimmy DeHart, however, became Pitt's first ever four-time letterman around that time.

Following back-to-back losing seasons, Flint's Panthers returned to their winning ways by going 9-6 in 1919-20—capturing the Intercollegiate Tri-State League title. Pitt opened that season with a 26-25 loss to Ivy League member Yale before what the *Owl* described as a "record crowd" at Trees Gym.

The curtain fell on George Flint's Pitt basketball tenure with a 12-9 season in 1920-21, and Andy Kerr was hired to lead the team in 1921-22—it was his only season. Led by sharpshooter Lloyd Jordan, the Panthers were 12-8 that year and ended the season with a four-game winning streak.

Following the 1921-22 campaign, school officials decided to hire former football All-American and basketball star Henry Clifford Carlson as their next coach—a position he would hold for the next 31 seasons. During that span, the laughter rarely stopped.

ARTIST'S RENDERING OF A WUP BASKETBALL PLAYER. *Courtesy of University of Pittsburgh Athletics*

THE DOC CARLSON ERA: 1922–1953

> "**HE WAS QUITE A CHARACTER. HE MARCHED TO HIS OWN DRUMMER. HE DID A LOT OF THINGS THE WAY HE WANTED TO DO THEM.**"
>
> —Bernie Artman

> "**PLAYING FOR DOC CARLSON WAS A VERY UNUSUAL EXPERIENCE.**"
>
> —Lou "Bimbo" Cecconi

> "**A COOL HEAD WINS A HOT GAME.**"
>
> —Doc Carlson

From 1922 to 1953—in a time when our nation and the world faced catastrophic changes—"Doc" Carlson managed Pitt basketball operations. His coaching tenure outlasted that of seven of Carlson's former Panther football mentors and teammates. His presence and profound influence define Pitt basketball during those decades. Anyone who had the opportunity to speak with him always left with at least one great story to tell.

Born July 4, 1894, in Murray City, Ohio, Carlson played football, basketball, and baseball at Pitt. An All-American for Pop Warner's 1917 undefeated football team, Doc graduated in 1918, earned his medical degree from Pitt just two years later, then played one year of professional football for the Cleveland Indians. After Pitt football assistant and basketball coach Andy Kerr left to lead Stanford's football program in 1922, school officials hired the 28-year-old Carlson as the Panthers' new basketball coach.

"Coach Carlson has the ideal temperament for a coach," wrote the *Owl*, Pitt's yearbook. "He knows how to handle men and put the fight into them, and he knows how to teach football and basketball."

Carlson coached Pitt's freshman football team during the late 1920s. As intercollegiate athletics evolved, many coaches were assigned to multiple sports to contain university budgets.

Carlson's first team—1922-23—won its first five games, including a 26-23 win against Syracuse in Carlson's debut on January 5, 1923—the Panthers' first ever basketball win against SU. Pitt finished the

Continued on page 21

THE 1940-41 FINAL FOUR TEAM

Not until the 1938-39 season did the NCAA recognize an official national champion through tournament play. That year, the National Coaches Association hosted the first ever model for what would ultimately become the NCAA tournament. Oregon won the first tournament in 1939, followed by Indiana a year later.

The 1940-41 Panthers opened their season by winning four of six games during an extended road trip through Big 10 country. A victory at Duke in late January sparked a six-game winning streak that helped the Panthers finish the regular season with a 12-5 record. Doc Carlson and his players then waited for an invitation from either the NCAA or NIT (National Invitation Tournament).

"The NIT was the big tournament then," Panther John Swacus remembered more than 60 years later. "It was played at Madison Square Garden in New York City."

The NCAA proved to be "Option B" for a number of teams that season, including the Duquesne Dukes—who declined their invitation from the NCAA, opting to take their 17-2 record to the NIT. One coaching giant added a caveat to his school's nay to the NCAA.

"Personally, I'm not interested in any playoffs sponsored by the NCAA," Kansas coach Phog Allen noted in published reports.

In any event, the Panthers were grateful for the opportunity to continue their season, and headed to Madison Wisconsin—along with Wisconsin, North Carolina, and Dartmouth—for the four-team East Regional. Washington State, Creighton, Arkansas, and Wyoming comprised the West Region of the entire eight-team tournament.

The Panthers were an experienced club that season. The starting lineup consisted of five seniors—Eddie Straloski, Mel Port, George Kocheran, Sam Milanovich, and Jimmy Klein. The six-foot-four Milanovich was the tallest man on the squad. Straloski, Port, and reserve Larry Paffrath were Pitt's primary scoring threats.

THE 1940-41 PANTHERS—FRONT ROW, LEFT TO RIGHT: DOLF, SILVERMAN, SWACUS, AND ARTMAN; MIDDLE ROW, LEFT TO RIGHT: KOCHERAN, PORT, MILANOVICH, KLEIN, STRALOSKI, AND (RAYMOND) ZIOLKOWSKI; TOP ROW, LEFT TO RIGHT: RIAL, PAFFRATH, LOHMEYER, MALARKEY, AND COACH CARLSON. *Courtesy of University of Pittsburgh Athletics*

Continued from page 20

The Pitt team also had confidence. It had defeated Wisconsin 36-34 on the same floor to start the season back in December. Ed Raymond—known then as Ed Ziolkowski—remembered a humorous incident that occurred while he and his teammates were watching Wisconsin beat Dartmouth in the first game of the March 21 doubleheader.

"I remember this one young kid, a program vendor, came into our area, and he was aware that we were the Pitt players," said Raymond. "He came up and said, 'Buy your programs here! Names, numbers...and salaries of every Pitt player!" (The remark was in reference to Pitt's reputation as a football factory under former head coach Jock Sutherland, who had resigned following the 1938 season.)

"We [Pitt basketball players] all laughed about it," said Raymond.

Not to be distracted, the Panthers took the court and beat North Carolina, 26-20. UNC featured George Glamack, a two-time Helms Foundation National Player of the Year. Glamack—a six-foot-five center who was from Johnstown, Pennsylvania—was nicknamed "The Blind Bomber" because of difficulties he had with his eyesight, a handicap that didn't hurt his 20.6 scoring average that year. The win—Pitt's only basketball victory against the Tar Heels in the team's first century of hoops—set up a rematch with the host Badgers, a 51-50 winner against Dartmouth. The winner of that game would advance to Kansas City for the championship game against Washington State. Before playing Wisconsin, Doc Carlson made a promise to his players.

"He said to us, 'You fellas win this [Wisconsin] game, and I'll buy each and every one of you the biggest steaks you ever saw in your life when we get to Kansas City,'" remembered Swacus.

The Panthers started quickly, leading 18-14 at halftime, and 23-18 midway through the second half before the Badgers found themselves aided by a little home cooking.

"They jumped ahead of us, and when they did, the Wisconsin band started playing 'On Wisconsin,'" said Raymond. "Did that ever charge them up! Oh, did their fans yell and scream. The Wisconsin team was really fired up."

The Badgers pulled away for the victory, 36-30. They won the national championship with a 39-34 victory against Washington State in Kansas City.

It was a heady time for the members of Pitt's 1940-41 basketball team. The NCAAs were played only nine months before the bombing of Pearl Harbor, and all 11 Panthers fought in World War II. One player—Harry Matthews—was killed in action, but the remaining players returned home safely.

season with a 10-5 record, securing the first of many successful seasons for Carlson. The Panthers enjoyed winning records in three of their next four seasons as well, and, when the 1927-28 Panthers went undefeated (21-0), they were named national champions by the Helms Foundation. Although All-American Charley Hyatt was the marquee player, Sykes Reed, Lester Cohen, Stan Wrobleski, Jerry Wunderlich, and Paul Zehfuss were also major contributors to the title.

From 1927 to 1931, Carlson's teams amassed a record of 80-11. Following a 14-16 mark in 1931-32, the Panthers won three consecutive Eastern Intercollegiate Championships from 1932-1935. All-Americans Claire Cribbs and Don Smith were stars during those years. Cribbs, known as an outstanding ball handler and defender, came to Pitt from Jeannette, Pennsylvania. Smith, from nearby Bellevue, is remembered for his quick court instincts. On what was unofficially proclaimed "Don Smith Day," Pitt wrapped up the 1932-33 season with a 38-21 home win against Carnegie

CHARLEY HYATT WAS A THREE-TIME ALL-AMERICAN FROM 1927-1930.

Courtesy of University of Pittsburgh Athletics

TIM LAWRY CAPTAINED THE PANTHERS IN 1932.
Courtesy of Ed Lawry

Tech. The Panthers also finished that season with a five-game winning streak.

The basketball team moved into a new home when Pitt Stadium was completed in 1925. Original sketches and plans called for a double-deck 90,000-seat stadium and a 6,000-seat basketball facility, but when Pitt Stadium opened for football on September 26, 1925—Pitt defeated Washington & Lee, 28-0—it sat approximately 60,000. The basketball court, which was known as The Pavilion, held about 3,000. One memorable game from the Pavilion's early days featured Sykes Reed hitting a basket with two seconds left to give the Panthers a 41-39 win against Carnegie Tech late in the 1926-27 season.

Not all of the exciting games were played in Pittsburgh. Carlson, who wanted his players to see the country, was known to schedule long road trips—he's believed to be the first collegiate coach to take his team across the continent. In 1931-32, the Panthers played one stretch of 12 consecutive games

on the road, including games at Wisconsin, Indiana, Purdue, Butler, Kansas City, Colorado, Stanford, Southern California, and Syracuse. The players found themselves on the road for Christmas and New Year's Day.

Pitt basketball registered another significant "first" in 1932 when it played a basketball game against Pittsburgh-area rival Duquesne. On January 13, 1932 at the Pavilion, the Dukes defeated the Panthers, 28-21. The Panthers and Dukes played all their games on Pitt's home court until January 28, 1939—when Pitt's director of athletics, Jimmy Hagan, announced a cessation of basketball relations with Duquesne. There had been bad blood between the schools on the court, as well as during scheduling boxing matches between the schools. The Dukes won that final basketball game, 40-29. The programs would not meet again until 1953. Hagan then announced that Pitt, wanting greater freedom to schedule upper-level opponents, planned to withdraw from the Eastern Intercollegiate Conference.

Before leaving the conference, however, Pitt provided some more thrills for its fans. On January 20, 1934—in the middle of a 13-game winning streak—the Panthers snapped Notre Dame's 22-game winning streak with a 39-34 win at the Pavilion. Leading the charge that night was Skip Hughes, who scored seven straight points to key the comeback. Hughes later became a very successful coach at St. Francis (Pennsylvania) College—where he coached the legendary Maurice Stokes. A year later, the Panthers ended Duquesne's 24-game winning streak at the Pavilion. That year, 1935, saw Pitt win its final Eastern Intercollegiate title by defeating West Virginia, 35-22, in Morgantown on March 18, 1935, avenging a loss on the same floor just five days earlier.

Throughout the 1930s, Carlson continued to develop a reputation as a basketball innovator. Along with his ambitious road schedules, which prompted the *Owl* to call Pitt's schedule "Cook's Tour of the United States," Carlson developed the Figure Eight Offense—a scheme that emphasized passing and ball movement. It disdained outside shots.

"There have been times when Pitt has kept the ball moving at top speed for as long as 15 minutes without taking a shot at the basket," publicist Frank Carver wrote in a 1935 preview of the Pitt basketball team.

"You had to be in extraordinarily good condition to play for him, unless you were the center, in which case you just stood there," remarked Mickey Zernich. "The center didn't go anywhere."

"It [the Figure Eight] did everything for you," said Ed Raymond. "It told you where to go, it told you where to pass, it told you when to pass, and it told you the type of shot you were expected to take. For Doc Carlson, the majority of the time, that shot was a lay-up."

"In the Figure Eight, after you passed the ball, you went down the middle," explained John Swacus, who played for Pitt from 1940-43. "The defense would put its biggest guy right there in the middle, and as you went by, he would let you have it!"

Carlson abhorred zone defenses, which neutralized his Figure Eight. In a game at Penn State during the early 1940s, the Nittany Lions refused to discard the zone, and Carlson refused to attack it. To keep the crowd entertained, Carlson went up into the stands and began tossing bags of peanuts to the Penn State students.

"Against the man-to-man, the Figure Eight was very effective," Swacus said. "Against the zone, it wasn't as effective. Consequently, teams would use a zone against us, and that would make it tough."

"During those years it was a different type of ballgame," said Raymond, who had played his high school ball in Ambridge, Pennsylvania. "I had never had the opportunity to see Pitt play. Not everybody had cars, that's for sure, and there was no television at the time."

As a result, many high school players recruited by Carlson were shocked when he exposed them to his basketball philosophy.

THIS WAS HOW THE PITT PAVILION APPEARED IN 1992, 41 YEARS AFTER IT HOSTED ITS FINAL COLLEGE BASKETBALL GAME. *Courtesy of University of Pittsburgh*

PITT'S TWO NATIONAL CHAMPIONS

Long before the NCAA instituted a postseason tournament to declare an official national champion, the Helms Foundation—which also selected All-America teams—selected one team as the best in the land. Pitt's 1927-28 and 1929-30 teams held this honor.

An eternal optimist, Doc Carlson liked to preview each season by telling anyone listening that his team's goal was to "Win 'em all!" The 1927-28 Panthers did just that, winning all 21 of their games—the only undefeated season in the school's first century of basketball.

The Panthers, who were led by the nation's top two scorers—All-American Charley Hyatt and Stan Wrobleski—opened the season by winning four straight road games (Michigan, Chicago, Northwestern,

and Iowa) against Big 10 opponents, a factor that impressed the Helms pollsters at season's end. The Iowa game was particularly difficult—the Hawkeyes took Pitt into overtime, where the Panthers prevailed, 44-40. Pitt again was forced to come from behind to defeat a tough Notre Dame team 24-22 at the Pitt Pavilion. Hyatt scored the game-winning basket off a feed from Paul Zehfuss. It was the Panthers' only lead of the game.

Most of the Panthers from those teams were from western Pennsylvania—a trend that would continue at Pitt well into the 1970s. Hyatt was from Uniontown, while Wrobleski and his All-America backcourt mate—Sykes Reed—had been teammates at Braddock High School.

Hyatt concluded his stellar career in 1929-30, having led the Panthers to a 23-2 record—the only losses were on the road at Syracuse and West Virginia—and another national title. Pitt opened that season with 12 straight victories before losing to Syracuse. Hyatt averaged 12.6 ppg, an impressive figure for that era, while Zehfuss, center Lester Cohen, and Ed Baker—who also quarterbacked Pitt's football team—made major contributions.

The 1927-28 and 1929-30 Pitt basketball teams also started another tradition that would persist, first at Fitzgerald Field House and later at the Petersen Events Center. The Panthers were unbeatable at home— the '28 team was 10-0 at The Pavilion, while the '30 club won all 12 of its home contests.

PITT'S 1927-28 TEAM WENT 21-0, THE ONLY UNDEFEATED TEAM IN SCHOOL HISTORY. *Courtesy of University of Pittsburgh Athletics*

Doc Carlson dubbed his war-depleted 1944 team "The Tiny Toughies."

Courtesy of University of Pittsburgh Archives

"His [Carlson's] system held scorers back," said Raymond. "So many of us had been our teams' leading scorers in high school, but when we came to Pitt, boy—were we in for a surprise."

Some Pittsburgh-area basketball stars had done their homework and wanted no part of Doc Carlson.

"I didn't want to play that continuity offense that Doc ran," said Dick Groat, who left Pittsburgh to attend Duke University, where he became the College Basketball Player of the Year in 1952. "He never had any big people because he wanted players who could run his Figure Eight. I didn't want to play that style of basketball."

"He [Carlson] was a taskmaster," said Swacus. "He wanted things done right."

"He was a Doctor Jekyll and Mister Hyde," said Raymond. "He had a very competitive nature, which I think is one of the biggest things I learned from him, and that I've tried to use in my life."

As he gained a reputation for his unconventional methods—including the Fatigue Curve, a drill that required players to run in place for periods in order to measure heart rate—Pitt began sponsoring a basketball clinic before the first home game every season at the Pavilion. Capacity crowds would sit and listen as Carlson explained his ideas about the game, using players for demonstrations.

Doc Carlson and his Panthers took a different type of stage on February 28, 1940, when they were part of the first ever college basketball telecast. Pitt defeated Fordham, 50-37, in the opening game of a doubleheader at old Madison Square Garden. W2XBS showed the game to a New York audience, utilizing only one camera for its broadcast.

Carlson's Panthers had their difficulties in the late 1930s. One exciting win came against Duquesne on February 18, 1936, at the Pavilion. Pitt trailed 25-16 at halftime, but scored 22 unanswered points in the second half en route to a 46-41 victory. Pete Noon and Bob Johnson keyed that rally. The following year, Pitt claimed its first "City of Pittsburgh Championship" in its tri-rivalry with Duquesne and Carnegie Tech. After trailing 30-15 at halftime, "Jumpin'" Joe Garcia made a last-second shot to give the Panthers a 51-50 win against the

ABOVE: GROUND WAS BROKEN FOR PITT'S NEW FIELD HOUSE IN THE EARLY 1950S. AT LEFT, WITH PICK, IS PITT ATHLETICS DIRECTOR TOM HAMILTON. STANDING IN MIDDLE (WITH HANDS IN POCKETS) IS PITT CHANCELLOR RUFUS FITZGERALD, FOR WHOM THE BUILDING WOULD BE NAMED. NEXT TO FITZGERALD (WEARING GLASSES) IS DAVID L. LAWRENCE, FORMER PITTSBURGH MAYOR AND PENNSYLVANIA GOVERNOR. *Courtesy of University of Pittsburgh Athletics*

BELOW: CONSTRUCTION CONTINUES ON THE MEMORIAL FIELD HOUSE ON UPPER CAMPUS. *Courtesy of University of Pittsburgh Athletics*

Dukes, Garcia also sparked a 34-31 home victory against Notre Dame earlier that season.

Not all the games against bitter rivals had happy endings. On February 8, 1939, the Panthers made only six of 66 shots from the floor during a 41-22 loss to Penn State at the Pavilion. The next year, however, Pitt set a school single-game record for points scored in a 73-42 win against Carnegie Tech. Eddie Straloski, who later changed his name to Strall, scored 32 points—also a Pitt single-game scoring mark at the time.

The 1940-41 Panthers were one of eight teams invited to the NCAA's third ever postseason tournament. Pitt defeated North Carolina at Madison, Wisconsin as part of the East Regional, but a 36-30 loss to Wisconsin in the East final prevented Pitt from advancing to he championship game in Kansas City.

The attack on Pearl Harbor pushed America into World War II and sent tremors through the world of collegiate athletics. Schedules were cut back significantly—Pitt played only 15 games

in both the 1941-42 and 1942-43 seasons, 14 in 1943-44, 12 games in 1944-45, and 14 in 1945-46. The 1944-45 team went undefeated at home, including a 37-point performance by Oland "DoDo" Canterna in a win over Westminster. The *Owl*, taking its cue from the wave of patriotism that swept across the nation after Pearl Harbor, summarized Pitt's basketball prospects during the war years:

"Call them 'kids' or 'ice cream eaters,' or even 'rinky-dinks,' if you wish, but Uncle Sam will make them he-men Americans if and when he casts his priorities on them." (Carlson called his 1943-44 Panthers the "Tiny Toughies." The team consisted largely of sophomores and 17-year-old freshmen.)

Swacus remembers one generous act the University extended to its final-term seniors who were marching off to war. "Pitt gave all those seniors their diplomas in absentia," said Swacus. "That was important. In the Army, when you filled out your questionnaires, you were able to put down that you had graduated from college."

Swacus later used the GI Bill to attend graduate school. He later worked as a coach, teacher, and administrator for 37 years in the Franklin Regional School District in suburban Pittsburgh—thanks largely to a strong recommendation by Carlson.

Carlson celebrated his 25th year as Pitt's basketball coach in 1946-47. Fourteen years earlier, in 1932, he had been named Pitt's director of men's health services—a position he held until his retirement in 1964. He had offices at the Falk Clinic and inside the Cathedral of Learning. For many years, he

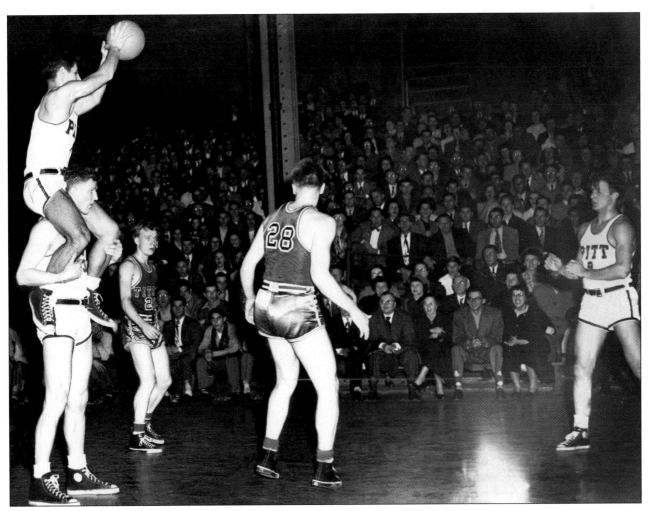

ANOTHER EXAMPLE OF DOC CARLSON'S SENSE OF HUMOR: THE 1948-49 PANTHERS HAD SEEN THE HARLEM GLOBETROTTERS PLAY IN CALIFORNIA. UPON RETURNING TO PITTSBURGH, CARLSON—WITH THE COOPERATION OF WESTMINSTER'S COACH—PULLED A TRICK PLAY THAT DEPLOYED BIMBO CECCONI ON TED GEREMSKY'S SHOULDERS. PITT WON, 50-41. *Courtesy of University of Pittsburgh Archives*

THE 1951-52 PANTHERS—FROM LEFT TO RIGHT: CLARENCE BURCH, MICKEY ZERNICH, DON VIROSTEK, DICK DEITRICK, AND ART BOYD. BURCH, OR "DUTCH," BECAME A TEACHER, ADMINISTRATOR, AND COACH. ZERNICH, DEITRICK, AND BOYD BECAME MEDICAL DOCTORS, AND VIROSTEK WAS A DENTIST.

Courtesy of University of Pittsburgh Archives

was a company doctor for Carnegie (Pennsylvania) Steel.

"I'm thankful that I knew him," recalled Swacus. "He gave me an opportunity to get an education, and that was the most important thing. He always helped his players out where he could. He lived in North Braddock, and that's where I came from. He removed my wife's tonsils. He was a physician in the community [North Braddock]."

While Carlson's coaching career approached its end during the late 1940s, his personality and eccentricities never subsided. During a 1948 loss at West Virginia, one overzealous fan, seated in the balcony section above the Pitt bench, dumped a bucket of water on Carlson. When the Panthers returned to Morgantown the following season, Carlson came prepared. In the locker room before his players took the floor, Carlson donned a raincoat, boots, and an umbrella and had the last laugh. Canterna made a last-second shot to send the game into overtime, where Pitt prevailed 34-32. That dramatic victory—in Pitt's regular season finale—

snapped West Virginia's 57-game home winning streak.

Unfortunately, that win was one of few during Carlson's final years of coaching—his teams suffered six consecutive losing seasons from 1946-1952. Change was in the air on the Pitt campus, and in the winter months of 1950-51, ground was broken for a new Memorial Field House—brainchild of Tom Hamilton, the school's athletic director and one-time football coach. Hamilton envisioned a multi-purpose facility that could house Pitt's basketball team, and serve as host facility for sports such as wrestling, gymnastics, and track, and be used as an indoor practice facility by the football team.

Pitt closed out the old Pavilion with a 74-72 victory against West Virginia on February 26, 1951. With the Panthers trailing at halftime, Hamilton took the public address microphone and predicted that Pitt would come back to win the game. A lay-up by Scott Phillips in the final seconds made Hamilton a prophet. A crowd of 2,365 witnessed the Pavilion finale—some drawn by the postgame

dance staged on the court—but there was little sentimentality on display after the game.

"There were no tears last night when they locked the doors on the Pitt Stadium basketball pavilion and threw the key away," wrote Chet Smith in *The Pittsburgh Press*. "The Panthers' Black Hole of Calcutta, home of Dr. Red [another of Carlson's nicknames] Carlson's teams since the early 1920s, can now go back to what it was originally intended to be—a cellar under the stadium. The Doctor and his boys will move into a sumptuous new field house next year."

Mention the Pavilion to any old-time basketball follower around Pittsburgh, and you'll find it was miserable.

"On cold nights I could judge the temperature by whether I was frozen to the knees or only the ankles, and by how much steam was coming off the players," Carlson remarked at the time of its closing.

"It was a terrible place to play," said Bernie Artman. "It was awful."

Mickey Zernich was one of three brothers (Wally and Steve were the others) to letter in basketball at Pitt; he was on the floor during the Pavilion's final game.

"His [Carlson's] orientation toward education was wonderful for colleges," said Zernich. "He helped me get into medical school. He talked to one of the people who would interview me. Doc Carlson was very strong in his attitudes and beliefs as far as

PITT'S NEW FIELD HOUSE WAS DEDICATED BEFORE A VICTORY AGAINST COLUMBIA ON DECEMBER 15, 1951. FROM LEFT TO RIGHT ARE: DR. HUBE WAGNER (A PITT FOOTBALL ALL-AMERICAN), DOC CARLSON, W.F. TRIMBLE (BUILDING CONTRACTOR), PITT AD TOM HAMILTON, AND CHANCELLOR RUFUS FITZGERALD.
Courtesy of Mickey Zernich

Artman had a front-row seat for some of Carlson's final follies on the basketball court—including one idea the coach told his players would "revolutionize the game of basketball."

"He called it the 'Ricochet Shot,'" Artman remembered. "He told us about it early one season. He'd been thinking about it over the summer."

The "Ricochet Shot"—according to Carlson—was the perfect way to dismantle the zone defense. Designed to overload the zone to one side of the court, a Pitt player—from behind what would later become the three-point arc—would throw the ball

Doc Carlson coached Pitt from 1922-1953.
Courtesy of Mickey Zernich

what he thought was right, and that was how he promoted things."

Bernie Artman—another Pittsburgher who played for Carlson in the coach's final years and whose brother, Bob, played for Pitt's 1941 Final Four team—appreciated the experience of playing for the venerable instructor.

"Doc Carlson was a good teacher about life," said Artman. "We'd go to a nice hotel in New York, and he made sure that everybody ate well and conducted themselves properly. We all dressed well on road trips."

"Our teams were very close under Doc Carlson," explained Swacus. "He made sure that we stuck together. He sensed that was very important to winning."

SIGNIFICANT WINS: THE CARLSON YEARS

1/5/22   PITT 26, SYRACUSE 23
• Doc Carlson's debut as Pitt's coach is a successful one.

2/15/24   PITT 31, PENN STATE 30
• Team captain H.C. Carr makes the game-winning shot in the final seconds.

2/18/28   PITT 24, NOTRE DAME 22
• All-American Charley Hyatt scores the winning basket at the buzzer.

2/7/31   PITT 35, NOTRE DAME 32 (OT)
• Tim Lawry keys a late rally to beat Irish team featuring Moose Krause.

2/8/35   PITT 35, DUQUESNE 34
• Victory by Pitt snaps Dukes' school-record 24-game winning streak.

2/11/41   PITT 56, WEST VIRGINIA 45
• Game delayed in second half after WVU's Scotty Hamilton decks Panther Eddie Straloski.

3/21/41   PITT 26, NORTH CAROLINA 20
(NCAA Tournament)
• Pitt's first ever NCAA tournament game is a winner.

3/5/49   PITT 34, WEST VIRGINIA 32 (OT)
• Panthers snap WVU's 57-game home winning streak.

2/26/51   PITT 74, AT WEST VIRGINIA 72
• Panthers top Mountaineers in final college game at Pitt Pavilion.

12/15/51   PITT 65, COLUMBIA 64
• First game at new Pitt Field House snaps long winning streak for Lions.

off the far side of the glass. A free-roaming Panther—standing alone under the basket—would rebound the ricochet and put the ball in for an easy bucket.

"We practiced it," said Artman. "Some guys would throw it completely over the banking board, some would throw it under the board, and some guys would hit the rim. Finally, we had a players-only meeting. We said, 'This is crazy. Let's just try to put the ball in the basket.'"

Finally, during a game at Carnegie Tech, Carlson decided to spring his invention. He called for the Panthers to run a play culminating with the Ricochet Shot.

"Mickey Zernich fired it over the board," said Artman. "The Carnegie Tech players and the fans had to be wondering what the hell we were doing. We players revolted. During a timeout, Doc Carlson was really upset with us. We told him we weren't going to do it. He walked off the floor and went inside the locker room. He calmed down a little and came back for the second half. 'Okay, do what you want,' he told us. So we never heard about the Ricochet Shot after that."

Zernich remembered another game when Carlson wasn't as forgiving. Following a particularly frustrating loss, Carlson was steaming in the locker room.

"One of the fellas took a shot he shouldn't have," said Zernich. "Doc came in the showers, fully clothed, looking for him. He had him against the wall and was yelling at the kid."

Zernich captained the Panthers in 1951-52, Pitt's first season at its new home—the Field House. On December 15, 1951, a stellar crowd of 3,378 braved a bitter Saturday night, to watch Pitt play powerhouse Columbia. The Lions entered the game—Pitt's opener—riding a 32-game regular-season winning streak. Tom Hamilton presented Carlson with a dedication ball during a pregame ceremony that included Pitt Chancellor Rufus Fitzgerald (for whom the Field House was eventually named) and W.F. Trimble (the building's contractor).

The Panthers upset Columbia 65-64 as Artman hit a lay-up with 15 seconds remaining. For the record, Pitt's Don Virostek registered the first field goal ever made at the Field House.

Pitt that first season finished 10-12 in its new home. The second campaign, 1952-53, turned out to be Carlson's last season as coach. His remarkable career ended with one final winning season—the Panthers went 12-11. On February 29, 1953, Pitt lost 73-53 at Penn State in his final game. Doc Carlson remained employed by Pitt until his retirement as director of Student Health Services in 1964. He died shortly thereafter—on November 1, 1964, at his home in Ligonier, Pennsylvania.

"By the end of his coaching career, he had developed a rotund belly," Artman said. "He even looked like Santa Claus. He used to tell us, 'Remember, Santa Claus only comes once a year, so you'd better be ready for him.' He could charm anybody."

Attending Pitt and playing basketball for Carlson was an eye-opening experience for Artman and his teammates.

"Going to Pitt broadened my horizons," he said. "I went to school with people who had just come back from World War II. There were students from poor walks of life, and students from affluent backgrounds. I grew up a lot in my years at Pitt."

THE FORGOTTEN YEARS: 1953-1968

"WE MADE 'EM SWEAT."
"YOU SHO' DID."

—Postgame exchange between Pitt coach Bob Timmons and Kentucky Governor Happy Chandler following UK's 98-92 NCAA tournament win over Pitt on March 15, 1957 in Lexington.

When Doc Carlson retired from coaching following the 1952-53 season, Pitt officials surprised everyone by naming 41-year-old Bobby Timmons the school's new basketball coach. Timmons, a Pittsburgh product, had grown up on the city's North Side and graduated from Allegheny High School in 1930. He had a history with Pitt—but not in the role he was being asked to pursue.

"I think many people were surprised when he [Timmons] was hired," said Bernie Artman, who began his playing career under Carlson, but finished under Timmons. "He didn't really know much about basketball, but he knew a lot about people—especially student-athletes."

His assessment was not entirely without merit. Timmons had lettered twice (1933 and 1935) in football at Pitt playing for legendary coach Dr. John Bain "Jock" Sutherland, but he did not play basketball. After graduating, he coached high school football in Pennsylvania and Ohio; then became an assistant football coach at Indiana University of Pennsylvania (IUP) and was eventually named head basketball coach there. He returned to his alma mater in 1946, and worked as an assistant football coach for several different staffs. Even after Timmons took over Pitt's basketball program, he remained a member of the football staff each season until November 1—when basketball practice commenced.

"He was kind of growing with us, too, at the beginning," remembered Don Hennon, who arrived at Pitt in 1955 and became one of the program's all-time greats.

"By the time I got to Pitt [in 1960], Bob was very well-versed in basketball, as far as Xs and Os," said Brian Generalovich, a star forward on two postseason teams from the early 1960s. "I came from Farrell High School, and Coach Timmons and I used to sit down and talk about things that [Farrell High School] Coach [Ed] McCluskey used to do, who was a well-known tactician."

Many think that the legendary McCluskey felt that perhaps *he* should have been coaching the Panthers during that era. McCluskey coached Farrell from 1949-77, winning seven Pennsylvania Interscholastic Athletic Association (PIAA) titles.

"McCluskey would have taken the Pitt job if it had been offered to him at that time," said Beano Cook, who was Pitt's sports information director from 1956-1966 and one of the basketball pro-

Continued on page 36

PITT VS. WEST VIRGINIA:
WILD, WONDERFUL, AND WEIRD

Pitt and West Virginia have met on a basketball court at least once per season since 1917-18. No other Pitt opponent can claim such frequency. Through the 2004-2005 season, West Virginia had defeated Pitt 91 times. Pitt claimed 77 victories. What happened off the court, at times, was even more interesting and entertaining as the games. Here are a few unusual moments from the basketball edition of *The Backyard Brawl*:

January 17, 1931
Pitt 17, West Virginia 15

The game, played at the Pitt Pavilion, illustrated the stubbornness of Pitt coach Doc Carlson, and his disdain for zone defenses. The Mountaineers were coached by Francis Stadsvold, a one-time All-Big 10 center at Minnesota. Stadsvold had his team come out in a zone, and Carlson refused to press the issue offensively. The partisan Pitt crowd booed and jeered, but neither coach was moved. The Panthers led at halftime, 7-2. The final score was 17-15 in Pitt's favor. No player from either team made more than two baskets. John Albright and Milt Cohen shared scoring honors for Pitt with four points each. All-American Don Smith was held to three points. Leo Dotson led the Mountaineers with five points.

February 11, 1941
Pitt 56, West Virginia 45

It was a rough night at the Pavilion for Pitt's Eddie Straloski. He was knocked senseless by WVU's Rudy Baric while driving for a basket in the first half, and smelling salts—administered by Doc Carlson—were needed to revive him. Later, after jostling with Mountaineer All-American Scotty Hamilton for a loose ball, Straloski attempted to toss the ball to the official. The ball inadvertently struck Hamilton in the side of the head. Without waiting for an explanation, Hamilton decked Straloski with a single punch to the face, causing fans and players to storm the court in anger. Hamilton was ejected from the game. A photographer tried to snap a picture of him, causing several of his angry teammates to chase the photographer into the stands. Officials from both schools had to take the floor to restore order, and play resumed after about 20 minutes. Hamilton made an appearance in the Pitt locker room after the game.

"This is the worst thing that's ever happened to me," Hamilton told reporters after the game. "I don't know why I did it. I hope you can understand how sorry I am."

"It was something that shouldn't have happened," said Pitt's John Swacus in an interview more than 60 years after the incident. "It wasn't meant to happen. Hamilton thought Eddie threw the ball at him deliberately, but he didn't. It wasn't a vindictive thing. Eddie was walking away from the play when he tossed the ball up."

March 5, 1949
Pitt 34, West Virginia 32

Why was Doc Carlson wearing a raincoat, boots, and carrying an umbrella as the Panthers took the floor for this game in Morgantown? The year before, a West Virginia fan seated in the balcony above Pitt's bench area doused the Panthers' eccentric coach with a bucket of water. This time, Carlson came prepared.

The Mountaineers appeared well on their way to their 58th straight victory at home, leading Pitt by nine points with three minutes to play. The Panthers rallied, however, to trail 32-30 with six seconds left. With the ball out under its own basket, the WVU player who accepted the inbounds pass had his foot on the baseline, turning the ball back over to Pitt. DoDo Canterna swished a shot at the buzzer to send the game into overtime. A lay-up by Sammy David was the only basket scored by either team, and the Panthers enjoyed a most satisfying 34-32 upset win.

February 2, 1963
West Virginia 68, Pitt 67

Pitt had lost 12 straight basketball games to the Mountaineers, but seemed to have halted that skid when Dave Roman hit a shot at the buzzer. His teammates mobbed Roman. Jubilant Pitt fans stormed the court to celebrate, but there was a problem—teammate Ben Jinks had called time out away from the ball.

"In the huddle, Coach [Bob] Timmons gave us two options, and we did both," Roman later explained.

The timer that night was Bobby Lewis, Pitt's baseball coach. "I think if Bobby had just let the clock expire, we would have had the win," said Roman. "But he recognized that time had been called, and he stopped the clock."

The Panthers misfired on their final shot attempt, and their losing streak against WVU had reached 13.

More than 40 years after the incident, Roman still hears about it.

"Mostly, people felt sorry for me," he explained.

January 14, 1970
West Virginia 67, Pitt 66

West Virginia's Wil Robinson was preparing to shoot a free throw when he had an unexpected visitor—one with gills. Pitt students had taken to throwing fish on the court during home games at the Field House, usually as a way of showing their displeasure with the play of the home team. This one was in protest of an official's call. The Panthers were assessed a technical foul, and

coach Buzz Ridl grabbed the public address microphone to ask the student body to refrain from such nonsense immediately. Pitt groundskeeper Leo "Horse" Czarnecki did the honor of cleaning the floor of its fishy residue.

"They [students] used to throw eels," Czarnecki said after the game. "But they're harder to clean up after."

March 7-8, 1975
ECAC Southern Division Playoffs

The good news was that the 1974-75 Pitt basketball team was topseed in the newly configured ECAC Southern Division Playoffs. The bad news was the site for the games—and Pitt's first-round opponent. The ECAC committee members picked West Virginia—there were no official league standings—as the No. 4 seed for the tournament at WVU Coliseum. Pitt lost to WVU, 75-73, and Panther players, fans, and officials were upset by much more afterward. WVU play-by-play announcer Jack Fleming, a West Virginia graduate and Morgantown native who was, at the time, employed by WTAE-TV in Pittsburgh, had been mocking and taunting Pitt coach Buzz Ridl from his broadcast station not far from the Pitt bench—according to Pitt eyewitnesses. The next night, after Pitt had beaten George Washington by 25 points in the consolation game, an overzealous Pitt supporter had a jar of urine dumped on Fleming's head while the announcer was broadcasting the WVU-Georgetown game.

Thereafter, when West Virginia visited Pittsburgh for basketball games at Fitzgerald Field House, Fleming—whose animosity toward Pitt was common knowledge—broadcast the games from a balcony sidewalk well above and behind the general seating area.

January 29, 1982
West Virginia 48, Pitt 45

Pitt had the last laugh on West Virginia during the 1981-82 season, defeating the Mountaineers in the conference's tournament champi-

PANTHERS SET A TRAP FOR WVU'S BOB HUGGINS DURING PITT'S LOSS TO THE MOUNTAINEERS IN THE 1975 ECAC SOUTHERN DIVISION TOURNAMENT IN MORGANTOWN. *Courtesy of West Virginia University Sports Communications*

onship game to receive an automatic bid to the NCAA tournament. Before that, however, the Panthers suffered a pair of bitter defeats to WVU during the regular season—Pitt's last as a member of the Eastern Eight.

Coach Roy Chipman had to be restrained in the closing moments of the first game, played at Fitzgerald Field House. With 14 seconds left, Panther Steve Beatty made a free throw that tied the game, but official Jack Prettyman—who was from West Virginia—called Pitt's Clyde Vaughan for a lane violation. Chipman went ballistic and drew a technical foul. The Mountaineers then put the game away.

"As soon as the ball left Steve's hand, I went for the rebound," Vaughan explained afterward.

Still upset after the game, Chipman called the violation ruling a "Mickey Mouse" call.

"You've got to be looking for something like that to make that call," Pitt's coach said. "My kids got cheated. If the Eastern Eight [Conference] doesn't like it, the hell with them."

January 15, 1983
Pitt 81, West Virginia 67

The game, played at Fitzgerald Field House, was Pitt's first against WVU as a member of the Big East Conference. That posed a problem before the game. A controversy arose over whether or not a shot clock would be used during the game. When West Virginia coach Gale Catlett noticed that shot clocks were in place at the ends of the court, he refused to allow his team to take the floor for the opening tip. Pitt associate athletics director Dean Billick was forced to fetch the game contract from his office upstairs at the Field House. The contract did stipulate that a 45-second shot clock would be used in the game, and a 40-second clock the following season for the game in Morgantown. The start of the game was delayed by about 20 minutes while all this was being sorted out.

Once the game started, the Panthers jumped out to a 12-0 lead, and went on to record a victory against that season's eventual Atlantic 10 champion. Six players—two from Pitt and four from West Virginia—fouled out.

For whatever reason, the rivalry seemed to cool after West Virginia joined the Big East for basketball in 1995. Strangely enough—through the 2005 event—WVU was the only Big East member Pitt had never played during the conference's postseason tournament.

JOE FENWICK SCORES IN PITT'S 74-62 UPSET OF PENN STATE IN 1954. *Courtesy of Joe Fenwick*

gram's staunchest, most outspoken supporters. "He told me that."

No one will ever know if Pitt's program could have reached greater heights during that period, but Timmons did lead the Panthers to three NCAA tournaments (1957, 1958, and 1963) and a National Invitation Tournament (NIT) appearance in 1964. Pitt's first six players to reach 1,000 career points played for Timmons. Seven of his 15 seasons produced winning records, and his final Pitt tally sheet read 174-189 overall.

Although Timmons fell in his 1953-54 coaching debut—a 78-69 loss to Michigan—his first victory was a thrilling 66-64 upset of Bradley. That win came in the opening round of the Steel Bowl—an annual regular-season four-team tournament that began in 1951 and was played in Pittsburgh each December through 1976.

Dutch Burch drained a shot in the final seconds to give Timmons his first win, but the exhilaration was short lived. The Panthers lost 75-46 to Duquesne in the championship game the next night. The Steel Bowl rekindled the Pitt-Duquesne rivalry—the schools had not met since the 1938-39 season. Pitt lost six straight games after the Steel Bowl and ended Timmons's first season with a 9-14 record highlighted by a pair of wins against West Virginia.

Pitt was 10-16 during Timmons's second season (1954-55), a schedule remembered for a 4,000-mile road trip that took the Panthers to Army, Navy, Tampa, Miami (Florida), and Puerto Rico—the first time a Pitt basketball team had played outside the continental United States. Pitt defeated Tampa, Miami, and Puerto Rico A&M during the extended road swing. Another highlight that year was Ed Pavlick's 40-point game against Ohio State. Sophomores John Riser and Bob Lazor were rising stars in Pitt's basketball program that was about to ascend under Timmons.

The Panthers won their first three games in 1955-56—Timmons's first winning season—and later won six straight games on their way to a 15-10 record. In 1956-57, seniors Lazor and Riser were joined by a newcomer to the varsity—five-foot-eight phenomenon Don Hennon, who had become the WPIAL's (Western Pennsylvania Interscholastic Athletics Association) all-time leading scorer two years earlier at Wampum (Pennsylvania) High School. The Panthers now had three legitimate scorers in their lineup.

After compiling a 15-9 record during the 1956-57 regular season, the Panthers were sent to Columbus, Ohio, to meet Morehead State in a first-round NCAA Midwest Regional contest—Pitt's first visit to the tournament since 1940-41. The Panthers prevailed, 86-85, on Milan Markovich's lay-up plus

Continued on page 38

JULIUS PEGUES: A PANTHER PIONEER

Thanks to a telephone call from Tulsa oilman E. Alex Phillips to Pitt's Director of Athletics Captain Tom Hamilton in the summer of 1954, Pitt was to welcome its first ever African-American basketball player. Pitt basketball coach Bob Timmons, however, wasn't aware of this until well after Pegues arrived on campus.

Phillips, who had attended Pitt before World War II, later served as a pilot on a Naval aircraft carrier under the command of Hamilton, who also coached the Pitt football team in 1951 and for part of the 1954 season. Pegues, who was the class valedictorian at Booker T. Washington High School, where his basketball teams lost only three times in segregated competition, had no definite plans lined up following his graduation in 1953. He took a year off from basketball, moving to Detroit, Michigan, to live with an aunt who was in poor health. He took some classes at Cass Technical, as well as Wayne State, but returned to Tulsa in the summer of '54.

"That summer, Alex and I were talking, and he said, 'Jules, I'll tell you what I'm gonna do. I'm gonna call Tom Hamilton [then Pitt's A.D.] and tell him I'm sending him a basketball player.' And that's what he did."

Phillips, a white man, was a familiar sight around Tulsa athletics. He loved sports, and would provide the same type of assistance to countless other black athletes who were hopeful of attending college on a scholarship.

"Where he [Phillips] grew up—Blacksburg, West Virginia—everyone was poor," said Pegues. "He wanted to help give young people a better chance in life. He had an appreciation for mankind, period. He did a lot to send black kids to colleges all across the country."

Pegues, with the help of Phillips, had tried to earn a scholarship from Carnegie Tech, literally down the street from the Pitt campus.

"I took a battery of tests," said Pegues. "You really had to score high for the scholarship. I did well, scoring in the 90s, but it was very competitive. I didn't get the scholarship."

Thus came the phone call to Hamilton.

"Tom Hamilton was the only person in Pittsburgh who knew I played basketball," said Pegues.

Phillips paid for Pegues's tuition during the first semester, and when Pegues reported for basketball practice with the rest of the players, he was awarded a full scholarship. His college coach had no qualms about welcoming an African-American to the squad.

"Bobby Timmons just wanted to win, and he put his best players on the floor," Pegues explained. "He was a super guy. He was kind and considerate. He treated everyone fairly. He treated everyone like they were human beings."

After starting every game for the Pitt freshman team in 1954-55, Pegues did the same for the varsity for three seasons (1955-58). A six-foot-three swingman, Pegues scored 1,050 points in his college career, averaging double figures in scoring all three years—including a 17.6 ppg average as a senior in 1957-58. He played on two NCAA tournament teams with the Panthers. He scored 15 points in Pitt's 98-92 loss to Kentucky in the '57 NCAAs played on the Wildcats' home court.

"We could have won that game," Pegues remembered. "We knew Kentucky was going to be slow. We were taking it up and down the court on them. They had not seen a team that could run the way we could."

Although Pegues isn't inclined to discuss the difficulties he had to endure as a black college basketball player during that era, one prominent Panther from that era remembers one incident clearly. Don Hennon began his collegiate career with a bang, scoring 34 points in a loss at North Carolina State on December 1, 1956. Another dramatic event took place about 90 minutes later.

"After the game we all went to eat at a restaurant [in Raleigh]," said Hennon. "I remember looking back, and they wouldn't let Julius into the restaurant. I can remember that very vividly."

Similar things happened a little closer to home, particularly when the Panthers were about to play, or were playing, West Virginia.

"I know that when we played West Virginia, people sent hate letters and made phone calls, calling him all kinds of crap," said Hennon. "He [Pegues] may have denied it, but I think they tried to scare or intimidate him. They didn't scare him, but I know they tried."

The Pitt-West Virginia rivalry was just as spirited on the court. One of Pegues's fondest memories from his playing career was the Panthers' 94-77 victory at the West Virginia Field House on February 25, 1956. The Mountaineers, who finished 21-9 that year and would win the Southern Conference Tournament a week after the loss to Pitt, had led 48-43 at halftime, but were outscored by the Panthers, 51-29, after intermission. Pegues, with 16 points and nine rebounds, was one of five Pitt players who scored in double figures. Bob Lazor had 21, followed by John Riser (19), and Joe Fenwick (16). Pegues, who usually drew the assignment of guarding the opponent's top scorer, had his hands full that night with Rod Hundley. "Hot Rod," as he came to be called, led all scorers with 40 points.

Pegues earned a degree in mechanical engineering from Pitt in 1959. He returned to Tulsa, and worked in the aeronautics industry for the next 41 years.

"The time I spent at Pitt, and in Pittsburgh, were some of the best years in my life," said Pegues.

Courtesy of University of Pittsburgh Archives

DON HENNON: PROLIFIC SCORER

Pitt's basketball program had never seen a player such as five-foot-eight shooting guard Don Hennon. He arrived at Pitt after a stellar career at Wampum (Pennsylvania) High School, where he was coached by his father, L. Butler Hennon. The younger

Courtesy of University of Pittsburgh Archives

Hennon scored 2,376 points during his scholastic career, and possessed an educated game, the beneficiary of his father's unconventional practice methods.

"He used a lot of gimmicks and things to teach fundamentals," explained Don Hennon. "They made learning fun. Practices became games more than drudgery."

For example, to make it easier for players to pass between defenders, Coach Hennon would have the defensive squad wear oversized mitts to disrupt the offense. He used

weighted balls. He outfitted his players in galoshes and popped the lenses from sunglasses—then put tape over the frames to make players concentrate better on ball-handling and shooting fouls.

When Hennon arrived at Pitt in the fall of 1955, he didn't figure to be surprised by anything third-year Pitt coach Bob Timmons had in store.

"Bobby Timmons was very easygoing," said Hennon. "He wasn't very rough. I don't think any two coaches are the same."

Hennon thrilled college basketball fans with his impressive arsenal of shots, using an array of jumpers, runners, and hooks to score 1,841 points for the Panthers. For 19 years, he was Pitt's all-time leading scorer. His season average of 26.0 ppg in 1957-58 was the best in school history during Pitt's first century. He was the first Panther to average at least 20 points per game in three different seasons. Billy Knight and Larry Harris also reached that milestone during the 1970s. Hennon's 24.2 scoring average also was the best in Pitt's first 100 years.

In many ways, Hennon remains Pitt's most prolific scoring machine. He was the program's first All-American in 25 years, a UPI first-team selection in 1957-58 and 1958-59. Other players selected to the first-team squad in 1958 were Wilt Chamberlain (Kansas), Elgin Baylor (Seattle), Oscar Robertson (Cincinnati), and Guy Rodgers (Temple). More importantly, he helped lead the Panthers to a pair of NCAA tournament appearances during his sophomore and junior years, playing within Timmons's structured system.

"I don't think he [Timmons] had anything special set up for me," said

Hennon. "It was just like anything else, you had to work your way into position to get your shot."

And shoot he did—Hennon topped 40 points in a single game on three occasions, including a 45-point outburst against Duke at the Pitt Field House in an 87-84 double-overtime win on December 21, 1957. He made 20 of 42 field goal attempts (both Pitt single-game records) and converted four of his five free throws. He scored 41 points against Ohio State on December 3, 1958 (a 73-70 Pitt win), and 41 versus Geneva in a 109-74 victory on February 24, 1958.

Despite his national reputation and sparkling basketball resume, Hennon understood that his basketball days were over once his college career ended, even if he did think about the NBA.

"I don't think I ever seriously considered playing pro basketball," he admits. "I thought about whether I would be able to make it, but I had already set my sights on going to medical school."

Hennon did follow his ambitious path, and later graduated from Pitt's School of Medicine. Dr. Don Hennon became a general surgeon at Pittsburgh's Allegheny General Hospital, Passavant Hospital, and Suburban General Hospital. His basketball career was honored in 1970, when he elected to the Helms Athletic Foundation Hall of Fame.

"I wanted to be a doctor," Hennon said. "I didn't know that I'd be a surgeon. I never worried about not being six foot six."

Hennon was the first Pitt player to have his jersey number (#10) retired, during a special ceremony at halftime of the January 13, 1968 Pitt-Penn State game at the Field House.

one with just 31 seconds left. Hennon scored 31 points, and Riser added 20. They were to face Kentucky next—in Lexington.

"That's the NCAA at work making money," said Beano Cook. "That was typical NCAA stuff."

Pitt, a 15-point underdog, threw a major scare into coach Adolph Rupp's Wildcats before succumbing, 98-92.

"We made 'em sweat," Timmons remarked to Kentucky governor Happy Chandler during a

SIGNIFICANT WINS: THE TIMMONS YEARS

2/22/56   PITT 94, AT WEST VIRGINIA 77
- Panthers outscore Mountaineers 51-29 in second half for comeback victory.

12/15/56   PITT 59, DUQUESNE 50
        (Steel Bowl)
- Pitt's first win against Dukes since 1938 gives Panthers their first Steel Bowl title.

3/11/57   PITT 86, MOREHEAD STATE 85
        (NCAA Tournament)
- Milan Markovich's three-point play gives Pitt its first NCAA tourney win since 1941.

12/21/57   PITT 87, DUKE 84 (OT)
- Don Hennon scores Pitt single-game-record 45 points.

1/30/58   PITT 86, ST. JOHN'S 73
- St. John's had been nation's last remaining undefeated team entering the game.

12/12/59   PITT 75, DUQUESNE 44
        (Steel Bowl)
- John Fridley's 20 points and Billy Mauro's 11 highlight surprisingly lopsided win.

12/2/60   PITT 81, PURDUE 80
- Panthers rally from 22-point deficit to win season opener.

2/13/63   PITT 69, AT WEST VIRGINIA 68
- Pitt's Brian Generalovich and WVU's Gale Catlett were ejected for fighting.

12/7/63   PITT 69, DUQUESNE 67
        (Steel Bowl)
- Panthers beat Dukes in hoops on same day Pitt football team beat Penn State by one point.

2/15/64   PITT 69, SYRACUSE 67
- Generalovich's late basket the difference against Dave Bing and Syracuse.

postgame handshake, as reported in *The Pittsburgh Press*.

"You sho' did," the *Press* quoted Chandler, phonetically.

"I think the kids underestimated Pitt," Rupp told reporters afterward. "They [Pitt] sure wouldn't quit. And that Hennon—somebody ought to send

[UK guard] Red Calvert a telegram and tell him that Hennon can shoot."

Hennon scored 24 for the Panthers, but top-scoring honors went to Riser (30), who also grabbed 13 rebounds. Riser converted 16-17 free throws before fouling out late in the game.

"Riser, he was a good ballplayer," said Hennon. "He really played well for us that year down the stretch."

GENTLE, MILD-MANNERED BOB TIMMONS RETIRED FROM COACHING FOLLOWING THE 1967-68 SEASON. *Courtesy of University of Pittsburgh Archives*

PITT

MEMBERS OF PITT'S 1957-58 TEAM INCLUDED, FROM LEFT TO RIGHT: JULIUS PEGUES, CHUCK HURSH, JOHN MILLS, JOHN MESHER, AND DON HENNON. *Courtesy of University of Pittsburgh Athletics*

Pitt's other senior starter, Lazor, was hampered by a leg injury. Still, at least one Panther wasn't overly impressed by Kentucky that night.

"I thought we could have won that game," said Hennon. "We were at a huge disadvantage, playing them in Lexington. We had maybe 50 or a hundred fans there. They had all the rest."

Kentucky's fans were so confident that the game did not sell out Memorial Coliseum. The announced crowd for the second-round game was just 11,200.

"I don't think they really had a great team that year," recalled Hennon. "It wasn't like some of the teams they had in years before, with Alex Groza, Ralph Beard, and those guys. They were fantastic

basketball players. The group that we played, they were just an average team, I thought."

Indeed. Kentucky lost to Michigan State in the next round—in Lexington. The Panthers dropped an 86-85 consolation-round decision to Notre Dame on St. Patrick's Day. Riser scored 34 points in his final Pitt appearance. He finished his collegiate career with 1,164 points. Lazor's three-year total was 1,175.

Pitt made it back-to-back NCAA appearances in 1957-58. The Panthers' 18-6 regular season, which included an eight-game winning streak, earned the team a spot opposite Miami (Ohio) in a first-round game at Evanston, Illinois. Miami—led by star center Wayne Embry—defeated the Panthers, 82-77.

DECEMBER 6, 1961

One of the highlights of the downtown Pittsburgh Renaissance during the 1960s was the construction of a sparkling, 12,000-seat, $22 million multipurpose civic auditorium. Pitt and Duquesne hosted a college basketball doubleheader at what was originally called...the Civic Auditorium. In time, *The Pittsburgh Post-Gazette* began referring to the domed structure as "Civic Arena," and the name stuck. Hockey enthusiasts have long called the home of the NHL's Pittsburgh Penguins "The Igloo." As of 2005, its official name was Mellon Arena.

The basketball doubleheader was sponsored by the Press Old Newsboys Fund for the benefit of Children's Hospital in Pittsburgh. Duquesne hosted Carnegie Tech in the first game, while Pitt met top-ranked Ohio State in the nightcap.

The Buckeyes, who had lost the NCAA title game to intrastate rival Cincinnati nine months earlier, and

lost to the Bearcats in a championship rematch three months later, brought a star-studded lineup to town. Their starting five included future pro greats John Havlicek and Jerry Lucas, plus Bob Knight. Another future college coach—Don DeVoe—also played for Ohio State. The official game program for the event listed Knight as "McKnight," as did a photo caption in *The Pittsburgh Press* the next day.

Pitt's lineup consisted of sophomores Brian Generalovich, Calvin Sheffield, and Paul Krieger, plus seniors Tom Maloney and Bob Sankey.

In previewing the contest, Pitt coach Bob Timmons sounded less than optimistic.

"I think the main difference between Ohio State and us is that they have three All-Americans and we have none," he said. "Maybe some of their greatness can rub off on our players."

After the Dukes disposed of Tech 78-40 in the first game, the crowd of 7,221 was treated to an exhibition basketball game between current members of the Pittsburgh Pirates baseball team and former Pirates. One of the current Pirates playing was Dick Groat, who had also played pro basketball in the NBA. The game was officiated by Pittsburgh Steelers Bobby Layne and Gene "Big Daddy" Lipscomb. Another celebrity who enjoyed the evening's festivities was former middleweight and welterweight boxing champion Sugar Ray Robinson, who was introduced to the crowd.

When the serious basketball resumed, Ohio State had little trouble with the Panthers, coasting to a 99-79 victory. Lucas had 23 points and 17 rebounds to lead the Buckeyes. Ben Jinks led the Panthers with 28 points.

The Panthers dropped to 10-14 in Hennon's senior season (1958-59), but the diminutive scoring machine averaged 25.5 points per game to conclude his brilliant career. The 1959-60 campaign was highlighted by the Panthers' shocking 81-80 upset of Purdue in their home season opener. Pitt had trailed by as many as 22 points in the game.

A new wave of talent arrived at Pitt in the early 1960s, poising the Panthers for another run at postseason play. Generalovich, Dave Roman, Dave Sauer, Ben Jinks, Tim Grgurich, Paul Krieger, and Calvin Sheffield formed the nucleus of NCAA and NIT teams in 1962-63 and 1963-64. Generalovich, a bruising 6-5 forward, had been a football and basketball star at Farrell, and Pitt coaches hoped that he would play both sports for the Panthers.

"[Assistant football coach] Steve Petro knew that I really wanted to play basketball, so that's when Coach Timmons first came to see me," said Generalovich. "He was a real gentleman, just a nice man. He was not an in-your-face guy."

As Generalovich remembers, Timmons also knew how to make the most of his contacts throughout the coaching fraternity.

"His friends were people like Lefty Driesell, Press Maravich, and Dudey Moore," said Generalovich, recalling the names of prominent basketball coaches. "Those were the people who used to get scouting reports for us, depending on the opponents we were about to play."

"He [Timmons] was always well-prepared," added Dave Roman. "He had great scouting reports on our opponents. Bob Timmons was a gentle giant. He didn't holler or yell, but everybody respected him, and everybody played for him. He always got the most out of his players."

If Timmons ever did have a problem imparting his message, Generalovich wouldn't hesitate to take matters into his own hands.

"Generalovich was our team leader," said Roman. "He would lead by example, but if someone wasn't hustling, he'd get in their face. He always gave

Continued on page 43

BEANO ON BASKETBALL

Though most sports fans recognize Carroll "Beano" Cook for his (sometimes) irreverent commentaries about college football, from 1956 to 1966 Cook angered a Pitt administrator or two during his tenure as his alma mater's sports information director. He entered Pitt as a sophomore in 1951 after transferring from Brown University. He graduated in 1954, and became the school's SID two years later. One of his greatest peeves was that he felt the university wasn't as committed to basketball as it should have been in those years. Beano offers his Pitt basketball memoirs in this February 2005 narrative.

I never thought I'd live long enough to see the day when Pitt played in a facility as impressive as the Petersen Events Center, and be ranked in the Top 20 every year. It's almost unbelievable.

Tom Hamilton was the Pitt athletic director who hired me in 1956. He had been a captain in the Navy who later coached the football team there, and at Pitt. He also cared more about wrestling than he did

about basketball, but you could say the same thing about the way it was at many schools in the '50s, including Penn State and Notre Dame. It was very discouraging for me because I always felt that if the administration had taken basketball seriously, and recruited hard, they could have had big-time basketball here a lot sooner. The feeling was— by a lot of people—that Pitt just didn't take basketball seriously.

Bob Timmons was the basketball coach in my years as SID. He was a great, great guy, and I'm not just throwing the word 'great' around. He was as fine a gentleman as you'd ever want to meet. He had played football for Pitt, and he was disappointed when Red Dawson was named the football coach in 1952. The administration made him the basketball coach almost as a consolation prize the next year. That's how Pitt did things in those days.

What helped Timmons early on was when he brought in Bob Lazor and John Riser, then what really was big was getting Don Hennon in 1955. Most people have heard the story about how I tried to arrange the picture of Hennon with Dr. Jonas Salk, who had discovered the polio vaccine. When I finally heard back from Dr. Salk, he didn't even know who Don Hennon was. That's nothing. Chet Smith, the popular columnist from *The Pittsburgh Press*? He never saw a Pitt basketball game while I was working there. He wrote that famous line, "If they played the NCAA Tournament in my backyard, I'd pull down the blinds." Harry Keck, the columnist for the *Sun-Telegram*: he never saw a Pitt basketball game. Al Abrams, from *The Post-Gazette*, he might drop by once a year. But those other guys never saw Hennon play.

It was so different then as far as the media. You didn't have 8,000 talk shows on TV and radio. Pitt basketball just wasn't important to many people. It was a bigger deal when Duquesne went to the NIT

than it was when Pitt went to the NCAA's twice in the '50s. The Pittsburgh Pirates and Duquesne basketball were big. Our best crowds for basketball were our

ROD HUNDLEY SHOOTS AGAINST PITT IN A 1950s GAME AT WVU FIELD HOUSE. PITT'S JOHN RISER (12) WAITS FOR THE REBOUND UNDER THE BASKET. *Courtesy of West Virginia University Sports Communications*

games with Duquesne and West Virginia. The Steel Bowl started when the Field House opened in 1951. We played Duquesne in the first round in '53. Duquesne had a great team. They won their first 22 games and ended the season ranked third in the country. Ed Pavlick scored the first basket of the game. Pitt was ahead, 2-0. Our students went wild. Then Dick Ricketts and Si Green went to work for Duquesne. The next time I looked up, we were down something like 19-2.

It was a shame Pitt and Duquesne didn't play each other for so many years. They didn't play at all during the 1940s. I'm not sure anybody really knows for sure why. For Duquesne to be mad at Pitt through the years was ridiculous. I think the

BEANO COOK. *Courtesy of ESPN*

DUQUESNE'S WILLIE SOMERSET (LEFT)
CHECKS PITT'S BEN JINKS DURING A 1961
STEEL BOWL GAME AT THE FIELD HOUSE.
Photo by Vic Kelley—Courtesy of Duquesne University Athletics

Continued from page 42

feelings were mutual, but I always felt it was more Pitt than Duquesne.

On the subject of Duquesne, December 7, 1963 was one of the best days of my life. We beat Penn State by one point in football in the afternoon, and beat Duquesne by two points in basketball that night. It would have been a disaster if we had lost those two games. That was the game where Horze Czarnecki, the groundskeeper, ruled that the Duquesne shot that would have tied the game at the buzzer was no good. Horse kept the clock at the games, and he convinced the officials to disallow the basket. That was for the Steel Bowl champi-

onship. U.S. Steel sponsored the tournament. After the game, Harry Stuhldreher—one of the Notre Dame "Four Horsemen" who worked for U.S. Steel in Pittsburgh—made the presentation of awards. All the Duquesne fans were booing. On the public address microphone, Harry said, "Don't blame me; I didn't make the call!" That's a true story. All the sportswriters loved Horse Czarnecki. They all wrote about him.

The one time I thought we got a raw deal was the NCAA tournament game at Kentucky in '57, Hennon's sophomore year. We only lost by six points, 98-92, but if we had played that game, that night, anywhere else but in the state of Kentucky, we would have won.

The games with West Virginia were interesting, especially at the old Field House in Morgantown. It had a second deck to it, like a balcony in a theater, and the press area was at the front on the overhang. I remember how Mickey Murfari, the Morgantown sportswriter who went to school with Jack Fleming at WVU, would stand up, lean over, and yell at the officials throughout the game. Jerry West played for West Virginia in the late '50s. Pitt never beat them while West was playing there.

Right after that, Timmons brought in a very good recruiting class in

1960. Brian Generalovich, Calvin Sheffield, Dave Sauer, and Paul Krieger were part of that class, and they were the basis of two postseason tournament teams, the NCAAs in '63 and the NIT in '64. After those guys left, things really got bad, and that's when I got out, in '65. I never would have survived the next few years, considering how bad both football and basketball became. I either would have been fired or committed suicide.

I don't know how many years I have left, but I do know one thing: If I could have one wish granted, it would be to see Pitt in the Final Four. I would die a happy man.

The All-Beano Teams
(1956-1966)

Beano's All-Pitt Team
Don Hennon
Brian Generalovich
John Riser
Bob Lazor
Julius Pegues
Calvin Sheffield
(sixth man)

Beano's All-Opponent Team
Jerry West—West Virginia
Rod Hundley—West Virginia
Jerry Lucas—Ohio State
Terry Dischinger—Purdue
Willie Somerset—Duquesne
Mark DuMars—Penn State
(sixth man)

his best effort. He battled under the boards and played great defense. He was a good shooter."

Generalovich also had a bit of Bobby Timmons in him.

"As big a star as Brian was, he was always very kind to me," said Bob Caldwell, who was a freshman when Generalovich was a senior (1963-64). "He would sit down and talk with me. He was a no-nonsense guy in practice. Everybody looked up to him. He set the tone at practice. There was no fooling around."

"You didn't want to make Brian mad," Roman added with caution.

Unfortunately, nobody told that to some of Pitt's opponents. One instance transpired at West Virginia on February 13, 1963, as the Panthers tried to avenge an earlier one-point home loss to the Mountaineers. During the game, Generalovich and West Virginia's Gale Catlett tangled as they fought for a rebound and punches were thrown. Both players were ejected. The story had a happy ending for the Panthers, who won the game, 69-68.

"Gale and I always seemed to draw each other whenever we'd go man-to-man," said Generalovich. "He was a tough, scrappy player."

THE 1962-63 PANTHERS EARNED AN NCAA TOURNAMENT BID. *Courtesy of University of Pittsburgh Athletics*

The 1962-63 season ended with disappointment for Generalovich and the Panthers—who took their 19-5 record to Philadelphia's Palestra for a first-round NCAA tournament tripleheader on March 11. Pitt's floor leader had suffered an ankle injury late in the season and remained doubtful for the NCAA opener.

"I did something I probably wouldn't do today," he remembered. "It was a spur on my left ankle, and

I knew it wasn't to get any better unless I had surgery, but I wanted to play so badly."

Generalovich, who played one year of football (1964) for Pitt while attending its dental school, took his problem to Pitt athletics director Frank Carver, suggesting he could take a shot [painkiller] so he could compete.

"He [Carver] said we'd better talk to my parents about it," Generalovich said. "My dad didn't want

me to do it, but I was practically begging. Finally, they said okay."

The statistics told the story for Generalovich and Pitt that night. The General had zero rebounds against New York University, led by the formidable one-two inside combination of six-foot-five Barry Kramer and six-foot-seven Happy Hairston. Generalovich fouled out with 8:48 remaining. Center Paul Krieger was disqualified as well. Kramer scored 37 points, Hairston added 29, and NYU shot 52 percent from the floor.

"I didn't contribute much in that game," remembers Generalovich. "I went out in the warmups and it felt like there was a piece of wood down where my ankle was. I could hardly feel it. I couldn't get comfortable."

"Kramer was just too much," Timmons told reporters after the game. "He has every move conceivable."

"Until tonight, I thought [Princeton's] Bill Bradley was the best I ever played against, but Kramer is better than I expected," added Pitt's Ben

Jinx, the Panthers' only senior. Pitt had defeated Princeton earlier that season, 71-62, to begin a six-game winning streak.

Pitt made its first NIT appearance at Madison Square Garden the following year (1963-64), losing 82-77 to Drake in what became Timmons's final winning season. Led by a strong senior class, the Panthers finished the regular season 17-7, highlighted by a 69-67 overtime win against Duquesne in the Steel Bowl finals at the Field House. Pitt clinched the win when an apparent game-tying shot by the Dukes' John Cegalis was disallowed when official timekeeper Leo "Horse" Czarnecki—a Pitt groundskeeper—ruled that the shot had been taken after the final buzzer had sounded. The officials deferred to Czarnecki's judgment. Pitt also split a pair of games against Eastern power Syracuse—a team that featured Dave Bing and Jim Boeheim.

The Panthers failed to win more than seven games during any of Timmons's final four seasons, and dissatisfaction with his program was growing. Crowds became sparse. Frank Gustine, who played

ACTION FROM A 1964 PITT-SYRACUSE GAME AT THE FIELD HOUSE—FROM LEFT TO RIGHT: DAVE BING, NORM GOLDSMITH, CAL SHEFFIELD, JIM BOEHEIM, DAVE SAUER, AND BRIAN GENERALOVICH.

Courtesy of University of Pittsburgh Athletics

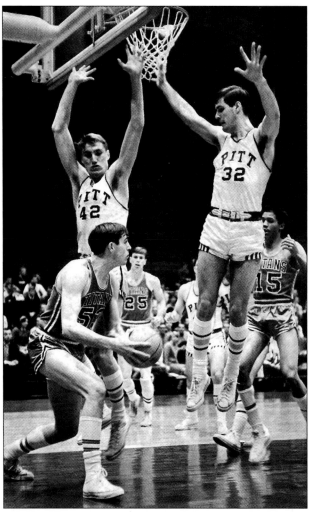

PITT'S CHARLES HUNT (42) AND TONY DELISIO (32) ON DEFENSE AGAINST WESTMINSTER DURING 1968 GAME IN PITTSBURGH.
Courtesy of University of Pittsburgh Athletics

for Timmons's last Pitt team (1967-68), remembers how the school's cheerleaders wouldn't even show up for some of the games. Those students who did attend home games took to throwing fish and eels on the court.

"I hate to say it, but I think he [Timmons] began to lose some of the discipline toward the end," said Bob Caldwell. "The players didn't go by the rules anymore. That was a crazy time in this country. You had the Vietnam War. There was a lot of rebellion going on. Kids were gonna do it their way. They didn't play with the same unity and togetherness. Kids were fooling around in practice. It was sad to see that happening. Under Brian [Generalovich] and

Dave Roman and those guys, it was serious, and we wanted to win. Later, some kids just didn't take it as seriously as others had before."

The Panthers went 25-67 during Timmons's final four seasons. The veteran coach, however, maintained his sense of humor. After Pitt defeated Carnegie Mellon 85-74 in the coach's farewell game on February 28, 1968, Timmons admitted to reporters what he'd said to his team as they trailed the Tartans by six points at halftime.

"In the locker room I told the players, 'I can't tell my grandkids I lost to CMU in my last ballgame,'" said Timmons.

Timmons resigned following a 7-15 season in 1967-68. The *Owl* summarized the mood surrounding Pitt basketball near the end of the coach's 15-year tenure.

"Timmons received sharp criticism that his non-aggressive recruiting policy had caused the dilemma," opined the *Owl*. "His answer was that he recruited as a gentleman and not as a professional like many other schools. Athletic director Frank Carver backed Timmons, saying that many of the team's opponents had lower academic standards and more athletic funds."

For his part, Timmons seemed to know that time had come.

"Coaching was getting to be no fun anymore," he said at the time of his resignation. "The fun sort of goes out of it when you get older, I guess. Get a little older, you lose the enthusiasm, and you don't have the patience."

Thirty-six years later—in an interview just three months before his death on April 29, 2004—Timmons offered more insight into some of the problems he faced as coach of the basketball Panthers. When he spoke of recruiting, he noted that Doc Carlson—his predecessor—would bring high school seniors to tryouts at the Pavilion. That practice had been outlawed by the NCAA by the time Timmons had become head coach.

"I had to fight to get money for scholarships and recruiting," he said. "When the NCAA put that rule in, you had to go out and look for players. I had to recruit kids locally. The administration didn't want to spend any money on basketball."

THE RIDL REVIVAL: 1968-1975

"WITH ALL THE PRESSURE THERE WAS IN COMPETING AT THAT HIGH LEVEL OF BASKETBALL, HE [BUZZ RIDL] NEVER DEVIATED FROM THE TYPE OF PERSON HE WAS. YOU APPRECIATE SOMEBODY WHO CAN DO THAT, AND THAT'S NOT JUST TALKING ABOUT XS AND OS, THAT'S LOOKING AT THE BIG PICTURE."

—Tom Richards

"I FEEL GOOD ABOUT WHAT WE'VE ACCOMPLISHED HERE. NOW, WHEN PEOPLE TALK ABOUT SUCCESSFUL PROGRAMS, THEY'RE APT TO SPEAK OF PITT."

—Buzz Ridl
April 4, 1975

Pitt basketball games were not included in the social agenda of most Pittsburghers during the mid- to late 1960s. Crowds were generally sparse at the Field House, and four consecutive losing seasons were reason enough for coach Bob Timmons to call it quits after the 1967-68 campaign.

Frank Carver's long career as an athletics administrator was ending, but his last major hiring was a good one. Carver enticed 47-year-old Charles "Buzz" Ridl to Pittsburgh following an 11-year term at tiny Westminster College in New Wilmington, Pennsylvania. Ridl, later named to the Helms Hall of Fame for NAIA basketball coaches, had directed the Titans to an overall record of 216-90, and his 1961-62 squad was voted the top small college team in the nation. Ridl had no reservations about leaving the cozy, secure hamlet of New Wilmington for the uncertainty of metro Pittsburgh.

"He felt that he had done as much as he could do at Westminster," said his wife, Betty, who met her future husband while both were undergraduates at

Continued on page 49

BILLY KNIGHT: THE RELUCTANT SUPERSTAR

Folks just can't seem to find enough nice things to say about Billy Knight, the All-America forward who led Pitt to a school-record 22-game winning streak and 25-4 season in 1973-74. Knight may be the most unassuming superstar athlete Pitt has had. Happiness for Billy Knight was a box of popcorn (which he consumed in massive quantities), a soft drink, and a sporting event to watch.

"To outsiders, he was the star, but to us, he wasn't like that," said Kirk Bruce. "My locker was next to his for three years, so I knew what was going on. He was the type of person who made everyone around him feel as if he were the star. There wasn't anybody he wouldn't joke with, from a freshman to the senior who never played."

"He was a great guy, just a super guy to be around," added Kent Scott, who was a senior when Knight joined the varsity as a sophomore in 1971-72.

"Mooney—Knight's nickname— was the superstar, but you didn't feel that among the team," said his coach, Buzz Ridl. "They just accepted Billy as Billy, and everything just flowed around him. And Bill, with his personality, it made it easy, too. He's just a real fine person."

"Billy never flaunted his status," said Mickey Martin, Knight's sidekick at forward.

Although Pitt faced stiff competition for Knight's services during the youngster's senior season at nearby Braddock High School, the six-foot-six Knight was certain that he would attend Pitt. Carl Morris, a former high school teammate, already played for the Panthers.

"I spent a lot of time on the Pitt campus with Carl," Knight explained. "I had gone to Pitt games before I was recruited."

That, plus the fact that Knight, who was one of 11 children, didn't want to go too far from home, sealed the deal for Pitt. The results were smashing, as Knight became the first player in Pitt history to lead the team in both scoring and rebounding in three different seasons (1971-74). The silky smooth forward was the complete package.

"He was advanced beyond his years," observed Scott. "He could do it all. He was our best rebounder, and he was our best inside player. He could do just about anything he wanted to do with the ball."

"He had an uncanny ability to hit the open shot," added Kirk Bruce, who started at shooting guard for the 25-4 team. "He had a good

Courtesy of University of Pittsburgh Archives

scoop move under the basket. He could power it inside. He was one of the best baseline players in college basketball. He wasn't just a scorer; he rebounded the heck out of the ball, and he could pass very well."

"He was like a quiet assassin," said Tom Richards, the point guard in 1973-74. "He didn't make a lot of noise and he didn't want a lot of fanfare, but he just went about his business and put up incredible numbers."

In some ways, Knight was almost a mirror image of his coach, Buzz Ridl.

"He had the same type of personality that Buzz had," Richards agreed. "He just did what needed to be done, and went about his business without calling attention to himself."

"In a lot of ways he was like Coach Ridl," added Kirk Bruce. "He never got rattled. He always kept an even keel. His demeanor allowed him to have the type of consistency he had."

Following his stellar collegiate career, Knight was a first-round pick of the ABA's Indiana Pacers in 1974, while the Los Angeles Lakers took Knight in the second round of the NBA Draft. He signed with Indiana, and played 11 seasons of professional basketball, first in the NBA, later with the NBA. He later went on to a career as an executive with several teams.

By 2005, Knight was general manager of the Atlanta Hawks. Through it all, he remembers his college days fondly.

"I wouldn't trade my experiences at Pitt for the world," he said.

"I'm proud to see who he's become, and what he's done," said Richards. "He's a class act."

BUZZ RIDL (FAR RIGHT) WITH FIVE MEMBERS OF HIS 1972-73 TEAM—FROM LEFT TO RIGHT: KEN WAGONER, MICKEY MARTIN, BILLY KNIGHT, JIM BOLLA, AND BILL SULKOWSKI.

Westminster in the 1930s. "He was ready for a new challenge."

One Pittsburgh newspaper, noting the bleak Pitt basketball situation, called the job "Mission Impossible."

Ridl, however, was not fazed.

"It's like starting all over again, but I'm looking forward to the challenge," he said at the time of his hiring. The players Ridl inherited in the fall of 1968 had suffered through nothing but losing seasons—the coach faced a dearth of talent.

"I knew they [Pitt] weren't very good, and I certainly saw that there was an opportunity to play," said Kent Scott, a six-foot-three sharp-shooting guard from Raytown, Missouri—one of Ridl's first recruits. "The players weren't the caliber of player, quite frankly, that Pitt wanted over the long run."

"He was very straightforward and sincere," added Mike Paul, "but his system was very difficult to learn, and the defenses were complex. Some of the offensive schemes were certainly different."

Ridl went through a period of adjustment himself, weeding through the players to discover who was prepared to commit to his plan. Following a pair of losses at the Hurricane Classic in Miami, he dismissed several veteran players that first season for violations of team rules.

"It was a little tough for him that first year," Scott remembered. "I had a lot of allegiance to Coach Ridl. I bought into his style of play, which was very fundamental, emphasizing good shooting and defense. I waited patiently in the wings."

To assist in the recruitment of better shooters and defenders, Ridl retained Tim Grgurich,

BUZZ RIDL CAME TO PITT FROM WESTMINSTER COLLEGE. *Courtesy of University of Pittsburgh Athletics*

Timmons's lone full-time assistant coach in his final season. From the Pittsburgh ward of Lawrenceville, about a 10-minute drive from the Pitt campus, Grgurich knew the city like the back of his hand, and chiefly he would attempt to attract and recruit many of western Pennsylvania's finest basketball players to Pitt throughout the 1970s.

The Buzz Ridl Era officially began November 30, 1968 with a 74-66 loss to Rutgers at the Field House. A crowd of 1,340 came out to see the new-edition Panthers. Pitt led 32-28 at halftime, but Rutgers moved ahead for good with 12 minutes remaining. It was the first of 20 losses that season—the first time that any Pitt team had lost 20 games.

The 1968-69 Panthers played 16 of their 24 games away from the Field House—including a 120-79 loss at LSU on January 31, 1969. In that game, Tigers' scoring whiz Pete Maravich scored 40 points—four below his season average at the time.

A rare highlight of Ridl's first season occurred January 28, 1969, when the Panthers upset West Virginia 90-87 at the Field House, snapping a nine-game losing streak against their bitter rival. WVU had defeated Pitt in 20 of their 22 previous meetings. Pitt had been averaging just 45 points per game entering the contest, and scored its last 19 points in the game on free throws. Mike Riggle and Tom Withers—a pair of Hoosiers—made 10 of 13 foul shots down the stretch to seal the victory for the Panthers. Pitt won only one game the rest of the season—a 30-point home victory against Carnegie Mellon—finishing with a seven-game losing streak, including a four-point loss to CMU.

"That [losing to CMU] was a fitting end to a losing season," said Billy Downes, one of Pitt's guards that year.

Ridl incorporated some much-needed talent in 1969-70, including Scott, Mike Paul, six-foot-eight sophomore center Paul O'Gorek (the tallest player

THE AMOEBA DEFENSE

When Fran Webster came to rejoin Buzz Ridl as an assistant coach at Pitt for the 1969-70 season, he brought with him a defense called the "Amoeba." He had even written a book about it.

"It was a combination of man-to-man and zone, keyed off certain things in the game, such as where the opposing team brought in the ball from out-of-bounds," said Kirk Bruce.

Tom Richards, Pitt's starting point guard from 1973-73, tried to make a modern-day parallel to describe it.

"In today's terms, it was kind of a match-up zone, with some unusual slides, or shifts, defensively," he said. "That's what really caused part of the confusion. In the early '70s, there weren't many match-up zones. Teams would think we were playing man-to-man, but because of the slides which weren't very conventional, and didn't involve traditional defensive thinking, passing lanes that appeared to be open were actually enticements for the offense to throw a pass, and the defender would step in and cover from an unusual position."

Cleve Edwards, who played for Ridl from 1969-72, and later coached at Pitt and at the University of Nevada-Las Vegas, offered per-haps the most confounding description of this most confounding defensive scheme.

"If people who are watching a basketball game tell you someone's using the Amoeba, they're wrong," said Edwards. "You never knew whether it was a man (to-man), or

FRAN WEBSTER DESIGNED THE AMOEBA DEFENSE. *Courtesy of University of Pittsburgh Athletics*

zone. If you say it's the Amoeba, then it's not."

Whatever it was, Pitt's teams of the 1970s were able to frustrate opposing teams. Like much of coach Buzz Ridl's system, learning its fine points took time.

"My freshman year [1972-73], it took us [Richards and Keith Starr] that whole year to really get it," said Richards. "Fortunately for us, we came into a situation where there were some pretty mature players already in place, but the complexity of the defense's trapping aspects forced the ball to certain situations."

There were a few instances when both Pitt and its opponent seemed baffled by the defense.

"We played down at Davidson [a 90-63 win in 1973-74], and their players were arguing back and forth while they had the ball," remembered Jim Bolla. "'It's a zone,' one would say. 'No, they're in man-to-man,' another guy would yell back."

"There were times when we'd be totally confused out there," admitted Kirk Bruce. "But by the time the opponent figured out what they thought we were doing, we'd work it out ourselves."

Pitt continued using the Amoeba defense when Tim Grgurich replaced Buzz Ridl as coach in 1975. Grgurich eventually took the tricky defense to UNLV when he left Pitt to become an assistant to Jerry Tarkanian following the 1979-80 season.

in Pitt history to that point) and (Robert Morris) junior college point guard Cleveland Edwards. The Panthers stumbled early, losing six of their first seven games, but began to jell in January, winning five of six games, the only loss coming at St. John's, 67-58. Ridl, who had authored a book titled *How to Develop a Deliberate Offense*, couldn't have imagined what was about to happen as Syracuse visited the Field House on February 13, 1970, a rare Friday night home game.

"They [Syracuse] kept trying to press us, but it wasn't working," said Kent Scott.

What an understatement. Pitt scored 61 points in the second half en route to a school single-game scoring record in a 127-108 victory.

"That's an incredible number of points, especially without the three-point basket," said Scott, who led Pitt with 28 points. "It was like a track meet back and forth, and so many of the buckets were lay-ups."

"It certainly was out of character from the way that we normally played," Mike Paul remembered.

With a 9-12 record heading into the final three games of the season, the Panthers needed to win all of them to finish the season at .500. Pitt easily dispatched Westminster and Carnegie Mellon to set up a grand finale at the old West Virginia Field House on March 3, 1970.

Continued on page 54

1973-74: A MAGICAL SEASON

Expectations weren't that great when Pitt's players and coaches convened for the start of basketball practice in the fall of 1973, Buzz Ridl's sixth season. The Panthers had gone 12-14 the year before but returned most of their key players, including senior forwards Billy Knight and Mickey Martin. However, when the Panthers dropped their season opener at West Virginia, 82-78, it was no great surprise.

The second game of the season, at Rutgers, may have provided a hint that something exceptional was about to happen. With the Panthers leading 36-21 late in the first half, the game was halted when a parade of African-American students staged a sit-in demonstration on the court. Pleas from Rutgers officials and star player Phil Sellers were ineffective, and the game never resumed. The officials ruled a forfeit to Pitt, and the Panthers were on their way to a school-record 22 consecutive victories. Several sellout crowds filled Fitzgerald Field House to watch the hottest team in town. The Panthers reached as high as No. 7 in the national polls. Most of the players were from the Pittsburgh area, and Pitt came within one win of reaching the Final Four in March.

"I can always develop a feel for why some teams are better than others," said Ridl during an interview in 1994, a year before his death. "When they're good, it's nice to have shared it with them."

Ridl pointed to the 1972-73 season as evidence that his next team had the ability for greater success.

"We had so many close games that were almost wins the year before," he said. "As you're looking to improve as a team, sometimes it doesn't always show in the record. Instead of losing by big margins, you're coming close."

The 1973-74 Panthers routed many of their opponents, including key wins against Duquesne (82-65), Florida State (82-60), Connecticut (83-63), Duke (62-46), Penn State (83-61), Syracuse (71-56), and George Washington (96-56). Pitt's talented cast of shooters—along with the befuddling Amoeba Defense—created havoc for opposing players and coaches.

"As a group of kids, it took us about a year to understand that defense," said point guard Tom Richards. "We just understood much better exactly what it was we were supposed to do. The thing that made the Amoeba very good was also the thing that made it very hard to learn."

Richards came to Pitt from Moon (Pennsylvania) High School, in the western suburbs of Pittsburgh. His back-court mate, Kirk Bruce, was from the South Hills. Center Jim Bolla was from Crafton. Knight (Braddock) and Martin (Baldwin) rounded out the all-local starting five.

"We had great cama-raderie," said Bruce, who later coached Pitt's women's basketball team. "We had inner-city kids; we had farm kids, but none of that mattered. It was just a very good blend of players and personalities."

Much of the credit for the team's unity went to its trio of coaches— Ridl and assistants Fran Webster and Tim Grgurich.

"They all brought something different to the table," explained Richards. "One of the things I remember most about Buzz was that, when things were chaotic, he had a very calming effect. Gurg, on the other hand, had kind of a Jekyll and Hyde relationship with the players. He was the one who would be in your face, screaming, at practice. On the other hand, I'd jump off a bridge for him. He related to the kids very well. He was a Pittsburgh person. Coach Webster helped Coach Ridl so much with the flow of the game, in terms of making adjustments. He was able to see what needed to be changed. And he was the architect of that defense."

As the wins mounted, the team began attracting the attention of the rest of college basketball. Pitt appeared in the Top 20, and its first postseason tournament bid since 1963-64 was all but assured.

"A lot was made about the streak, but the coaches and players didn't

talk about it that much," said Billy Knight. "We didn't put any undue pressure on ourselves. The coaches just wanted everybody to do the best that they could possibly do, then whatever happened, happened."

"We got some pretty good publicity out of it, but I don't recall that we ever paid a whole lot of attention to it," said Ridl. "The only thing that

PITT'S 1973-74 TEAM WAS HONORED 25 YEARS LATER ON JANUARY 23, 1999. FROM LEFT TO RIGHT: FRAN WEBSTER, MRS. BETTY RIDL, BILLY KNIGHT, AND MICKEY MARTIN. *Courtesy of Sean Brady*

bothered me is that we won 22 straight, but we should have won 24. We lost at West Virginia in the opener in a game we had every reason to win, but we had the streak end when we lost at Penn State [February 23, 1974] at the buzzer. I often think that would have been fun—to have been 24-0!"

Heroes were everywhere that season, especially when they were needed most. In a key road game at Virginia on January 2, Mickey Martin couldn't play because of illness. Willie Kelly, a six-foot-six sophomore walk-on who had come to Pitt on an academic scholarship stepped in to score 12 points in the Panthers' 80-71 win.

"That one [Virginia] game really gave us a lot of confidence, as far as winning away from home," explained Ridl. "From then on, the team just seemed as if it couldn't wait to get out on the floor to play. We weren't as concerned with the other team as much as we were concerned with just playing our game. That's one of the big hurdles, I think, a team has to get through."

Knight had to get through a lingering shoulder injury in the days

MICKEY MARTIN SCORES AGAINST WEST VIRGINIA. *Courtesy of University of Pittsburgh Athletics*

Continued from page 52

leading up to a crucial Eastern showdown with Syracuse on February 9 at Fitzgerald Field House. He responded with a 24-point, 19-rebound performance in the Panthers' 15-point victory—a game covered by Curry Kirkpatrick of *Sports Illustrated*.

The winning streak came to a dramatic halt two weeks later at State College, where Penn State nipped the Panthers, 66-64, on a last-second top-of-the-key jumper by Ron Brown. Pitt had a chance to win the game seconds earlier, but Knight was called for traveling when the score was tied at 64.

"It was a questionable call, but that's the way it goes," said Knight. "The referees do a great job. I'm sure all the Penn State people thought it was the right call. Just as the Pitt people thought it was the wrong call. But I don't feel that we were cheated out of anything that day."

As it turned out, the 22-game winning streak was followed by a two-game losing streak. Pitt's post-Penn State malaise continued when South Carolina drubbed the Panthers, 67-50, four nights later in Columbia. The Panthers righted themselves four days later in the season finale, avenging the season-opening loss to West Virginia with an 83-78 win against the Mountaineers in the final home appearance for seniors Knight and Martin.

The Panthers received an at-large bid to what was then the 32-team NCAA Tournament, and were assigned to meet St. Joseph's in a first-round game at the WVU Coliseum in Morgantown, where Pitt had never won a game. The Panthers defeated the Hawks, 54-42, setting up a trip to Raleigh, North Carolina for the Sweet 16. Knight, who had been in a shooting slump late in the season, broke out for 34 points to lead Pitt to an 81-78 win against Furman, setting up an East Regional final against the host team, North Carolina State.

"That was a tough situation, having to play North Carolina State right there on their home court," said Ridl. "That's not done anymore. The NCAA would not permit that."

"We knew [playing at N.C. State] was a tough proposition," said Knight. "They had David Thompson and [7-4] Tommy Burleson on that team. Our biggest guy was [6-8] Jim Bolla, and he banged and battled with Burleson and used as much of his physical presence as he could, but Burleson was the one who really hurt us, because of his superior height."

The Panthers hung with the Wolfpack during the first half. Then, in a most unexpected way, the momentum swung entirely in favor of the home team. Thompson, N.C. State's high-flying small forward, became tangled with Pitt's Lew Hill when leaping for a rebound. Thompson crashed to the floor, hitting his forehead with a sickening thud. He lay motionless. He was carried from the floor.

"We felt we had a real shot at them until that point," said Richards. "We had been surprising people all year; it would have fit the script perfectly for us to have won that game. But the place just went crazy when he came back to the bench in the second half, and we got kind of a strange feeling."

After trailing 47-41 at halftime, the Panthers were blitzed after intermission, and Pitt's magical season ended within one game of the Final Four—N.C. State 100, Pitt 72.

"I'm sure if we played them again, we would have played them a little differently," said Ridl. "You learn a little bit about a team after you play them for the first time."

Pitt's 25-4 season played out against a much different college basketball cultural backdrop. During the regular season, only one game—South Carolina—was televised. ESPN and the Big East Conference were still a few years away, and there weren't nearly as many talk shows and media outlets to spread the word about what those Panthers accomplished.

"The only regret I have in the difference of eras is that, today, it's so easy to catch things on TV or tape," said Richards. "I would love to have that season on tape, if only because it's something I could share with my kids. But people still come up to me and tell me how well they remember that season."

THE 1973-74 PANTHERS WON A SCHOOL-RECORD 22 CONSECUTIVE GAMES. *Courtesy of University of Pittsburgh Athletics*

SIGNIFICANT WINS: THE RIDL YEARS

1/28/69   PITT 90, WEST VIRGINIA 87
- Pitt had lost nine straight basketball games to the Mountaineers.

2/13/70   PITT 127, SYRACUSE 108
- Panthers establish school record for most points in a game.

3/3/70   PITT 92, AT WEST VIRGINIA 87
- Kent Scott's 32 points wipe out 19-point deficit in last game ever at WVU Field House.

12/29/70   PITT 70, DUQUESNE 58
(Steel Bowl)
- Upset victory in first round snaps Duquesne's 20-game winning streak at Civic Arena.

2/11/72   PITT 109, SYRACUSE 99
- Billy Knight scores 33 points as Pitt tops century mark against Syracuse again.

12/7/73   PITT 82, DUQUESNE 65
(Steel Bowl)
- Knight hits for 32 points as Panthers are on their way to a 25-4 season.

2/9/74   PITT 71, SYRACUSE 56
- Capacity crowd, *Sports Illustrated* at Field House for Pitt's 19th straight win.

12/18/74   PITT 65, MARQUETTE 58
- Pitt's lone win against a ranked opponent during Buzz Ridl's tenure.

1/13/75   PITT 84, NOTRE DAME 77 (OT)
- One day after Steelers' first Super Bowl win, Panthers rally from 15 down in second half.

2/15/75   PITT 71, VIRGINIA 70
- Mel Bennett's 22 points and 15 rebounds set up Keith Starr's winning basket in final seconds.

"That's probably the most memorable game—personally—for me, because it was the last game of my sophomore year, and we were fighting to turn our program around," said Scott. "It also was the last basketball game ever played at West Virginia Field House. They had balloons in the rafters and were planning a post-game celebration."

The Panthers were contributing to the Mountaineers' celebration plans, falling behind by 19 points in the first half before finally turning the tables on their hosts.

"Everything just started to click," said Scott. "You hear talk in sports about being in a zone? Well, I was."

Scott scored 23 of his game-high 32 points in the second half, and Pitt shocked the Mountaineers, 92-87.

The WVU postgame agenda was abandoned.

Freshmen weren't eligible for varsity competition until 1972, but Pitt's recruiting class of 1970 included four local players who would play important roles in a special season with the Panthers several years later. Billy Knight (Braddock), Mickey Martin (Baldwin), Jim Bolla (Canevin), and Ken Wagoner (Beaver Falls) were freshmen on campus when the new decade began, and prospects were brighter for Ridl as he began his third season.

The 1970-71 Panthers won three of their first four games, setting the stage for a Steel Bowl meeting with the Duquesne Dukes—the more popular college basketball team in Pittsburgh. Duquesne had won 20 straight games at the Civic Arena, but Pitt pulled off one of its most significant upsets in years, defeating the heavily favored Dukes, 70-58.

"We went into that game with the hope of playing UCLA the next night," said Duquesne's Jarrett Durham in a 2005 interview. "At that time, UCLA was the Duke of today. Losing to Pitt was embarrassing. Duquesne was *the* college basketball team in Pittsburgh then, and we weren't supposed to lose to Pitt."

"This was my biggest win at Pitt," Ridl told reporters afterward.

Ed "Buzzy" Harrison—a six-foot-four sophomore swingman from Laurel Highlands (Pennsylvania) High School—led the Panthers with 25 points. Unfortunately, the Steel Bowl would be the zenith of Harrison's collegiate career. He became an academic casualty after that season, and never played another game for Pitt.

"Buzzy was a great player," said Mike Paul. "One season and that was it. What an athlete. He was very similar to [future Pitt star] Jaron Brown in size and strength—a very heads-up player."

A Civic Arena sporting event record crowd of 13,535 came the next night to see how far Ridl's

JIM BOLLA CONTESTS A SHOT BY WEST VIRGINIA'S STAN BOSKOVICH DURING A 1974 GAME. LEW HILL (23) IS UNDER THE BASKET. *Courtesy of West Virginia University Sports Communications*

revival had come. Pitt's opponent in the Steel Bowl championship game was UCLA—the defending national champion. Some of Pitt's players took advantage of an opportunity to watch the Bruins and their legendary coach, John Wooden, during a pre-tournament practice at the Pitt Field House the day before Pitt played Duquesne.

"We [Pitt players] hung around to watch them practice, which was probably a mistake," said Kent Scott. "We were in awe."

Awestruck or not, the Panthers found themselves tied with the Bruins, 40-40, with 15:35 to play.

That's when the Bruins decided to flex their muscles.

"They [UCLA] were shooting a free throw, and I was just observing all this," said Scott. "One of them, Sidney Wicks or Curtis Rowe, said across the lane, 'Uh, it's time to get going here.' They put us away after that."

The all-senior front line of Wicks, Rowe, and center Steve Patterson was too much for the Panthers—UCLA won, 77-64. Wicks and Rowe scored 26 points each, but the performance represented how far Pitt's rebuilding program had come in just over two seasons.

Pitt's chances for a 1971 postseason bid were extinguished when the Panthers dropped their final three games—all road contests—to Penn State, West Virginia and Georgia Tech. However, the final 14-10 record was the program's first winning season since 1963-64.

With four starters returning, plus the additions of sophomores Billy Knight and Mickey Martin, optimism abounded as the 1971-72 season approached. Even the coach was talking big.

"We're not hiding any longer," said Buzz Ridl. "We're going after it. We hope to be in a postseason tournament."

Following a road win at Gettysburg to open the season, a Field House record crowd of 5,522 came to watch Ridl's fourth Pitt team host coach Dean Smith's North Carolina Tar Heels. UNC had a distinct western Pennsylvania flavor that season; three of its starters—Dennis Wuycik (Ambridge), George Karl (Penn Hills), and Steve Previs (Bethel Park)—had played their high school basketball for Western Pennsylvania Interscholastic Athletic League (WPIAL) high schools.

Yet, the brightest name on the Field House marquee was Pitt's Billy Knight—who had been one of the nation's most prized recruits two years earlier. Knight did not start, but entered the game with seven minutes gone. Pitt held its ground against the mighty Tar Heels, but ultimately succumbed 90-75. Knight finished with 12 points. Scott, who was so impressed by UCLA the year before, was even more impressed by what the Tar Heels had to offer.

"They had Bobby Jones and Bob McAdoo," Scott recalled. "I thought to myself, 'This is the most talented bunch of players I have ever seen together on one floor.'"

There was no postseason invitation for Pitt in 1971-72. The Panthers were wildly inconsistent, dropping four in a row after winning four straight in January. Knight had an excellent sophomore season, averaging 21 points per game, including a season-high 33 in a 109-99 win against Syracuse, but Pitt's 12-12 record overall was a step back for Ridl's program.

Three starters were gone—Scott, Paul, and O'Gorek—but Billy Knight was back for his junior season in 1972-73. Two talented freshmen—point guard Tom Richards and guard-forward Keith Starr—were eligible for varsity play, and both made contributions by season's end. Richards, who once scored 63 points in a game for Moon (Pennsylvania) High School, became a three-year starter; while Starr, who eventually grew to six foot seven, was versatile to play at the point or work inside.

Pitt alternated wins and losses through its first six games that season, including an embarrassing 63-54 home loss to Wittenberg. The Panthers took a 3-3 record to Los Angeles for games against

UCLA and Pepperdine on back-to-back nights. UCLA was the first stop, but Buzz Ridl and Billy Knight nearly missed the game altogether.

"I got lost," said Pitt radio broadcaster Bill Hillgrove, whose rental car included Buzz and Betty Ridl, Knight, and sports information director Dean Billick. "I made a wrong turn and couldn't find Pauley Pavilion. We got there 22 minutes before tip-off."

The easy-going Knight refused to be flustered. He made 17 of 32 shots and scored 37 points—then a new Pauley Pavilion record for points by an oppos-

CARL MORRIS (22) BATTLES NORTH CAROLINA'S BOBBY JONES IN A 1971 GAME AT PITT. DENNIS WUYCIK (44) AND BOB McADOO (35) OBSERVE.
Courtesy of University of Pittsburgh Athletics

PITT DEFEATED WEST VIRGINIA IN THE LAST GAME PLAYED AT THE OLD WVU FIELD HOUSE ON MARCH 3, 1970. *Courtesy of West Virginia University Sports Communications*

finished the season ranked (No. 16) by a national wire service poll for the first time in school history reached the NCAA tourney Elite Eight.

ing player. Unsurprisingly, the Bruins won the game, 89-73—their 50th consecutive victory en route to 88 in a row.

Although Knight reached his offensive peak in 1972-73 (23.1 points per game), Pitt fans were grumbling after the two consecutive 12-win seasons, but Ridl refused to be rattled. Pitt, arguably, was on the verge of its most remarkable basketball season ever. The 1973-74 Panthers won a school-record 22 consecutive games en route to a 25-4 record. Pitt

Pitt returned three starters in 1974-75—which turned out to be Ridl's final season. Tom Richards and Kirk Bruce provided a strong backcourt, while rugged six-foot-eight senior Jim Bolla provided plenty of inside muscle. Two impressive freshmen were poised to make an immediate impact as well. Melvin Bennett was an emotional six-foot-seven center from Pittsburgh's Peabody High School, while Larry Harris was a smooth six-foot-six small forward from Lorain, Ohio with a great shooting

touch. Both would be important factors in Pitt's first season without Billy Knight and Mickey Martin.

"I've always said those two guys—Harris and Bennett—are the two best true freshman basketball players I've ever seen at Pitt," said Kirk Bruce, who was a senior that year. "Melvin had an energy level that was unbelievable. And Larry—I remember the first day of practice—I said to myself, 'This guy can really shoot the ball. Holy heck!' Most freshmen, they struggle at times, but those guys never did. They were consistent."

Although the freshmen didn't struggle, the 1974-75 Panthers did, especially early. Pitt lost three of its first four games, including a bitter 100-94 loss to Duquesne in the opening round of the Steel Bowl—a game in which Bennett had 17 points and 19 rebounds. Pitt took an incredible 101 shots in the contest. Penn State upset a despondent Pitt team in the consolation round the following night, leaving the Panthers at 1-4. There was no time to panic; the coach wouldn't allow it.

"In highly stressful situations, he was always the model of calm," said Tom Richards. "There was just a peacefulness about him, even in chaotic situations, and I think that transferred to the players. Buzz taught people that you needed to maintain your poise in the face of chaos."

Pitt rebounded to defeat St. Joseph's at home, setting up a much-anticipated battle at Fitzgerald Field House with No. 7-ranked Marquette, which had lost the NCAA title game to North Carolina State the year before. Keith Starr registered a rare triple-double—13 points, 11 rebounds, 11 assists—and Bolla made seven of eight free throws down the stretch to clinch Pitt's 65-58 upset.

"It was Jim's finest hour," Ridl told reporters.

Al McGuire, a loser in what turned out to be his only appearance as a head coach in Pittsburgh, offered Pitt praise.

"They [Pitt] were stronger than us, more physical," he said.

The Panthers regressed in late December, losing three straight, including a 72-66 loss to Jim Valvano-coached Bucknell on the road. Two nights later, Digger Phelps brought his Notre Dame

MELVIN BENNETT LEFT PITT FOR THE PROS AFTER HIS FRESHMAN SEASON (1974-75).
Courtesy of University of Pittsburgh Athletics

Fighting Irish to meet Pitt at the Civic Arena. Leading by as many as 15 points, the Irish appeared to be in control in the second half, but Pitt rallied to force the game into overtime—where the Panthers prevailed, 84-77.

"Even when we were up by 15 points, I didn't like the tempo of the game," said Phelps after the game. "I turned to my assistant [coach], and said I didn't like it."

Keith Starr led Pitt with 22 points and 10 assists. Larry Harris added 15 points, and Jim Bolla contributed eight points and six rebounds.

Such heroics defined the Panthers' play at the Field House toward the end of Ridl's tenure. Pitt was undefeated (25-0) at Fitzgerald during the 1973-74 and 1974-75 seasons.

Pitt won 10 of 11 games to finish the regular season and captured the No. 1 seed for the ECAC Southern Division playoffs that were scheduled for the WVU Coliseum. Unfortunately, the Panthers' opening-round opponent in the four-team tournament—Georgetown and George Washington were the other teams—was No. 4 seed West Virginia.

Politics aside, Pitt headed to Morgantown looking to win two games and receive an automatic return bid to the NCAAs. The Panthers fell far behind in the second half, then rallied, but ultimately came up short—losing a heartbreaking 75-73 decision to the Mountaineers, despite Mel Bennett's 22 points and 21 rebounds.

The Panthers focused their frustration on George Washington in the following night's consolation game, winning 89-64. To the delight of the Pitt players and fans who waited to watch WVU play Georgetown for the NCAA bid, Georgetown defeated the Mountaineers on a last-second shot, 62-61. The dramatic ending finished West Virginia's season, while the Panthers received a berth in the NIT.

In the opening round of the 1975 NIT, Pitt defeated Southern Illinois 70-65 to set up a second-round match-up with Providence, which was coached by future Big East Conference Commissioner Dave Gavitt. The Friars won easily, 101-80—ending Pitt's season at 18-11. Slightly more than two weeks later, Ridl told an assembly of reporters in his office's reception area that he was retiring.

"Coaching limits you," he said, "and there are some things my wife and I would like to do."

Buzz and Betty Ridl had brought a homey, folksy, family feel to Pitt's basketball program. There was a Christmas tree in the team's locker room. The coach's wife was a visible figure on the Panthers' basketball scene—even to the point of serious work.

"Buzz always included me in everything," Betty Ridl explained in a 2005 interview. "I went along when he scouted games, and he'd have me chart shots, rebounds, or whatever."

On bus trips, Mrs. Ridl's homemade cookies were a favorite snack of the traveling parties. She also knitted bow ties for the players and staff members. She has nothing but fond memories of her husband—who died in April 1995.

"He [Buzz Ridl] was just a very selfless person," she said. "He was always a very thoughtful person. It was never about himself. He thought about the other guy."

The young men who played for Ridl remember him in similar fashion.

"He prided himself on taking players he could coach," said Kirk Bruce. "There were no bad guys on our teams, and that didn't happen just by luck. He wanted to have players he knew would be able to learn what he wanted and needed to teach them."

Ridl's grandfather-like aura belied a hidden motivation.

"People wonder how he would get his point across because he didn't yell much," observed Kenny Wagoner, a reserve guard on the 1974 team. "But he had his way of letting you know where you stood. You did things his way, or you didn't do them. It was that simple."

"I felt very blessed that I had a chance to play for him," said Tom Richards. "He was the consummate gentleman. At the same time, I don't think people realized how intense a competitor he was. As I get older, my opportunity to have played for Buzz becomes more special. You appreciate what a fine person he was."

"He wasn't a yeller or a screamer, as everybody knows," added Bruce. "He didn't get mad very often. It was a rarity when he did, but it got your attention. He was a tough, tough man. He was in great shape. He never appeared to be tired. He was always ready, always alert."

SETBACKS, RESURGENCE, AND RESIGNATION: 1975–1980

"**THEY LOOK LIKE YESHIVA'S JUNIOR VARSITY. ONE OR TWO HAVE THE BODY AND CARRIAGE OF ATHLETES. THE REST ARE BUG SIZE. MAJOR COLLEGE BASKETBALL PLAYERS? SOME DON'T EVEN RESEMBLE MAJOR COLLEGE STUDENTS.**"

—Jeff Samuels, *The Pittsburgh Press*, describing Tim Grgurich's first (1975-76) Pitt basketball team

"**THE CREDIT GOES TO THE PLAYERS, NOT TO THE COACHES. WE JUST SIT THERE AND WATCH THEM PLAY.**"

—Tim Grgurich, after Pitt upset No. 3 Duke on February 10, 1979 at Cameron Indoor Stadium

In the 1970s, Jackie Sherrill and Tim Grgurich were each 33 when they became the head coaches of Pitt's football and basketball teams, respectively. Unlike Sherrill, who had grown up in Oklahoma and Mississippi before going off to play college football for Bear Bryant at Alabama, Grgurich had never strayed far from his Pittsburgh roots. In a sense, he had been preparing to become Pitt's basketball coach since the day he arrived on campus as a freshman in 1960. After paying his dues as an assistant coach, he ascended to the job in April 1975, replacing the retired Buzz Ridl—who had been his boss. There was no search for a replace-

ment—Grgurich was named Pitt's new coach the same day that Ridl announced he was leaving.

"I had mixed emotions," said Tom Richards, who had one year of eligibility remaining when Grgurich took control of the program. "I really loved playing for Buzz, but I was excited for 'Gurg' because I thought he had earned it."

Richards had up-close knowledge and perspective. A shooting guard in high school, Ridl and Grgurich envisioned the six-foot sharp-shooter as a point guard in college. Grgurich and Cleve Edwards—a sidekick of sorts to Grgurich throughout his career—went to work with the fledgling

Continued on page 63

SAM "BAM" CLANCY

Sam Clancy was one of the most important basketball recruits in school history. When the six-foot-six, 240-pound Clancy picked Pitt over North Carolina State in the spring of 1977, he was coming to a reeling program. The Panthers had endured back-to-back losing seasons, including the 6-21 debacle of 1976-77.

"The school I'm going to doesn't expect to lose," Clancy told *The Pittsburgh Post-Gazette* shortly before announcing his college choice.

Clancy made Pitt coach Tim Grgurich's day when the news became official, and he was true to his word: Pitt posted four straight solid winning seasons during his career, and he left the program as the only player to reach a minimum of 1,000 in both points (1,671) and rebounds (1,342).

"He [Clancy] was a guy who took the program to another level," said Larry Harris, who was a senior (1977-78) during Clancy's freshman season. "He helped get the Pitt basketball program headed in the right direction. Pitt went from being an okay team to a pretty damned good one."

A starter at power forward to begin his career, Clancy soon served notice that a new era of Panthers basketball was dawning. Point guard Pete Strickland recalled an incident from one of Clancy's earliest games as a freshman.

"I got clocked on a highball screen," said Strickland. "Next thing you know, Sam is between me and the guy who hit me. Sam ran straight up from the low post, and he was there. I remember thinking to myself, 'Oh boy, things are going to be different around here. This is great!' I knew we weren't going to be pushed around anymore, because my sophomore year—when we were 6-21—we had been."

A hulking specimen who never lifted weights before coming to college, Clancy became one of the program's most dominating inside pres-

ences. He often outrebounded players who were much taller, using his unique blend of strength, power, quickness, and jumping ability. To Clancy's way of thinking, it was no big deal:

"If someone is good at getting position and boxing out, he can be six feet tall and be a good rebounder," he said. "Getting good position comes from experience and learning the science of rebounding. For

Courtesy of University of Pittsburgh Athletics

instance, 90 percent of your bank shots will come off the front of the rim. If a shot comes from the left side of the basket, the majority of rebounds will comes off the right side and vice versa."

"He was a guy who understood the game very well," said former Duke star Jim Spanarkel, who played against Clancy once in college. "He always reminded me a little of Paul Silas, who played for the [Boston] Celtics. He knew how to use his body and position himself to take advantage of what he had, which was a lot of talent."

Clancy averaged double figures in rebounds in each of his four seasons, and grabbed 20 in a victory against Duquesne at Fitzgerald Field House during his freshman season.

"He was one of the greatest rebounders I've ever seen or played with," explained Strickland. "He was a tremendous college basketball player, and he was as good a teammate—and I've had great teammates—as I've ever been around. He was totally devoted to the team concept, and to you as a teammate."

"He was such a strong person, both physically and mentally," said teammate Ed Scheuermann, the Panthers' six-foot-11 center whose injury-plagued career forced Clancy to play center for much of his career. "He was a great leader."

"He was even a better person than he was a player," said Cleve Edwards who, like Clancy, had been a basketball standout at Pittsburgh's Fifth Avenue High School, and was an assistant coach under Grgurich. "He enhanced the ability of the players around him. Even though he was the star, you could never tell that. He was outspoken, but he also led by example."

While new coach Roy Chipman was being introduced as Pitt's new coach following Grgurich's surprise resignation in 1980, Clancy was a member—albeit for a brief time only—of Pitt's powerhouse football team. He went out for spring practice in 1980, where he was deployed as a defensive end, but gave it up at the conclusion of spring drills to concentrate on basketball.

Clancy's senior season was a special one. After being shifted to power forward, he was a first-team All-Eastern Eight selection and led the Panthers to the league's tournament championship by defeating Duquesne 64-60 at the Civic Arena in the title game. Following an NCAA first-round win against Idaho, Clancy's remarkable collegiate basketball career ended with a second-round loss to Dean Smith's North Carolina Tar Heels.

Ironically, Clancy's professional career in sports was in football. He had been a standout at Fifth Avenue, where he admits he did it "for fun, because some of my friends were

Continued from page 62

on the team." Clancy played 11 seasons of professional football and went on to become an assistant coach in the NFL. But it's his basketball legend—on and off the court—that most Pitt people remember.

"He was a good person," said Edwards. "If he liked you, there was nothing he wouldn't do for you. Sam never alienated his teammates; he blended right in."

"Sam was more impressive as a person than he was as a player," said teammate Terry Knight. "He could remember your mother's name and how she was sick ten years ago, and that impressed me more than the things he could do on a basketball court. And he could do some amazing things on a basketball court."

TIM GRGURICH WAS ALWAYS ANIMATED ON THE SIDELINE. *Courtesy of University of Pittsburgh Athletics*

point guard during the summer months before classes began.

"They spent hours and hours with me before my freshman year, just to get me ready to make the transition from shooting guard to point guard," Richards recalled. "I don't know how the NCAA would have felt about that today. The Field House, the outdoor courts at Upper St. Clair, Carnegie Mellon, camps I traveled to…wherever there was a

hoop. Cleve's job was to beat the hell out of me. Gurg's job was to teach me how to be a point guard. Through brute force, they turned me into a point guard."

Richards, who started his first collegiate game at point guard on December 22, 1972 at UCLA, had a classic love-hate relationship with his coach and mentor.

LARRY HARRIS MADE MORE BASKETS (803) THAN ANY PLAYER IN PITT'S FIRST 100 YEARS OF BASKETBALL. *Courtesy of University of Pittsburgh Athletics*

"He [Grgurich] used to call me things I can't repeat," said Richards. "My dad would come to practice and sit in the stands. He used to say to me, 'How can you take it when he's calling you those names?' I said, 'Dad, Gurg's my guy. I know he's yelling at me because he wants me to be a better player, and I know he'd do anything for me.' And that was true."

That was the essence of Pitt basketball and its young coach throughout the second half of the '70s. Grgurich's teams never had much height, weren't blessed with more than one or two good shooters, and were rarely deep, but they compensated by playing tenacious defense, scrapping and clawing, diving for loose balls, as their coach had done during his playing career as a Panther. His players, for the most part, listened to him.

"He [Grgurich] was absolutely devoted to the game and to his players," said Pete Strickland, a point guard from Washington D.C.'s DeMatha Catholic who was one of Grgurich's first recruits in 1975. "He really lived and breathed Pitt basketball. I never once questioned whether he was wholly and completely behind me. He was a great teacher of the game. I came from a great teacher in Morgan Wooten [at DeMatha], but was fortunate to land next to another."

There was plenty of optimism heading into Grgurich's rookie season. He inherited a program that had posted back-to-back winning records and had gone to the NCAA (1973-74) and NIT (1974-75). From Ridl's last team, Grgurich could look forward to having his point guard, Richards, back for his senior season. The team's other top returning starter would be another senior, six-foot-seven Keith Starr, easily the most versatile player on the roster. At center, there was six-foot-seven Melvin Bennett, who had been a major force as a true freshman. One of Grgurich's incoming recruits was six-foot-11 center Kelvin Smith, who—along with teammate and fellow Pitt recruit Wayne Williams—had led Pittsburgh's Schenley High School to the Pennsylvania state championship the year before. A third straight postseason tournament appearance appeared well within the program's gasp, but it wasn't to be.

"It was a comedy of errors," Richards recalled in a 2005 interview.

Shortly after Grgurich accepted the job, Bennett announced that he was turning pro. He was taken in the first round by the ABA's Virginia Squires. In Pitt's only exhibition game before Grgurich's first season, Starr suffered a serious knee injury, and played only a few minutes in a game against Notre Dame. Then, two weeks before the season opener, Richards broke his right (shooting) wrist and was ineffective for most of the season. Years later, Richards admitted he should have redshirted, but

KEITH STARR (LEFT) AND TOM RICHARDS BOTH HAD SIGNIFICANT INJURIES AS SENIORS (1975-76).
Courtesy of University of Pittsburgh Athletics

didn't so out of loyalty to Grgurich. The final blow came shortly before Pitt's first game, when Smith was declared academically ineligible.

Against that backdrop, Grgurich and the remaining players attacked the 27-game schedule, and that's why Jeff Samuels's demeaning description must be taken in context. The words were written the day after Pitt's one-point loss to Duquesne in the first round of the Steel Bowl at Civic Arena. It was Pitt's third game of the season, and the largely partisan Duquesne crowd already smelled blood and eagerly awaited an opportunity to embarrass Pitt.

"The natural tendency when the Pitt Panthers take the floor is to snicker, and that's probably what a lot of fans were doing when Pitt's band of shrimps came out to battle the giants from Duquesne," Samuels also wrote.

Duquesne, led by its outstanding junior guard, Norm Nixon, walked off the floor a 75-74 winner only after Pitt's Willie Kelly missed a medium-range jumper at the buzzer that would have given Pitt the win.

"I think we really fooled 'em," Grgurich told reporters afterward. "I don't think they [Duquesne] thought we were that good."

And despite all the setbacks, Grgurich's first team surprised many people in 1975-76. Pitt defeated Syracuse, West Virginia, Penn—coached by Chuck Daly—and Penn State (twice). The Panthers were competitive throughout the season, losing only one game by more than 20 points. One important early victory came on December 13, 1975, when Richards—bad wrist and all—threw in a 40-foot desperation shot from the wing to extend Pitt's Field House winning streak to 27 games in a 72-71 defeat of Ohio University.

"I thought, that first year, Gurg got everything he possibly could out of that team," said Larry Harris, who was the team's leading scorer as a sophomore that season.

"That may be as good a coaching job as I've ever been around," said Strickland. "I've never been around a team that worked any harder than that team. He [Grgurich] just wouldn't let us quit. It became like a Marine Corps experience. That was a special team in my career, just because of the way we worked and the way we bonded."

"There were so many things that went wrong that year, you had to really wonder, 'Was this a fair

FEBRUARY 10, 1979

Even the team's most prominent player was surprised by the Panthers' stunning 71-69 victory against Duke before a disbelieving crowd of 8,564 at rowdy Cameron Indoor Stadium on February 10, 1979.

"We just wanted to give them a good game," Sam Clancy admitted.

Instead, Clancy and the rest of the Panthers dealt Duke its only home loss of the season. The Blue Devils were ranked No. 1 in the nation by the preseason Associated Press Poll but they were 16-3 and ranked third when Pitt traveled to Durham for a rare February non-conference game.

"That was a great win," said Clancy. "That was the best win we had in my four years. The most disappointing thing was that the game wasn't on TV."

Coach Tim Grgurich used only six players that night: Clancy, Sammie Ellis, Terry Knight, Carlton Neverson, Wayne Williams, and Pete Strickland. The Panthers were at a severe height disadvantage—Duke's lineup boasted three All-Americans in six-foot-11 Mike Gminski, six-foot-eight Gene Banks, and six-foot-seven Jim Spanarkel. Pitt, with the six-foot-seven Ellis being the tallest starter, countered with quickness and tenacious defense to upset the Blue Devils' rhythm.

The Panthers outscored Duke 10-2 in the final minutes of the first half to take a 37-32 lead at intermission. The second half was a seesaw affair, and with 3:05 remaining and the score tied at 69, Duke coach Bill Foster ordered his team to stall. With no shot clock in college basketball then, Grgurich instructed his team to sit back in a zone defense.

"They were doing us a favor by holding the ball," said Clancy.

With under a minute to play, Grgurich switched the Panthers to man-to-man. With about 10 seconds left, Clancy intercepted a pass from Bob Bender that was intended for a back-cutting Spanarkel.

Clancy had one thought in mind: "I wasn't much for dribbling, but I went the length of the floor. I wanted that basket bad."

With Gminski in hot pursuit, Clancy stopped and missed a short jumper. Gminiski, however, mistimed his jump, and Clancy was able to get the offensive rebound and subsequent lay-up with two ticks left on the clock. With Pitt leading 71-69, Foster called timeout.

"In our huddle, we were all jumping around on tiptoes, that's how excited we were to have the lead," said Strickland. "Gurg told us exactly what Duke would do. He drew it. He said, 'They'll get the ball to Gminski right here. He'll take the shot. Square up and get your hands up.' So we went out there, still all excited, running around. They threw it in to Gminski, and nobody was near him! He took one dribble and took a long shot, but missed. I got the rebound. There were about 19 people in our travel party, and we were all screaming. That place [Cameron] was absolutely silent. They were in shock."

"The only feeling you can have better than this is winning the NCAA championship," Clancy said afterward

Clancy finished the game with 23 points and 11 rebounds. Ellis scored 17 points, and Terry Knight added 13. Williams had six steals to go with

his 10 points, and he and Strickland masterfully directed Pitt's offense against Duke's pressure.

"The credit goes to the players, not to the coaches," said Grgurich, after his team's seventh consecutive victory. "We just sit there and watch them play."

In Pittsburgh to broadcast the 2005 Pitt-Connecticut game at the Petersen Events Center, CBS commentator Jim Spanarkel remembered Clancy's performance that night.

"He came in and kicked our butts on the boards," said Spanarkel. "We [Duke players] knew who he was, knew he was a great college player, but we didn't think he could come down to Cameron and do what he did against us that night."

The victory had added significance for Clancy, who had developed a special friendship with Gene Banks. Two years earlier, at the 1977 Roundball Classic in Pittsburgh, Clancy and the Philadelphia-product Banks had teamed to lift the Pennsylvania All-Stars to a stirring 98-92 victory against Kelly Tripucka, Albert King, and the rest of the United States All-Stars before a record crowd of 16,649 at the Civic Arena. Banks contributed 20 points and 10 rebounds, and was voted the game's MVP. Upon being presented his trophy after the game, he took the public address microphone and announced he was giving the trophy to Clancy, who had 14 points and 12 rebounds.

---

assessment of Gurg's first year as a head coach?'" Richards asked.

A big part of Pitt's 12 victories that year was Harris, who went from being a complementary role player as a freshman to Pitt's go-to guy as a sophomore. He averaged 22 points per game, including

39 against Syracuse and 34 in a road loss to Virginia. Harris understood and accepted his additional burden.

"That was just the way it was for me," he explained. "There wasn't anybody with enough

NATHAN "SONNY" LEWIS TRANSFERRED TO POINT PARK COLLEGE DURING HIS SOPHOMORE SEASON WITH THE PANTHERS.
Courtesy of University of Pittsburgh Athletics

experience—other than me—to be able to handle that."

"All the adversity before that season enabled some of the second-level players—guys like me—to become first-level players," said Terry Knight, Billy's younger brother. "Everybody took advantage of the opportunity that year."

Having survived all the trouble that first season, Grgurich and his staff—assistants Fran Webster and future NBA head coach Bob Hill—looked forward to 1976-77, when a much-ballyhooed recruiting class would be coming to Pitt. Michael Rice, Ed Scheuermann, Nathan "Sonny" Lewis, and David Washington comprised one of the most celebrated basketball recruiting classes in school history, and Grgurich, for one, couldn't wait for the season to begin.

"Gurg was talking about Top 20 and this, that, and the other," remembered Scheuermann, a six-foot-11 center from Baldwin (Pennsylvania) High School, the same school that produced former Pitt basketball star Mickey Martin and future Panthers' football coach Dave Wannstedt. Martin and Wannstedt, in fact, were both members of Baldwin's Class of '70, where they were basketball teammates. "But that [1976-77] season turned out to be a major disaster."

Harris had another superb season, again averaging 22 points per game, with single-game highs of 39 (at Maryland) and 35 (Duquesne), but the veteran Panthers had a difficult time meshing with all the newcomers. There may have been a hint of animosity between the factions.

"I think Gurg may have thought, 'Well, I have a different type of player, maybe I gotta coach 'em differently,'" Strickland theorized. "The truth is, as a coach, you just have to be who you are, and I think Gurg recognized that. We were all trying to adjust to talented newcomers. I was a sophomore, but I thought, 'Hey, these guys are talented, but they still have to prove themselves.' Gurg learned from that experience."

"What I remember about that season was that we always seemed to have two or three freshmen who didn't know or understand where they were supposed to be on the court," said Harris.

Lewis, a six-foot-two swingman who possessed phenomenal jumping ability, showed flashes of excellence, but his personal style clashed with Grgurich's standards, and he would eventually transfer from Pitt to Point Park College in January 1978. Rice, a powerful six-foot-eight forward from Maryland, enjoyed a productive freshman season (10 points and eight rebounds per game), but was declared academically ineligible after that season, and never played another game for Pitt. Washington, a five-foot-ten junior-college point guard, saw limited duty that season and transferred away from Pitt at the end of the school year.

In that season of lowlights, there were a couple of highlights. The first occurred on February 2, 1977, when the Panthers shocked nationally ranked Cincinnati 65-64 at the Field House on a last-sec-

Continued on page 69

OF PANTHERS AND DUKES

The best thing to happen to Pitt's basketball program—a 1981 invitation to join The Big East Conference—was the worst thing to happen to the fierce Pitt-Duquesne basketball rivalry.

THE 1979 PITT-DUQUESNE GAME DREW A CROWD OF 10,205 TO THE CIVIC ARENA. EVEN LARGER CROWDS CAME IN SUBSEQUENT SEASONS. *Courtesy of Duquesne University Athletics*

The Eastern Collegiate Basketball League, of which Pitt was a charter member, opened for business in the 1976-77 season. Duquesne, West Virginia, Villanova, Penn State, George Washington, Rutgers, and Massachusetts were the other members. The conference was renamed the Eastern Athletic Association (Eastern Eight) the following year, before finally settling as the Atlantic 10 in 1982-83. But from 1976 through 1982, Pitt and Duquesne staged one of the most thrilling sporting events around town.

"The Eastern Eight was really good for the city because it brought the schools together, and Pitt and Duquesne got to play each other twice," said Pitt coach Tim Grgurich.

Adding to the rivalry, particularly during the late 1970s, were the two head coaches, Grgurich and Duquesne's Mike Rice—alums of their respective schools who had played against each other during the early 1960s.

"Both coaches [Rice and Grgurich] were very similar in personality and coaching styles," explained Ray Goss, a Duquesne graduate who began broadcasting Dukes' games in 1968, and was still behind their play-by-play microphone in 2005. "Both were very intense individuals."

The animosity between the schools was genuine. John Cinicola was an assistant coach to Duquesne's Red Manning before becoming the Dukes' head coach in 1974. As the program's chief recruiter, he and Grgurich—then an assistant to Buzz Ridl—were regular combatants in the recruiting wars of western Pennsylvania, a fertile recruiting basketball ground at the time.

"Tim and I never spoke," said Cinicola. "It wasn't until the [Eastern Eight] Conference was formed, and we both became head coaches, that we had to open up to each other."

"I hated losing a kid to Duquesne," Grgurich admits.

The frenetic nature of the rivalry also produced this quirky bit of trivia that seems entirely fitting for former coaches Grgurich and Rice: Grgurich's last game as Pitt's coach was a two-point loss to Duquesne in 1980; Rice's final game as Duquesne's coach was a two-point loss to Pitt in 1982.

Throughout the 1970s, it was common to see Pitt's players at the Civic Arena watching the Dukes play, and Duquesne players visiting Fitzgerald Field House to observe the Panthers. They kept closer tabs throughout the summer months, often meeting at the Field House or Pittsburgh-area playgrounds.

"Most of the players were local," said Garry Nelson, who played at Duquesne. "The Pitt guys would have a team; Duquesne would have a team; and you would play hard. We'd get into a fight now and then, but they weren't things which carried outside the boundaries of the basketball court."

The rivalry was extremely competitive—and close—while both schools were members of the Eastern Eight.

"I think we played them eight times, and there must have been seven fights," said Larry Harris, who played for Pitt from 1974-1978, and later served as an assistant coach at Duquesne.

The rivalry lost its luster, however, when Pitt switched conferences, and both schools went their separate ways. As members of the Eastern Eight from 1976-1982, Pitt held the series edge, 9-7. After leaving for The Big East, the Panthers won 21 of the next 24 games in the series.

"I think Pitt certainly did the right thing [joining The Big East] for itself,"

PITT'S WAYNE WILLIAMS HOUNDS DUQUESNE'S B.B. FLENORY IN A 1978 GAME AT THE FIELD HOUSE. *Courtesy of Duquesne University Athletics*

said Red Manning. "The biggest impact came in recruiting. Before the Big East, Duquesne certainly could go head to head against Pitt in

stage for overtime by swishing a corner jumper with seven seconds remaining in regulation time.

"It's finally coming up, maybe not roses, but at least violets for Grgurich," wrote Bob Smizik in *The Pittsburgh Press*, "who has been the victim of some incredible bad luck since he took over the Pitt job three season ago."

Pitt enjoyed a pair of impressive back-to-back Eastern Eight wins late in the season. The Panthers defeated Villanova, 97-81, on February 20, 1978, then toppled Duquesne on Senior Night, 72-65, two nights later. Clancy, who had predicted after the Villanova game that "my best performance is coming up Wednesday against Duquesne," backed up his bold claim with 20 points and 20 rebounds against the Dukes.

After defeating George Washington 85-83 in the first round of the Eastern Eight Tournament at the Civic Arena, Pitt's season ended in heartbreaking fashion the following night. Villanova's Rory Sparrow hit a game-winning shot at the buzzer to send the Wildcats into the championship game against West Virginia the following night. Pitt's season ended 16-11—a 10-game improvement from the season before. It also marked the conclusion of Harris's stellar career as a Panther. He scored 1,914 points, and his 803 baskets were the most by any Pitt player in the Panthers' first 100 years.

"He [Harris] was an extraordinary talent," said Strickland, who played three seasons with Harris. "What a shame the three-point shot hadn't been put in yet. . . . He had unbelievable range."

"There's no denying he could shoot the ball," added Richards, who played two seasons with Harris. "Larry was a great shooter. As he got older, one of the things that made him an even better player was his ability to put the ball on the floor and create his own shot, but if you got him an open look [at the basket], look out!"

With Harris gone, Pitt would have to become a more balanced club in 1978-79—what turned out to be Pitt's best team under Grgurich. With the oft-injured Scheuermann forced to take a redshirt because of ankle and thumb injuries, Pitt went to a smaller, quicker lineup that thrived defensively. Two important newcomers were added before the season: Carlton Neverson was a six-foot-five wing player

SIGNIFICANT WINS: THE GRGURICH YEARS

2/7/76   PITT 71, SYRACUSE 67
- Pitt's fourth straight home win in the series with Syracuse.

2/2/77   PITT 65, CINCINNATI 64
- Larry Harris's buzzer-beater shocks No. 12 Bearcats.

2/27/77   PITT 64, AT DUQUESNE 56
- 5-20 Panthers spoil Norm Nixon's last home appearance for rival Dukes.

1/14/78   PITT 86, SYRACUSE 81
- Larry Harris scores 22 of his game-high 30 points in second half against No. 8 Orange.

2/8/78   PITT 87, AT WEST VIRGINIA 76
- Panthers defeat Mountaineers for the first time at WVU Coliseum.

2/16/78   PITT 89, MARYLAND 86 (OT)
- Ed Scheuermann's 23 points and 14 rebounds doom Lefty Driesell's Terps at Civic Arena.

2/20/78   PITT 97, VILLANOVA 81
- Panthers win rescheduled Eastern Eight game following flu outbreak at Villanova.

2/10/79   PITT 71, AT DUKE 69
- Sam Clancy's game-winning steal and lay-up hand Duke its only home loss of season.

3/1/79   PITT 77, VILLANOVA 64
         (Eastern 8 Tournament)
- Panthers avenge bitter regular-season loss to Wildcats one week earlier.

1/16/80   PITT 55, DUQUESNE 53
- Panthers beat Dukes for fourth straight time in Eastern Eight league play.

from New York City who had transferred to Pitt from Elmira (New York) College; and six-foot-seven Sammie Ellis, another transfer from Middle Georgia College. Both became starters that season, and were crucial to the Panthers' 18-11 season.

Pitt's basketball program also established an historical footnote during the 1978-79 season when Grgurich fielded Pitt's first ever all-black starting

although undersized—frontcourt. The combination keyed a nine-game winning streak from January 25 through February 17, but Pete Strickland remembers a particularly bitter loss—an 84-79 overtime defeat to Jeff Ruland and the Jim Valvano-coached Iona Gaels on January 22 as a turning point in the season.

"No way we should have lost that game," said Strickland. "I really thought we got homered that night, but that was the type of thing that used to happen in those days. After the game, Gurg came in the locker room and said, 'Great game, guys. If you keep playing like that, we'll be fine. We won't lose too many the rest of the way.'"

The coach was right. Pitt defeated rivals Penn State (twice), Duquesne (twice), and West Virginia along the way. One of the most memorable games was the victory against the Dukes at the Civic Arena on February 1, 1979. It was the first meeting between Clancy and Duquesne's six-foot-seven star big man Bruce Atkins, who had played at Wilkinsburg (Pennsylvania) High School. Clancy and Neverson played the entire 40 minutes, and Ellis fouled out with 6:43 remaining, but the Panthers climbed out from a nine-point second-half deficit to defeat the Dukes, 89-83. Clancy and Terry Knight each scored 23 points for Pitt, while Ellis added 20. Atkins finished the game with 25 points and 12 rebounds. Clancy scored eight straight points during one stretch of the second half to lead the comeback, and Pitt's aggressive defense held Duquesne without a point in the last 3:41 of the game.

Nine nights later, Pitt recorded its biggest win of the Grgurich years, a shocking 71-69 upset of third-ranked Duke at Cameron Indoor Stadium.

The 1978-79 Pitt team lost eight games by five points or fewer, but still had an excellent chance to make the NCAAs. The Panthers defeated George Washington 85-80 in the first round of the Eastern Eight playoffs at the Field House, then toppled Villanova in the semifinals 77-64 before a crowd of 15,208 at the Civic Arena. That set up a championship game meeting with Rutgers—led by star center James Bailey. The Scarlet Knights had defeated Pitt at the Field House eight nights earlier. A sellout crowd wasn't enough to get the Panthers into March

SAMMIE ELLIS SHOOTS AGAINST VILLANOVA AT THE CIVIC ARENA DURING THE 1979 EASTERN EIGHT TOURNAMENT. *Courtesy of University of Pittsburgh Athletics*

lineup. Terry Knight, Sammie Ellis, Dwayne Wallace, Sam Clancy, and Wayne Williams took the court for the beginning of the Panthers' 78-75 overtime loss to Cincinnati at Fitzgerald Field House. Knight scored 32 points in that contest.

Pitt led the nation in rebounding during much of that season, and outrebounded its opponents by 10.6 rebounds per game. Clancy, Knight, and Ellis comprised an exceptionally quick and agile—

Madness—Pitt lost, 61-57. Pitt also failed to get an invitation from the NIT.

With a veteran team returning for the 1979-80 season, but little depth, the Panthers raced to a 14-3 record. They won their first four games before losing at Cincinnati on a buzzer shot on December 19, 1980. After losing at home to Syracuse 73-66, Pitt traveled to Hartford for the Connecticut Mutual Classic. The two-day tournament had a significant historical twist, although nobody could have predicted it at the time. In a 2004 interview, Grgurich remembered what happened:

"These people approached us and said they were part of a new cable network called ESPN, and that they were going to do a lot of college basketball games. They did our games at our Christmas tournament at the University of Connecticut. That was the start."

It was Pitt's first on-air experience with the now-mega sports network.

Pitt won that tournament with wins against Cal State-Fullerton and Connecticut, with Sammie Ellis taking home the Most Valuable Player trophy, but after winning eight of nine games, the Panthers were upset at Cleveland State on January 23, 1980, starting a malaise that the team couldn't shake. Consecutive losses to Duquesne, Penn State, and West Virginia followed, and the Panthers lost four of five games to end the regular season. The only win was a 62-53 defeat of Villanova on February 20, 1979.

For the third straight season, Pitt defeated George Washington in the opening round of the Eastern Eight tournament but couldn't get past Villanova—another team Pitt was meeting for the third consecutive time in the semifinals—at the Civic Arena. Pitt's 17-11 record did earn the Panthers an invitation to the NIT, and tournament officials paired Pitt and Duquesne at the Civic Arena in early March.

"Even if there were no stakes at all, a Duquesne-Pitt game could still be a matter of putting two strange alley cats into a bag and shaking it," wrote Russ Franke in *The Pittsburgh Press*.

NIT officials knew what they were doing. A crowd of 12,385—the largest of any of the tour-

LENNIE MCMILLIAN SCORES IN A 1980 WIN AGAINST EASTERN KENTUCKY. *Courtesy of University of Pittsburgh Athletics*

nament's first-round games—came to the Civic Arena to watch the Dukes win the rubber match with Pitt, 65-63. The three Pitt-Duquesne games played during the 1979-80 season were decided by just five points. They also typified Tim Grgurich's five-year period (1975-80) as Pitt's head coach. The Panthers lost 15 games by two points or fewer during that time.

The Panthers had a chance to tie the game late, but sophomore point guard Dwayne Wallace—who broke into the starting lineup late in the season—missed the front end of a one and one with five seconds left to play.

Nobody other than Tim Grgurich knew it that night, but the young head coach had just directed his final game at Pitt. Less than 24 hours later, he walked into Pitt's athletics administration offices on March 7, 1980, and submitted his resignation. He had won 69 games and lost 70 in his five seasons but had three consecutive winning seasons at the end, the first time Pitt had done that since the early 1960s. On the surface, it was a shocking decision, but the players who represented Pitt during those years remain steadfastly supportive of their coach.

"He [Grgurich] never said a bad word about us to the press," said Strickland. "It was always his fault. As a player, you came to respect him for that. You loved him because he was so devoted to you."

"It was all Grgurich," said Sam Clancy, when asked why he chose to attend Pitt in 1977. "I felt like he was someone I could trust."

"Gurg had as much to do with my decision to go to Pitt as any single person," said Tom Richards. "To this day, I consider him one of my closest friends.

Loyalty was the byword with Gurg. That was how he operated. If you were loyal to Gurg, he would take a bullet for you. In some ways I think that became almost a problem for him, because he was so loyal, and others didn't reciprocate."

"I made a lot of great friendships during my years at Pitt, and some of those I will treasure for the rest of my life—especially with Coach Grgurich," said Larry Harris.

"He cared more about the kids probably before coaches started caring about the kids," added Terry Knight. "There were some people who might have thought, 'He's too much into the kids, and not into the game as much as he should be.' I still believe in Gurg."

Almost 25 years after leaving Pitt, Grgurich had this to say in retrospect:

"It was a wonderful time to be a head coach," he said. "We won some games we probably shouldn't have, and we lost some games we probably shouldn't have."

Smizik, his former Pitt classmate, summarized Grgurich this way—one day after the coach's resignation: "He does not bleed blue and gold, but he probably thinks he does."

Grgurich's resignation also marked the end of an era in Pitt basketball. For most of its first 75 years, men with Pitt backgrounds had coached the teams that were composed primarily of players from western Pennsylvania. With the Pittsburgh area about to dry up as a basketball recruiting ground and an invitation from another conference on the horizon, the face of the program was about to change dramatically.

Transitions: 1980–1986

"**The first time we played Georgetown at the Capital Center, I remember we stopped during warmups to look at them. 'Hey, there's Patrick Ewing. That's Ralph Dalton.'**"

—Joey David
Discussing Pitt's first season of Big East
competition in 1982-83

"**I reached the decision [to retire from coaching] when my nine-year-old came home and asked if I was going to jail for illegal recruiting.**"

—Roy Chipman
December 18, 1985

March 1980 was one of the most tumultuous months of Pitt's basketball history. A popular coach, Tim Grgurich, had quit after three consecutive winning seasons. Upgrades and improvements to Pitt's program weren't happening fast enough (or at all) according to Grgurich's way of thinking.

"Tim felt that he wasn't getting the support from the administration that he wanted," said Dean Billick, Pitt's associate athletics director at the time. "I can see where he felt that way, and to some degree he may have been right. It was a matter of resources, it was a matter of money, and the money wasn't

there. Yet, the physical side of it—the facility, the offices, and so forth—were not what they needed to be. That's clear. A new building needed to be put up long before it was put up."

Pitt's search for a new basketball coach had a decidedly eastern Pennsylvania flavor to it. Villanova's Rollie Massimino, Penn's Bob Weinhauer, and 41-year-old Dr. Roy Chipman—the head coach at Lafayette—emerged as the three finalists. There was also a surprise applicant; his name was Tim Grgurich.

In the weeks after the coach's resignation, many of Pitt's players had maintained contact with

Grgurich, pleading with him to try to get his old job back. Complicating the matter was the fact that Sam Clancy, the team's top returning player, had decided to give football a shot, and participated in spring drills with Pitt's nationally acclaimed football team that month. His future with the basketball team was uncertain. So determined were Pitt's basketball players to have Grgurich back, they went straight to the top, arranging a meeting with Chancellor Wesley Posvar at his office inside the Cathedral of Learning.

"Chancellor Posvar gave us a lot of lip service about how important basketball was to the university, and how committed the university was to it," remembered Ed Scheuermann, who played his final season (1980-81) for Roy Chipman. "He told us that they were going to bring in a good coach for us. We told him, 'Hey, we already had a good coach.' But we all felt a very strong loyalty to Pitt. When Gurg quit, we understood why."

Unbeknownst to the players, Billick, who chaired the search committee to find the new coach, had already been instructed not to consider Grgurich's application, which left Massimino, Weinhauer, and Chipman. Massimino was the first to visit Pitt's campus, where he spent time at Posvar's home.

"I think we felt pretty strongly that we were going to get Rollie," said Billick. "Rollie indicated that he wanted to go back and talk to his wife, which was perfectly reasonable."

Massimino said thanks, but no thanks. Scratch one candidate.

"It wasn't like we were offering the moon," Billick recalled. "Pitt wasn't loaded with money at that time. The basketball program wasn't bringing in a ton of money, but we were offering a decent package, I thought."

Weinhauer also visited Pittsburgh, and Pitt officials had met with Chipman during that year's Final Four in Indianapolis. Weinhauer was offered the job, but wouldn't commit. Finally, at the Dapper Dan Roundball Classic on March 28, with both Weinhauer and Chipman seated in different parts of the Civic Arena, Billick went looking for Chipman to extend Pitt's offer. Between games of the double-header, Billick staged an impromptu press confer-

ROY CHIPMAN WAS NAMED PITT'S COACH ON MARCH 28, 1980.
Courtesy of University of Pittsburgh Athletics

ence to introduce Roy Chipman as Pitt's new basketball coach.

Born in Cleveland, Ohio, Chipman attended high school in Freeport, Maine. He graduated from Maine, then taught and coached basketball at Winthrop (Maine) High School. Chipman, who had a doctorate in physical education, coached at Hartwick College for nine seasons before becoming head coach at Lafayette for three years before coming to Pittsburgh. In 12 seasons at the collegiate level, he had never had a losing season. The new coach breathed a sigh of relief when Sam Clancy decided to concentrate on his senior year as a basketball player, but there was a period of adjustment for the veteran players who had become attached to Grgurich.

Dwayne Wallace, who became the starting point guard late in his sophomore year—Grgurich's final

Continued on page 78

Pittsburgh's Knight to Remember...

1973-74 PITT BASKETBALL

The media guide cover from the 1973-74 season spotlights All-American Billy Knight and Pittsburgh's skyline. *Courtesy of University of Pittsburgh*

Jerome Lane (left) and Charles Smith were an All-America duo in the 1980s.
Courtesy of Bruce Schwartzman

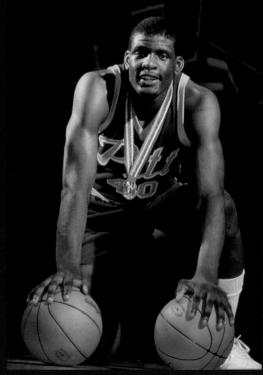

Sam Clancy was a member of the United States team that won the gold medal at the 1979 Pan American Games. *Courtesy of University of Pittsburgh*

Jerome Lane led the nation in rebounding as a sophomore in 1986-87. *Photo by Mike Drazdzinski*

Charles Smith was the Big East Player of the Year in 1987-88. *Courtesy of University of Pittsburgh*

Paul Evans directed Pitt to five NCAA tournament appearances. *Photo by Mike Drazdzinski*

Pitt's heralded 1987 recruiting class posed for this picture in October 1990. Inside the circle is Sean Miller. Above Miller, and proceeding clockwise are Brian Shorter, Darelle Porter, Bobby Martin, and Jason Matthews. *Courtesy of Michael E. Haritan*

Brian Shorter led the Panthers for two seasons in scoring and three times in rebounding.
Photo by Chaz Palla

Sean Miller was a four-year starter at point guard.
Photo by Chaz Palla

Ralph Willard (background) and son Kevin were the only father-son combination in Pitt's first 100 years of basketball.
Courtesy of University of Pittsburgh

Bobby Martin anchored the middle following the departure of Charles Smith in 1988.
Courtesy of University of Pittsburgh

Julius Page flies high against Duquesne in 2001 at Mellon Arena in Pittsburgh.
Courtesy of William McBride

Mark Blount (30) and Kellii Taylor (in air) put the pressure on Georgetown's Victor Page during a 1997 game.
Photo by Harry Bloomberg

A capacity crowd fills Fitzgerald Field House for the December 12, 1998, game between Pitt and No. 1

Vonteego Cummings was one of Pitt's best players at creating his shot. *Courtesy of University of Pittsburgh*

Brandin Knight cuts down the net following Pitt's 2003 Big East Tournament title game victory against Connecticut. *Photo by Harry Bloomberg*

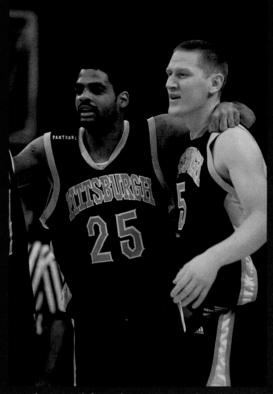

Ricardo Greer (left) and Donatas Zavackas share one of many happy moments during the 2001 Big East Tournament in New York. *Photo by Harry Bloomberg*

Jaron Brown contributed mightily to Pitt's great run from 2000-2004. *Photo by Harry Bloomberg*

Ben Howland was named Coach of the Year by several sources following the 2001-2002 season. *Courtesy of University of Pittsburgh*

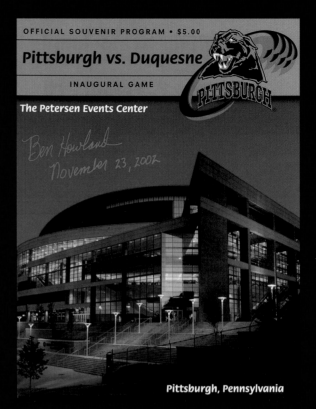

Pittsburgh vs. Duquesne

INAUGURAL GAME

The Petersen Events Center

Ben Howland
November 23, 2002

Pittsburgh, Pennsylvania

The demolition of Pitt Stadium in early 2000 cleared the way for a new basketball facility on campus. The Cathedral of Learning is framed in one of the stadium's last remaining archways. *Photo by image Point Pittsburgh*

The souvenir program from the inaugural basketball game highlights the new Petersen Events Center. *Courtesy of University of Pittsburgh/CIDDE*

The Petersen Events Center is packed during Pitt's win against Syracuse in 2005. *Courtesy of University of Pittsburgh*

Carl Krauser gives his customary tribute to his native Bronx after a made basket or free throw.
Photo by Joe Kapelewski/CIDDE

Coach Jamie Dixon (center) instructs the Panthers.
Photo by Joe Kapelewski/CIDDE

From left to right: Levon Kendall, Carl Krauser, Antonio Graves, and Chris Taft participate in a unique pregame ritual during home games in 2004-2005. *Photo by Image Point Pittsburgh*

Chris Taft slams it home as West Virginia's Kevin Pittsnogle
(34), Tyrone Salley (4), and Mike Gansey watch.
Courtesy of University of Pittsburgh/CIDDE

Chevon Troutman goes for two against St. John's in a 2005
game at the Petersen Events Center.
Photo by Joe Kapelewski/CIDDE

The Panthers have enjoyed a significant home-court advantage since the Petersen Events Center
opened in 2002. *Courtesy of University of Pittsburgh/CIDDE*

JOINING THE BIG EAST

Pitt's decision to accept a 1981 invitation to join the Big East Conference changed forever the face of the university's basketball program. Before then, the vast majority of Pitt's coaches and players had come from western Pennsylvania and neighboring states. Since 1982, virtually all of the key figures for Pitt's teams arrived in Pittsburgh from outside the region.

"I think everybody knew that Pitt was primarily a football school [before joining the Big East], and the emphasis had been there," said Dean Billick, Pitt's associate athletics director who was in the middle of the discussions about jumping from the Eastern Eight to the more visible Big East Conference. "I, in particular, felt there wasn't any reason why we couldn't do both [football and basketball]. Schools around the country were starting to prove that. I was trying everything I could, within the administration, to improve our basketball program."

Pitt had joined the Eastern Collegiate Basketball League—renamed the Eastern Eight the following year—in 1976-77, but except for the fabulously popular and successful postseason tournament held at the Civic Arena from 1978-82, the league did little to enhance Pitt's program outside the Pittsburgh area. In most cases, Pitt appeared on television no more than one or two times a season before becoming a member of the Big East. Rivals Duquesne, West Virginia, and Penn State also were charter members of the Eastern Eight.

"The Eastern Eight was actually on board before the Big East," said Tim Grgurich, Pitt's coach when the Eastern Eight was formed. "Back when we, as coaches, would go to the league meetings, we would talk about a lot of the things which were so important to get the league going, like a major television contract, but the athletic directors just didn't seem to want to make it work."

The Big East was formed in 1979, largely through the efforts of Dave Gavitt, the Providence basketball coach who became the league's first commissioner.

"The Big East Conference was put together primarily with schools in metropolitan cities for television," Billick explained. "Pitt fit that mold, and Penn State's basketball program did not at the time. That's what I've been told."

Villanova, another charter member of the Eastern Eight, was the first league member to bolt, accepting an invitation from the Big East after the 1979-80 season. Then, during the fall of 1981, Pitt officials were courted not only by Gavitt, but also by Joe Paterno, then Penn State's athletics director as well as football coach, who had an idea of his own for an all-sports conference composed of Eastern schools. Pitt, Penn State, West Virginia, Temple, Rutgers, Boston College, and Syracuse all heard the proposal.

"Those were schools that all met in a series of meetings regarding an Eastern conference," Billick remembered. "There were difficulties with revenue sharing, as I recall. At that time, Pitt had been very successful in football, and everybody knew that Pitt had to be a part of that to make it [all-sports conference] work. It was very serious, with him [Paterno] directly. I was involved in those meetings with Joe, and with representatives from Penn State and the other schools."

Pitt wasn't the only Eastern power interested in the Big East during that time.

"Penn State was also involved in discussions—let me say that," Billick said. "Penn State was a different entity with its basketball program, and was in a different location."

When all the proposals were heard, Pitt officials decided to join the Big East, retaining its independent status in football until the Big East added football in 1991.

"Dave Gavitt came to town and talked with the Pitt administration," said Billick. "I was part of that, but so was the chancellor [Dr. Wesley Posvar]. Ultimately, Pitt chose to go in that [Big East] direction. It would be hard to fault the results of that, which have been pretty good."

At the press conference to welcome Pitt, Gavitt proclaimed that its new conference status would make a ticket to a Pitt basketball game the hardest ticket to get in town. He was right.

"Immediately, it had an impact on attendance," remembered Billick. "The Field House was jam-packed. Students were beating on the back doors to get in. We'd make arbitrary

BIG EAST COMMISSIONER DAVE GAVITT (MIDDLE) WELCOMES PITT AD CAS MYSLINSKI (FAR LEFT) AND COACH ROY CHIPMAN DURING A 1981 PRESS CONFERENCE.
Courtesy of University of Pittsburgh Athletics

decisions about how many we would let in and how many we couldn't. We were trying to sit people on the running track. As I look back on it now, it was almost dangerous, but it was an incredibly electric atmosphere."

Pitt also enjoyed the national exposure that the Big East provided as the 1980s developed. Pitt basketball, the Big East Conference and ESPN all emerged as major players in America's sporting culture during that decade.

CLYDE VAUGHAN WAS ROY CHIPMAN'S FIRST RECRUIT TO PITTSBURGH. *Photo by George Gojkovich—Courtesy of University of Pittsburgh Athletics*

DWAYNE WALLACE WAS THE POINT GUARD FOR BACK-TO-BACK NCAA TOURNAMENT TEAMS. *Photo by Keith Srakocic—Courtesy of University of Pittsburgh Athletics*

season—considered transferring. "I had thought about leaving, but when I thought about the core guys we had coming back, I thought we could make a difference. My loyalty to the team and to Pitt helped me decide to stay."

Still, the differences between the new coach and former coach were obvious to the players.

"Gurg had more of a hard-nosed, blue-collar philosophy that was a lot like Pittsburgh at that time," said Wallace. "Chipman was more of an Ivy League type. I thought that he didn't care too much for Grgurich's guys."

"Grgurich's guys" included seniors-to-be Clancy, Scheuermann, Carlton Neverson, Lennie McMillian, and Dave Olinger, plus lightning-quick guard Darrell Gissendanner, who would be a junior. Reggie Warford, one of Chipman's hired assistant coaches at Pitt, refuted Wallace's claim.

"I don't think that was necessarily the truth," Warford said. "Roy was a competitor, and he knew that, even after he took the job, that some of the

players had wanted their old coach back. But that wasn't a long-lasting thing. We brought in a transfer that year, a point guard by the name of Billy Culbertson, who provided some good competition for Dwayne at practice. Dwayne was a nice player. He had a great bank shot, he could do some things, and I think Roy saw that. Roy was looking down the road because Neverson, Clancy, Scheuermann, and McMillian were all seniors that first year, so he needed to get some competition going at different positions."

Still, it was a difficult time for some of the older Panthers to adjust to their new coach and his personality.

"He [Chipman] was different from Gurg," Warford said. "You can't get to know someone in a year as well as from knowing someone from three or four years."

The players Chipman inherited were noted for their talents at the defensive end of the court—a fact Chipman came to realize early in his tenure.

THE 1981-82 PANTHERS WON THE LAST EASTERN EIGHT TOURNAMENT CHAMPIONSHIP.

Courtesy of University of Pittsburgh Athletics

"We thought that those guys were excellent defensive players, not as good offensively," Warford said. "I thought Roy brought a lot of things, offensively, out of those guys that weren't there before."

Warford knew all about Clancy, having played against him when Clancy was preparing to play for the United States team in the 1979 Pan-American Games in Puerto Rico. "I knew what kind of player Sam was; he was a beast," said Warford.

Clancy, who had played center his first three seasons, was moved to power forward by Chipman. Pitt would play a three-headed center, composed of Scheuermann, freshman Steve Beatty, and sophomore Paul Brozovich, who left Pitt after Chipman's first season and transferred to Nevada-Las Vegas—where Grgurich had become an assistant coach under Jerry Tarkanian. Added to the mix for Chipman's inaugural season was Clyde Vaughan, a six-foot-four scoring forward from Mt. Vernon, New York who had been recruited primarily by Chipman's other assistant coach, Seth Greenberg.

"Chipman installed a spread 1-3-1 defense that first year," said Scheuermann. "By the time we got

the hang of it, as the season went along, it turned out to be a pretty effective defense for us."

How effective was apparent in Pitt's second game of the season. In Roy Chipman's debut, the Panthers had defeated St. Francis (Pennsylvania) 91-70 at Fitzgerald Field House on November 29, 1980. Pitt traveled to Olean, New York, to meet St. Bonaventure, which featured freshman point guard Norman Clarke. It was a perfect time to put the 1-3-1 to use. The Panthers forced Clarke into 11 turnovers and ran away with an 84-68 victory. It was the Bonnies' worst loss at the Reilly Center since the building opened in 1971.

"With arms so long they could maybe tie their shoelaces without bending their knees, and hands so quick they could catch a butterfly, Carlton Neverson and Lennie McMillian led a ferocious Pitt defense that hounded and harried St. Bonaventure," wrote Bob Smizik in *The Pittsburgh Press*.

But back-to-back losses at the Show Me Classic in Missouri followed that win, and Pitt was plagued

Continued on page 81

CLYDE

Clyde Vaughan played his first two seasons in the Eastern Eight, then finished his collegiate career during Pitt's first two years in the Big East, but—by any conference—he was a model of excellence and consistency. He was the prize recruit of new coach Roy Chipman's first recruiting class in 1980, and he led the Panthers in both scoring and rebounding for three straight seasons (1981-84). Despite those accomplishments, Vaughan failed to earn first-team All-Conference honors in either league.

Recognizing a potential publicity bonanza, Pitt officials were able to arrange to have Vaughan photographed with comedian/actor Rodney Dangerfield, who was appearing at the Stanley Theater in downtown Pittsburgh. The photo went off without a hitch, and Pitt's sports information office sent out copies of the two performers who suffered from lack of respect.

"He [Dangerfield] was nice about the whole thing," Vaughan remembered many years later. "It was neat getting to meet him like that."

Fortunately for Pitt, new coach Roy Chipman and assistant coach Seth Greenberg were able to convince the six-foot-four, 210-pound scoring forward from Mt. Vernon, New York to visit Pittsburgh, even after he had decided to go to DePaul.

"I visited Pittsburgh, saw some people that I knew and really liked the place," said Vaughan. "Everything just came together, and I really felt Pittsburgh was the best place for me."

Panther fans would agree. Pitt went to the NCAAs as champions of the Eastern Eight tournament in Vaughan's freshman and sophomore seasons, but skeptics questioned how successful he would be playing against the upscale competition he would face every night in the Big East. It didn't take long for Vaughan to prove he was up to the new level of play.

"I think I finally earned the respect of the coaches," said Vaughan. "They knew what I could do. I also knew by the way they set up their defenses to stop me."

"Clyde was a scorer," said Dwayne Wallace, Pitt's point guard during Vaughan's first two collegiate seasons. "He wasn't as much a shooter as he was a pure scorer. He could score from anywhere on the court. My job was to make sure he got the ball in position where he could score."

When Vaughan got the ball in position to score, he usually did. He finished his career with 2,033 points, second behind only Charles Smith (2,045) in Pitt's first 100 years. He had four games of 30-plus points, all during his senior season.

"I felt like I had an unbelievable work ethic until I met Clyde Vaughan," admitted Curtis Aiken, who joined Pitt's program in 1983-84, when Vaughan was a senior. "We used to work out together. I never met anyone who worked harder than Clyde Vaughan."

Aiken and Vaughan roomed together on the road that year, with Vaughan taking Aiken under his wing, helping the freshman make the adjustment to big-time college basketball at the highest level. Aiken appreciates and understands what Vaughan accomplished—how and why.

"His basketball record at Pitt speaks for itself," he said. "The way he got it done was because nobody outworked him."

"He has a nose for the basketball," said his coach, Roy Chipman. "He's

got long arms, a big body, and great anticipation. When he puts his arms up he's like a six-foot-seven guy."

Vaughan was the team's unquestioned go-to guy. He was at his best in pressure situations, as evidenced by his performance in the Eastern

RODNEY DANGERFIELD MET CLYDE VAUGHAN DURING A 1983 VISIT TO PITTSBURGH. *Courtesy of University of Pittsburgh*

Eight tournament when he led the Panthers into the NCAAs. His late-game heroics were on display at the 1981 Far West Classic in Portland, when he hit a long jumper in the final seconds to lead Pitt to a 55-54 win against Tennessee on December 29, 1981.

"Clyde was a guy who would take over a game," said Joey David, a teammate of Vaughan's for two seasons (1982-84). "He would come to us and say, 'Get me the ball. I'm taking this game over.' We wouldn't ask any questions. We just got him the ball and he took care of things. He worked like crazy on his game. A far as scoring goes, I don't think there was anyone better, as far as being able to take the ball underneath or at any spot away from the basket and score."

by inconsistency throughout much of Chipman's first season. Then, in what would become the pattern for his first two Pitt teams, the Panthers came together late in the season, peaking at just the right time. Pitt won three of its last four games, the only loss coming in the season finale at Rutgers, a 61-60 defeat in which Wallace missed a top-of-the-key jumper, which was in and out at the buzzer.

The same two teams met three nights later at Fitzgerald Field House in a first-round Eastern Eight playoff game. This time Pitt won 67-62, setting up a semifinal round game with No. 1 seed Rhode Island at the Civic Arena. A crowd of 16,241 jammed the Arena on March 6, 1981 to see Pitt beat the Rams, 74-45, and Duquesne outlast West Virginia, 55-50. That set up a Pitt-Duquesne rubber match for the conference title. Pitt and the Dukes had split a pair of regular-season games with each team winning at home. This game would be played on the Dukes' home court. Pitt's defense carried the Panthers into the NCAAs for the first time since 1974. McMillian and Dwayne Wallace both earned All-Tournament honors following Pitt's 64-60 win. McMillian was named tournament MVP. Again, Pitt's defense was the difference.

"They should outlaw [Lennie] McMillian and [Carlton] Neverson," Duquesne coach Mike Rice joked with reporters after the game. "They have hands coming out of their ears. I've never seen hands like McMillian's. They score almost all their points on steals."

Duquesne turned the ball over 29 times, and Pitt maintained control of the game in the second half after opening an early 12-point lead.

Wallace, who blossomed during his last two seasons at Pitt, was the hero in the Panthers' NCAA opening-round victory against Idaho in El Paso, Texas. He hit the game-winner with three seconds left in overtime to give Pitt a 70-69 win, and a spot against Al Wood, James Worthy, Sam Perkins, and the rest of the North Carolina Tar Heels two days later. Pitt lost, 74-57, but Clancy left the floor to a standing ovation from the crowd, having finished his outstanding college career.

Wallace and Gissendanner were the only key holdovers from the Grgurich years when Chipman prepared for his second season (1981-82). Chipman

FRESHMAN ANDRE WILLIAMS WAS A KEY CONTRIBUTOR IN 1981-82. *Courtesy of University of Pittsburgh Athletics*

added two key freshmen from New York City, point guard George Allen and six-foot-eight Andre Williams. Roosevelt Kirby, a six-foot-seven junior-college transfer from Midland, Pennsylvania, was ticketed to take Clancy's position. Something else happened before that season: Pitt accepted an invitation to join the Big East Conference the following year (1982-83), but would play its final season in the Eastern Eight (1981-82) first.

Continued on page 83

MARCH 6, 1982

Clyde Vaughan, who apparently wasn't good enough to earn first-team All-Eastern Eight honors in 1981-82, had to settle for being the league's No. 1 prognosticator, and the conference tournament's Most Valuable Player.

Playing in its final game as a member of the Eastern Eight, Pitt defeated top-seeded West Virginia 79-72 in an emotionally charged tournament championship game before a crowd of 16,056 at Civic Arena on March 6, 1982. The crowd was split evenly between Pitt and WVU supporters, and the Panthers were energized not only by the enthusiasm of the fans, but by comments Mountaineers' coach Gale Catlett had made just 10 nights earlier.

It was then, after WVU had just won its 23rd straight game, and secured a season sweep of Pitt in the regular season, when a Pittsburgh writer asked Catlett if Pitt would continue scheduling West Virginia. With Pitt changing conferences the following season, it might not be able to accommodate the Mountaineers. After wondering aloud who Pitt was to be dictating policy to West Virginia, Catlett proposed a question for his interrogator:

"They're a mediocre program, right, right?"

Unaware of Catlett's comments, in another part of the WVU Coliseum, Clyde Vaughan was predicting that Pitt and WVU would meet in the Eastern Eight finals ten days hence. Then, after Pitt easily disposed of Rutgers 60-47 in the Eastern Eight semifinals on March 5, Vaughan told everyone that Pitt would beat the Mountaineers in the championship round the next night.

Vaughan wasn't the only Panther with added incentive. Senior point guard Dwayne Wallace, who led the Eastern Eight in assists that year, failed to earn any league honors. Pitt officials suspected—correctly—that some league coaches were snubbing Pitt because it was abandoning the Eastern Eight. As it turned out, two coaches failed to vote for any Pitt players for any honors, a clear and obvious slight. Vaughan had finished tied for first in scoring and third in rebounding. Two Pitt freshmen, George Allen and Andre Williams, made significant contributions that season, but failed to make the Eastern Eight All-Freshman squad.

West Virginia was led by its dynamic point guard, Greg Jones, the Eastern Eight Player of the Year who captured the same honor the next season in the renamed Atlantic 10 Conference. Vaughan and Wallace couldn't wait to get their third shot at WVU.

"I had a chip on my shoulder," said Wallace. "I felt like I was one of the best point guards on the East Coast at that time. Greg Jones was good, but I thought he was a

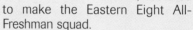

one-dimensional player. I looked at a lot of film, and I studied his tendencies. We felt like if we could take away his greatest asset, which was quickness, that we could beat them. We wanted to force him to go to his left, because he didn't like to put the ball in his left hand."

The Mountaineers quickly grabbed an 8-2 lead, but after Vaughan and Wallace warmed up, there was little West Virginia could do to stop them. Defensively, Pitt coach Roy Chipman started the game in a 2-3 zone before switching to his trademark 1-3-1. "We didn't want to use the 1-3-1 right away, because I thought we'd tire ourselves out," Chipman explained after the game.

"They [WVU] didn't know what to do with that defense," Vaughan added. "We knew that zone gave them trouble in the past and it gave them some more."

Vaughan made 10 of 13 shots from the floor and finished with a game-high 21 points. Wallace made seven of eight shots for 20 points. He also distributed seven assists. He was named to the All-Tournament team.

After the game, at the official postgame press conference, Catlett was gracious but brief in his remarks.

"Pitt played a heck of a game," he said, "and I congratulate them. Vaughan and Wallace were outstanding."

About one second after asking if there were any questions, Catlett interjected a quick 'Thank You', then headed for the exit.

"Maybe they [Eastern Eight] will invite us back," Chipman quipped.

"For a mediocre team, I think we played pretty well," said Vaughan.

ROOSEVELT KIRBY REBOUNDS IN FRONT OF WEST VIRGINIA'S PHIL COLLINS (53) DURING THE 1982 EASTERN EIGHT TOURNAMENT FINALS. *Courtesy of University of Pittsburgh*

ROY CHIPMAN CELEBRATES A SWEET VICTORY AGAINST WVU IN THE LAST EASTERN EIGHT GAME.
Courtesy of University of Pittsburgh

The new-look Panthers opened the 1981-82 season with a 78-62 loss at Alabama-Birmingham, but came back to win their next five games—all at home. A four-game losing streak in early January left the Panthers at 8-6, but Pitt won eight of 10 late in the season to position itself well for its final appearance in the Eastern Eight tournament in Pittsburgh.

"Pitt looks good," observed Rhode Island coach Claude English after his Rams lost to Pitt 81-67 on February 18, 1982 at Fitzgerald Field House. "The doctor [Chipman] is bringing them together at the right time, just like he did last year."

One of the key elements in Pitt's late-season surge was the play of Clyde Vaughan, who—along with Wallace—emerged as the team's top offensive threats. Vaughan averaged 18 points per game as a sophomore to go along with 9.5 rebounds. Wallace averaged 11.4 points and an Eastern Eight-leading 6.2 assists per contest. They were crucial to Pitt's efforts to get past No. 1 seed West Virginia and return to the NCAA's.

Playing a first-round Eastern Eight playoff game for the fourth consecutive year, Pitt squeaked past

Duquesne, 66-64, then defeated Rutgers, 60-47, setting up the third shot at WVU in the title game. The Mountaineers had beaten Pitt twice during the regular season and entered the championship game with a 26-2 record, but Pitt—energized by critical remarks made by Mountaineers' coach Gale Catlett earlier—beat West Virginia, 79-72, in front of a sell-out crowd at the Civic Arena.

DARRELL GISSENDANNER (WITH BALL) BLOSSOMED LATE IN HIS CAREER. *Photo by Keith Srakocic—Courtesy of University of Pittsburgh Athletics*

83

TRANSITIONS

1980–1986

SIGNIFICANT WINS: THE CHIPMAN YEARS

3/7/81   PITT 64, DUQUESNE 60
(Eastern Eight Tournament)
• Victory in Eastern Eight title game earns Panthers automatic NCAA tourney berth.

3/13/81   PITT 70, IDAHO 69
(NCAA Tournament)
• Dwayne Wallace's jumper in final seconds wins it for Panthers.

3/6/82   PITT 79, WEST VIRGINIA 72
(Eastern Eight Tournament)
• 26-2 Mountaineers had beaten Pitt twice in the regular season.

1/22/83   PITT 78, SETON HALL 68
• Pitt's first conference win in the Big East.

2/1/83   PITT 72, ST. JOHN'S 71
• Pitt makes 12 of 14 shots in second half to humble 18-1, No. 4 Johnnies.

2/7/83   PITT 85, SYRACUSE 74
• Panthers' fourth straight conference win in inaugural Big East season.

2/19/83   PITT 65, GEORGETOWN 63
• Panthers conclude string of Big East upsets at Field House in February.

1/16/84   PITT 63, ST. JOHN'S 61 (OT)
• First league win after 0-3 start in the Big East.

3/2/85   PITT 85, VILLANOVA 62
• Pitt routs eventual national champion after Rollie Massimino benches his starters.

2/7/86   PITT 85, VILLANOVA 71
• Panthers force defending national champs into 19 turnovers.

MARCH 2, 1985

With 17:20 remaining in Pitt's March 2, 1985 regular-season finale against Big East rival Villanova, Wildcats coach Rollie Massimino did a strange thing: he benched his five starters. The Panthers were ahead at the time, 48-27, and the Fitzgerald Field House crowd was frenzied. Massimino was adamant, and Pitt went on to rout Villanova, 85-62.

"I told them at halftime [with Pitt leading 40-23] I'd give them three minutes more to play as well as I wanted them to play, or they were coming out," Massimino explained to bewildered reporters after the game.

What was a great way for Pitt to end its home schedule wasn't very good theater. CBS was televising the game, and at least one Pitt official took some degree of exception to Massimino's ploy.

"I would hesitate to tell Rollie how to coach his basketball team," said Dean Billick, Pitt's associate athletics director. "But from a league [Big East] point of view, it might not have

been in the best interests of the league—especially on national television. He did everything but throw up the white flag. But it's his basketball team, and he's won more games against us than we've won against him."

The loss to Pitt, Villanova's ninth defeat of the season, was its first that season to a team not rated in the nation's Top 20 on game day. The Wildcats were 18-8 entering the game, so Massimino must have been confident that his team still would receive an NCAA bid a week later on Selection Sunday. Still, Pitt's players were somewhat confused, if not focused.

"When all the starters went out, I felt it was time to bury them," said Panther Charles Smith. "I still don't understand his tactic."

At least one Panther thought he knew what the wily coach was thinking. There was a good chance Pitt and Villanova would meet five nights later in the opening round of

the Big East Tournament in New York City.

"If we play them Thursday night now, they're going to come out twice as hard, and we have to come out four times as hard," reasoned Pitt's Matt Miklasevich. "It was a strategic retreat."

Smith and Darryl Shepherd were a combined 16 of 22 from the field. They scored 18 and 16 points, respectively. Ed Pinckney, Villanova's leading scorer, was held to two points in Pitt's runaway romp.

Sure enough, Villanova did meet and beat Pitt 69-61 at Madison Square Garden on March 7. After losing to St. John's in the next round, Villanova ran the table all the way to the 1985 national championship, ending the season with a memorable 66-64 win against Georgetown in the title game at Lexington, Kentucky.

Pitt also earned an NCAA bid that year, but fell to Karl Malone and Louisiana Tech, 78-54, in a first-round game in Tulsa, Oklahoma.

Pitt's season—and final game as a member of the Eastern Eight—was a 99-88 loss to Pepperdine in an NCAA opening-round game played at Washington State University.

The Big East Conference move generated enthusiasm that paid immediate dividends. Pitt picked up a pair of guards during the next two recruiting seasons. Curtis Aiken was a six-foot sharpshooter from Buffalo, New York, and Joey David was a six-foot-four guard from nearby Upper St. Clair (Pennsylvania). His father, Sam David, had played for Pitt in the late 1940s. Family ties wouldn't have been enough, however, to entice Joey David to attend Pitt. He had other intentions.

"I didn't want to play in the Eastern Eight or Atlantic 10," said David. "I was being recruited by ACC [Atlantic Coast Conference] schools, Pac 10, Southeastern Conference, and Big 10 schools. I wanted to play big-time basketball."

Enter the Big East.

"That [Big East] really sold me on Pitt," David explained. "That—along with being able to play that brand of basketball and still be able to have my family and friends see me play."

Aiken was all set to go to Kansas. He had been recruited by former Boston Celtics great JoJo White, who was then an assistant to Ted Owens in Lawrence. Then, Owens was fired, and White knew he wouldn't be in Kansas anymore.

"I started looking closer at the Big East," said Aiken. "Pittsburgh was a place that was close. I wanted to go to a place where I could help build a program. I thought Pitt was a well-kept secret at the time."

It also helped that Pitt assistant Reggie Warford had an aunt who was a social worker in Buffalo. She was acquainted with Aiken's grandmother, who had raised the rising basketball star. It was a good fit for Aiken, who was impressed during his visit to the city.

"When I drove through the Fort Pitt Tunnel, I thought to myself, 'Wow, this is a real city, with a lot of nice people.' It surprised me that more top players in the country weren't considering Pittsburgh. I knew that when I got there it was going to be a challenge to attract more top-notch players there because that's the way you build programs—you need talent."

Aiken was the first of four blue-chip prospects to come to Pittsburgh from outside Pennsylvania over the next two years. Charles Smith, a six-foot-10 prize from Bridgeport, Connecticut, and the six-foot-five Demetreus Gore, a scoring machine from Michigan, enrolled one year after Aiken. A year later, six-foot-six Jerome Lane left Akron, Ohio, to become a Panther—giving Pitt probably its greatest cumulative group of recruits in any three-year period.

"It [attracting talented players] wasn't as hard as I thought," said Aiken. "I was able to convince Charles [Smith] to come, and Demetreus Gore, and then Charles convinced Jerome Lane, and then the rest is history."

Pitt entered the Big East in 1982-83 under Roy Chipman. The Panthers' first conference game was at Syracuse on December 27, 1982, during holiday break. Even with many students away from campus, 23,668 were inside the Carrier Dome to watch the Orange defeat Pitt, 87-66. Vaughan had 26 points and 11 rebounds for the Panthers. For his part, Chipman said he found the crowds at West Virginia to be more hostile to his team.

"At least they didn't throw anything at us here," he told reporters after the game.

Pitt lost its first four Big East games before winning for the first time, a 78-68 home victory against Seton Hall on January 22, 1983. Following a loss to Boston College three days later, the Panthers won four straight, including home upsets of St. John's (72-71) and Syracuse (85-74). Suddenly, Pitt basketball was a happening in Pittsburgh.

"For the first time in the city, you had some of the best basketball teams in the country coming to Pittsburgh," David recalled. "The Field House was alive. It was packed for all those games. There was no doubt who the best basketball conference in the

GEORGE ALLEN WAS A KEY NEW YORK CITY RECRUIT. *Courtesy of University of Pittsburgh Athletics*

country was. It was the Big East. It was a very exciting time in Pittsburgh."

The biggest surprise of all was February 19, 1983, when Pitt upset Patrick Ewing and the Georgetown Hoyas, 65-63, at Fitzgerald Field House. "The fairy tale continues," wrote Bob Smizik in *The Pittsburgh Press* the next day. "The basketball team from which so little was expected continues to produce what five weeks ago would have been considered miracles."

With every inch of the Field House occupied, the Panthers rallied from seven points down with four minutes to play to upset the No. 14 Hoyas. Vaughan had 22 points and nine rebounds. Billy Culbertson added 10 points and eight assists. The Panthers limited Ewing to 11 points and 11 rebounds. Pitt finished the season at 13-15, Chipman's first losing season as a head coach, but served notice to the rest of the conference that it would be a major player sooner rather than later.

Aiken arrived at Pitt in 1983, and the Panthers finished the season with an overall record of 18-13, advancing to the third round of the NIT before losing to Notre Dame 72-64 in Pittsburgh. The Panthers had won at Notre Dame during the regular season. Clyde Vaughan finished his career by averaging 20.8 points per game during his senior season. He was named a member of the All-Big East second-team. He had individual highs of 37 (Boston College), 34 (Florida State in the NIT), and 33 (St. Francis) in his final season.

The 1983-84 Panthers also upset St. John's for the second straight season at home, beating Lou Carnesecca's Redmen in overtime, 63-61, on January 16, 1984. Pitt had lost its first three conference games, but it was able to win even though Vaughan was nursing an injured ankle. George Allen keyed Pitt's efforts in the second half. Chris Mullin scored 26 points for St. John's. Carnesecca showed his displeasure by kicking a folding chair into the crowd at one point.

Youth was served for the 1984-85 Pitt basketball team, Chipman's fifth season at Pitt. Smith and Gore arrived as freshmen, and Smith led the team in scoring with 15 points per game. Gore tied with Aiken for second (9.2 ppg). Pitt also returned to the NCAAs that year after finishing the regular season with a 17-12 record. For the third straight year, however, Pitt failed to get past the first round of the Big East tournament at Madison Square Garden—a problem that would plague Pitt teams long after Chipman's departure as coach.

After losing their first three Big East games during the season, the Panthers went 8-5 the rest of the way to finish at .500 for the first time. The 1984-85 Panthers also had the unique distinction of playing two different teams—Georgetown and St. John's—that were ranked No. 1 in the country on the day of the game. Pitt lost both of those road contests. Pitt's season ended with a 78-54 loss to Louisiana Tech in the first round of the NCAAs in Tulsa, Oklahoma. The Panthers' cause was hindered by an injury to Smith, who was slowed by a wrenched left foot.

Jerome Lane joined the program in 1985-86, and expectations were high for Chipman's sixth season. The Panthers started quickly, winning their first four games before suffering an 83-73 loss at Xavier

THE LURE OF THE BIG EAST ATTRACTED JOEY DAVID TO PITT IN 1982.
Courtesy of University of Pittsburgh Athletics

on December 7. Pitt beat Robert Morris three nights later, but lost at West Virginia 74-63 on December 14. Warford, who played racquetball with Chipman regularly, sensed that something was bothering the coach.

"There were a lot of things going through his mind at that time," Warford recalled.

The most obvious matter involved a published claim by Villanova freshman Doug West that a Pitt

WHEN BUFFALO'S CURTIS AIKEN CHOSE PITT IN 1983, IT STARTED AN UNPRECEDENTED INFLUX OF TOP-FLIGHT NON-PENNSYLVANIA TALENT TO PITT.

Courtesy of University of Pittsburgh Athletics

him to get out of coaching, but it was his decision, his life."

"Roy Chipman will never coach basketball another day after this season," he told reporters. "I've asked myself if I want to coach basketball when I'm 55 years old, and the answer is no. The damn game has become far too important. There are things a lot more important than a football or basketball game, and it's about time people realized that."

Pitt's players were surprised—and confused—by Chipman's announcement, but their comments seem to validate their coach's decision, even if the early-season announcement seemed ill-timed. Chipman, it turned out, may have been a victim of his own recruiting successes.

"Once we got some Top 20, Top 30 players in the program—*Parade* All-Americans—I just thought it was overwhelming for him [Chipman]," said Curtis Aiken. "Coming from where he came from [Hartwick and Lafayette], he really had to teach those guys the fundamentals. I don't think he was accustomed to the type of talent we had, and how to coach it."

"He [Chipman] was probably coaching at a level one step higher than I thought he would be at his best," added Joey David. "We needed someone who really understood the superstar-type mentality, particularly on the bench. We did not have very good team chemistry. We always had guys yapping about playing time, upset about not playing. We'd win games, and guys would be in the locker room complaining about their minutes [played]."

The Panthers were 5-2 at the time of Chipman's announcement and won their next four games—including the championship of the Sugar Bowl tournament in New Orleans, but the team dipped to 6-10 in Big East play and slumped badly down the stretch. Pitt lost seven of its last nine games in the regular season.

David didn't like what he saw. "We had a problem with a lack of discipline from the get-go," he said. "Let alone now to have a coach who's said he's not going to be here next year. Well, I was a senior, and we [seniors] were coming out playing hard.

"We had some kids who were extremely talented in Charles Smith, Demetreus Gore, Jerome Lane,

trustee had offered him $10,000 to sign with the Panthers—a claim Chipman and other Pitt officials denied vehemently. Pitt's coach wouldn't talk about that charge directly, but he shocked most Pittsburghers on December 18, 1985 when he held a press conference to say he was walking away from coaching at the end of the 1985-86 season.

"I tried to talk him out of it," said Warford, "but he was determined. I didn't think it was time for

and Curtis [Aiken]. To tell those kids you're not going to be their coach next year, and then try to tell them to do something made it a very difficult task for Coach Chipman. It wasn't much fun toward the end of that season. I really wish he wouldn't have made that announcement until after the season. It wasn't the best thing for the team. It really hurt that team a lot."

Aiken, who was a junior that season, remembers it this way:

"I liked Roy Chipman. I thought he was a great person, but I know—to a man—that we were very confused after he told us he was quitting. You're always taught never to quit. For him to tell us that he was no longer going to be our coach was very confusing. It took a while for our players to get over it. That affected our season, obviously. We were almost playing as if we were already looking forward to next year."

Following another first-round loss in the Big East tournament (a 57-56 overtime decision to Georgetown), Pitt accepted an invitation to play at Southwest Missouri State in the NIT. The Panthers committed 27 turnovers and lost, 59-52. Chipman's final season ended with a 15-14 record. He became philosophical as the clock wound down on his coaching career.

"With 13 seconds to go, you figure it's over," he told reporters after the game. "There is no place to go; there is no sub-NIT. This is as far as it goes. This is the dance, and it's over."

Following that season, Chipman stayed in the Pittsburgh area, and went to work as a vice president for marketing for a Bridgeville (Pennyslvania) manufacturer of cardboard containers. He died of liver and colon cancer in 1997 at the age of 58.

Dean Billick, the man who led the search for Pitt's new coach in 1980, remains adamant that Roy Chipman was the right man for the job.

"Roy Chipman turned out to be an outstanding choice," said Billick. "He did a great job for Pitt. He made the transition very well from the Eastern Eight to the Big East. I'm not sure any of us realized how big a step it was. It wasn't as if the administration threw a ton of money into the program and said, 'Okay, we're going to a different level, we have to go fight Patrick Ewing and John Thompson, Louie Carnesecca, Jim Boeheim and all those great schools.' It's not as if we put another $400,000 or $500,000 into the program. That didn't happen."

Big East Champs ...
And Beyond: 1986–1994

"Let's get this straight: Pittsburgh is into basketball now? The Pittsburgh of Chuck Noll and Mario Lemieux and Andrew Carnegie? The University of Pittsburgh? Ditka to Dorsett to Marino, the football Pittsburgh?"

—Curry Kirkpatrick
Sports Illustrated, March 1988

"Coach [Paul] Evans had his way of doing things. He was very rigid in his system, which is a good thing. Like all 18- to 22-year-olds, I thought I knew everything at the time. When you're upset, whom do you blame? The coach. But he did an outstanding job. He helped me grow up."

—Sean Miller
February 13, 2005

"Can Anybody Coach These Guys?" That was the headline in a 1986 *Sport Magazine* feature article about the Pitt basketball program during its search for Roy Chipman's replacement, who had announced his retirement from coaching several months earlier. The new coach would be inheriting a talented nucleus that included Curtis Aiken, Charles Smith, Demetreus Gore, and Jerome Lane. The cynics around college basketball would say that was both the good news and the bad news.

As he had done six years earlier, Dean Billick, Pitt's associate athletics director, chaired the search to find Pitt's new basketball coach. This time it would be done under the watchful eye of a new AD—Ed Bozik—who had replaced Cas Myslinski in 1982. The search quickly became a two-man race.

"It came down to [Cleveland Cavaliers coach] George Karl and Paul Evans," Billick remembered. "Paul was the hot candidate around the country that year. He had been doing an outstanding job at the U.S. Naval Academy, where he had recruited David Robinson. The reason we went in Paul's direction was that Paul had head-coaching experience on the collegiate level, which we thought would be an advantage for him in recruiting. As it turned out, he won an awful lot of games for Pitt."

Paul Evans coached Pitt's basketball teams for eight seasons (1986-1994), during which time the program received unprecedented attention from both fans and the national media. The Panthers went to five NCAA tournaments under Evans's direction, the most by any Pitt coach in the school's first 100 years of basketball. His teams won 28 games against ranked teams. Pitt established a national reputation.

Who was Paul Evans? Why did some of his players at St. Lawrence, one of his previous coaching stops, decide to nickname him "The Mad Doctor"?

At Ithaca College ('87), Paul Evans had been a three-sport athlete. He ran track and played some football and basketball. Talented with a trombone, he almost majored in music before the coaching bug bit him. He rose through the ranks the hard way, without having served as an assistant at a Division I-

AD ED BOZIK (CENTER) WELCOMED NEW BASKETBALL COACH PAUL EVANS (FAR LEFT) AND FOOTBALL COACH MIKE GOTTFRIED IN 1986. *Courtesy of University of Pittsburgh Athletics*

JANUARY 15, 1989

Coach Billy Tubbs and his No. 3-ranked Oklahoma Sooners brought their brooms with them to Pittsburgh, hoping to beat Pitt for the third straight time in as many years as the teams collided at filled-to-capacity Fitzgerald Field House on January 15, 1989. The game was telecast nationally by CBS.

Paul Evans and his Panthers had come up excruciatingly short in two previous shots at Oklahoma. The Sooners defeated Pitt 96-93 in an NCAA second-round game in March 1987, denying the Panthers a trip to the Sweet 16. The following year, Pitt visited Norman for the first of two scheduled regular-season games. Oklahoma nipped Pitt again, 86-83.

"That was a tough afternoon," remembered Larry Eldridge, Pitt's publicist who had made the trip to Norman with the team. "Sean Miller, who was a freshman, was growing a mustache—and not a very good one—and shot an air ball early in the game. The crowd got on him pretty bad. It was a very vocal crowd."

Pitt had been ranked in every Associated Press Poll during each of Evans's first two seasons (1986-87 and 1987-88), but failed to make the rankings at any point of Evans's third season. The Panthers were understandable underdogs going into the Oklahoma game, but came away with one of their most satisfying wins of the Evans Era, a 99-91 upset that left Tubbs anxious to get away from Pittsburgh afterward.

"Tubbs had made a disparaging remark about the Big East when Oklahoma had won the game the year before," said Eldridge. "I was waiting to hear what he had to say this time. He stiffed us. He didn't show up [for the postgame press conference]."

Newspaper accounts of the game did credit Tubbs as follows: "Pitt pretty much whipped us physically and emotionally."

Pitt sophomore Brian Shorter was a tower of strength for the Panthers that day, scoring 37 points. He shared game-high honors with Oklahoma's Mookie Blaylock. Rod Brookin added a career-high 24 for the Pitt. Brookin, who fought weight problems throughout his career, lost seven pounds playing inside a steamy, cramped Field House.

"Maybe I need for us to play Oklahoma every Sunday," he jokingly told reporters afterward.

Evans was most impressed by the play of Shorter, who had been ineligible as a freshman in 1987-88.

"That's the player I recruited," said Pitt's coach. "He needs to dominate all games like he did today."

"They [Oklahoma] weren't contesting many of my shots," Shorter explained. "They were just standing there, and I shot over them."

A 9-0 run in the first half gave the Panthers a 31-25 lead—an advantage they never relinquished. Stacey King, OU's six-foot-eleven center, picked up his third personal foul with 6:18 left in the first half, and his fourth with 11:58 in the game. Pitt scored 55 points in the first half.

The victory, which snapped OU's 11-game winning streak, improved Pitt's season mark to 8-6. The Panthers had suffered disappointing early-season losses to Siena, West Virginia, and Duquesne.

"We're just young," Miller offered by way of an explanation for the team's roller-coaster first season without Charles Smith, Demetreus Gore, and Jerome Lane. Still, the 1988-89 Panthers ultimately advanced to the NCAA's for the third straight year under Paul Evans.

A school before being named coach at Navy as Chipman took the reins at Pitt. At Navy, his teams averaged 20 wins per season, including 26 wins per campaign (80-19) over his last three years. He was 41 when he accepted the Pitt job.

Paul Evans, however, also had a reputation as a hard-driving coach with a relentless style. His methods were somewhat reminiscent of L. Butler Hennon, the great high school basketball coach who mentored his son, former Pitt great Don Hennon, at Wampum (Pennsylvania) High School.

"He didn't get his doctorate in psychology; he got it in discipline," said Tony Ross, one of his players at St. Lawrence. "I hadn't known discipline before. You learned to respect him as a master teacher."

"He [Evans] has a knack for making the routine experience memorable," wrote Pitt publicist Larry Eldridge for one of Evans's Pitt basketball media guide profiles.

How Evans adapted to his new players (and vice-versa) was one of college basketball's most interesting stories. The 1986-87 Panthers soon realized how different their new coach was. Before a game against Duquesne, just before the team was about to leave its locker room, Evans wanted to do something to inspire his players to come out and play with more alertness. He turned out the lights in the room and fired a gun with blanks.

"The idea was to get them thinking like a sprinter coming out of the blocks at the sound of the starter's pistol," Evans later explained.

The players quickly sized up Evans's expertise shortly thereafter.

"He was certainly the best coach I ever played for in terms of Xs and Os and knowing the game, teaching the game," said Curtis Aiken, who was a senior during Evans's first year at Pitt. "I think he thought he was getting a bunch of thugs when he came here, and a bunch of guys who didn't listen and didn't understand what discipline meant. When he got here, it was quite the contrary.

"We were accustomed to a different style of coach [Chipman], who didn't necessarily get up in your face the way Evans did. I think that [Evans's style] helped us a little bit."

Methods aside, Evans's first season at Pitt was a smashing success. Pitt, 25-8, tied the school record for most victories in a season. It won the Rainbow Classic in Hawaii by defeating Kansas, Arkansas, and Wisconsin on successive nights. The Panthers established a school record for points (2,782) in a season and scoring average (84.3). Most importantly, the Panthers and Syracuse shared the Big East regular-season championship, even though Pitt won both games they played. The 1986-87 Panthers also had the distinction of sweeping two teams—Syracuse and Providence—that advanced to that season's Final Four. The win at Syracuse was Pitt's first road win against SU since 1961.

But in what also would become a sore spot during Evans's tenure, the Panthers failed to make the finals of the Big East tournament and were eliminated by Oklahoma in the second round of the NCAAs in Tucson, Arizona.

Aiken was gone, but Smith, Gore and Lane, complemented by forward Rod Brookin, plus talented freshmen Sean Miller, Jason Matthews, Darelle Porter and Bobby Martin, gave Pitt fans reason for high expectations in 1987-88. Pitt was ranked No. 4 in the Associated Press Poll at the start of the season, and the Panthers proved why—winning 13 of 14 games to start the season. The only loss was a 62-57 defeat at Georgetown on January 6, 1988. Pitt didn't lose again until an 86-83 loss at Oklahoma on January 23. In fact, during Evans's first two seasons, Pitt never lost back-to-back games.

Looking to avenge the loss to Georgetown, Pitt hosted the Hoyas at a sold-out (16,721) Civic Arena

DEMETREUS GORE FOUND MANY WAYS TO SCORE.
Courtesy of University of Pittsburgh Athletics

on February 20. The Panthers had lost five straight games to Georgetown until that day. Pitt prevailed, 70-65, in less than regulation time. With Pitt leading by that score and four seconds remaining, several fights broke out at once. According to the *Pittsburgh Press* account of the incident, Georgetown's Perry McDonald went at it with Jerome Lane, Demetreus Gore put a headlock on seven-foot Sam Jefferson, and Charles Smith—

while trying to play peacemaker—took a poke at Johnathan Edwards. The officials decided to call the game at that point. The late-game donnybrook provided great theater for the substantial television audience.

"The Big East, we should remember, is a television show first and a basketball conference second, and if violence isn't good for television, there ain't a cow in Texas," wrote *Pittsburgh Press* columnist Gene Collier, a writer known for his cynical, sarcastic leanings. During the mid-1980s, Pitt began moving some of its more attractive home games downtown to the larger, more spacious Civic Arena.

"The Big East wanted its big televised games to be in the big arenas because they were competing with the Atlantic Coast Conference (ACC), and they wanted the look on television of big arenas," said Dean Billick. "I know Georgetown and Syracuse were two games the Big East wanted us to play down there [at Civic Arena]. We didn't oppose that. It was good for us financially. We readily agreed to that."

On the court, the Panthers won an important game, getting the Hoyas off their back at the same time. Smith scored a team-high 25 points, including eight straight free throws in the second half.

"Smith, Pitt's six-foot-ten center, delivered the knockout punch when it mattered most…when both teams were playing basketball," wrote Gerry Dulac in the *Press*.

Georgetown coach John Thompson, recognizing a shift toward Pittsburgh in the Big East power structure, gave Pitt credit: "Pitt should win. They have a lot of experience, and you should win games when you have that."

The Panthers captured the Big East regular-season title outright by winning at Syracuse on the final day of the season, but not before being swept in two games by Seton Hall. The Panthers also lost Rod Brookin, an experienced scorer off the bench, to academics after the first semester.

After defeating Connecticut 75-58 in their first game at the Big East tournament, the Panthers were upset by Villanova 72-69 in the semifinals. With an extra day to regroup, Evans prepared his team for the NCAAs, where the Panthers drew Eastern Michigan in a first-round game at Lincoln,

Nebraska. Pitt shot 63 percent from the floor to win easily, 108-90. Smith collected 31 points while Gore scored a season-high 22. Lane was everywhere, scoring 22 points, gathering 17 rebounds, and handing out eight assists. That set up a second-round meeting with Vanderbilt on March 20, 1988.

Pitt led by four points with fewer than 10 seconds remaining, but Vanderbilt guard Barry Goheen hit a three-point basket to bring the Commodores to within one point, 62-61. Charles Smith converted a pair of free throws to increase the Panthers' lead to three with four seconds remaining. Vanderbilt had to go the length of the court. Goheen did just that, taking the ball—and matters—into his own hands, then drilling another three-pointer at the buzzer to send the game into overtime. Most observers wondered why Pitt hadn't fouled Goheen, who was known for late-game heroics.

"There are a lot of different ways to play that scenario," said Sean Miller. "The point is Barry Goheen had to make two dramatic three-point baskets, both off the dribble. If he shot those 10 times, with no defense, he might make two or three, at best. But he did a great job."

Still, there was overtime, and the Commodores had to play without their starting center, Will Perdue, who had fouled out near the end of regulation. It didn't matter. The shellshocked Panthers were unable to recover, and what might have been Pitt's most talented team in school history failed to reach the Sweet 16 for the second year in a row. Vanderbilt won, 80-74.

"That [Pitt] starting lineup was the most talented one I ever played against in college," admitted Goheen. "It's not even close."

The devastating loss brought the curtain down on the careers of Smith and Gore. Smith had started every game for four seasons at Pitt, and Gore registered 1,555 points in his four seasons. Lane, a junior, had another year of eligibility remaining. With Pitt's impressive group of freshmen that season and the addition of six-foot-six Brian Shorter expected the following season, Lane was uncertain about his immediate future.

"I liked that group so well, I wanted to come back [in 1988-89] and play my senior year," he said

Continued on page 95

PITT'S FAB FIVE

Individually, they came from near, not-so-near, and far away. Collectively, they formed what may have been Pitt's greatest basketball recruiting class ever.

Paul Evans was in his first season as Pitt's basketball coach in 1986-87. He and his chief recruiter, assistant coach John Calipari—aware that Curtis Aiken, Charles Smith, Jerome Lane, and Demetreus Gore were in

"It was August 7, 1987. As soon as he picked me up, we hit it right off. The only one of the group I had met before that was Bobby Martin. We were here together on our recruiting visit."

Pitt's returning veteran players made sure the celebrated newcomers were taken care of during that first season.

went to work establishing themselves on the court. Shorter was ineligible as a freshman, but the other four all made significant contributions as freshmen in 1987-88, when Pitt won the Big East regular-season title. As the season progressed, Miller and Matthews became entrenched as the Panthers' starting backcourt. When Smith, Gore, and Lane all left after that sea-

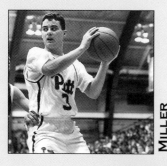
MILLER

MATTHEWS

MARTIN

the homestretch of their careers—went to work to attract more top-flight talent to Pittsburgh. Their efforts bore five supremely talented players, a starting five in itself.

Sean Miller, Darelle Porter, Bobby Martin, Brian Shorter, and Jason Matthews all signed letters of intent with Pitt in 1987. Miller was from nearby Beaver Falls, where he had played his high school basketball for his father, John Miller, at Blackhawk. Porter, a Pittsburgh City League product from Perry Traditional Academy, had the shortest path to campus. Martin arrived from Atlantic City, New Jersey (Atlantic City H.S.), while Shorter played his scholastic ball at Philadelpia's Simon Gratz before going to Oak Hill Academy for his senior year. Matthews (St. Monica High School in Los Angeles) made the longest journey, but quickly discovered how comfortable he would be in Pittsburgh.

"Darelle [Porter] picked me up at the airport," Matthews remembered.

SHORTER

PORTER

"Jerome Lane and Demetreus Gore would take Bobby [Martin] and me out to the movies, and let us kind of hang out with them and have a good time," said Matthews. "It was shocking that they wanted to hang out with a couple freshmen, and show us the ropes, but we really appreciated that. They were really good guys."

The freshmen also reveled in the company of each other.

"Our closeness was more so off the court, even though Brian Shorter couldn't play that first year," Matthews added. "We were extremely close. We did study hall together. All five of us were constantly together."

While the five became acclimated to life as college students, they then

son, the entire recruiting class became the team's starting lineup as sophomores in 1988-89, and again in 1990-91. Miller missed the 1989-90 season and red-shirted following foot surgery.

"We were all pretty good people," Miller said about that quintet. "Everyone worked hard and they did the right things off the court, and we did the right things on a daily basis. From a chemistry and character standpoint, we really had those things as a part of who we were."

Pitt's Fab Five left its mark in the rugged Big East Conference, a league that was one of college basketball's biggest stories in the 1980s. Its message made it all the way to California.

"When I was in high school, I was very much aware of the ACC and the Big East," said Matthews. "At the time, they were the best two conferences in the country. I was also looking at the Big Ten, but the Big East just seemed to be so exciting. I

Photos by Harry Bloomberg and Chaz Palla—Courtesy of University of Pittsburgh Athletics

Continued from page 94

went to Five-Star basketball Camp and met John Calipari. He was the one who recruited me."

Matthews finished his career as the Big East's most accurate three-point shooter ever. He was just as proficient from the free-throw line, where he made 34 consecutive attempts as a freshman. He scored a career-high 34 points in a win against Jacksonville as a sophomore.

Martin, who played behind Charles Smith as a freshman, showed his poise and maturity early that year when he hit a pair of crucial free throws to help seal Pitt's first win against West Virginia—at the WVU Coliseum—in nine years. In his junior season, Martin collected 27 points and 20 rebounds in a game against Georgetown.

Shorter, who played only three seasons, was a bullish inside presence who set a Pitt record for free throw attempts (23) in one game.

He was named the Big East Rookie of the Year as a sophomore in 1988-89. He led the Panthers in scoring twice, and was the team's leading rebounder three straight seasons.

Porter, who normally played the "three," or small forward position, showed his versatility by moving to point guard in place of the sidelined Miller in 1989-90. All he did that year was set a school single-season record for assists (229). As a senior, Porter registered a rare triple-double when he had 13 points, 10 rebounds, and 11 assists in a victory at Providence.

Miller was the only five-year man among the group. He left Pitt having played in three NCAA's and one NIT. He shot 91 percent from the charity stripe as a sophomore (1988-89) and was the school's career assists leader until Brandin Knight assumed that honor in 2003. Miller twice had 13 assists in a game.

As the years go by, the accomplishments of the 1987 recruiting class become more appreciated. In

1999, FOXSports.com ranked it among college basketball's all-time Top 25 recruiting classes. All five members of the class scored more than 1,000 points in their careers. Their combined numbers—7,044 points, 2,562 rebounds and 1,789 assists—don't tell the total story of what they did for Pitt's basketball program. More importantly, they helped maintain the Panthers as a national college basketball force after the departures of Curtis Aiken, Smith, Gore, and Lane.

"When you have a group of players who are also good people, I think that's what makes a class special," said Miller. "That's when you can really build from it.

"Going to Pitt was the greatest decision I ever made. There are so many people in Pittsburgh who helped me grow and mature more than people could ever imagine. That's what makes this place so special: the number of people who care."

in 2005. "It didn't seem that Paul Evans wanted me around. Even when I told him I was probably going to the NBA, he didn't try very hard to get me to stay."

Lane and Smith both were first-round NBA Draft picks, and Evans faced what figured to be a rebuilding year in his third season. Although their 17-13 overall record wasn't as impressive as Pitt's two previous clubs were, the 1988-89 Panthers were an exciting team to watch, sparked by sophomores Miller, Matthews, Martin, Porter, and Shorter. They struggled through the usual inconsistencies associated with inexperienced teams, losing at home to Siena 80-79 on November 28, 1988. They also dropped a double-overtime 84-81 decision to West Virginia at Fitzgerald Field House on December 10. Pitt's first visit to the newly opened A.J. Palumbo Center on the Duquesne campus also ended in disappointment as Pitt suffered an 80-76 loss to the Dukes—the first time Pitt had lost to Duquesne since 1982 and since joining the Big East Conference. The Panthers also endured an 88-62

loss to Arizona in the Fiesta Bowl Classic on December 30, 1988.

But the 1988-89 Panthers enjoyed just as many highlights. Pitt defeated four teams—Syracuse, Oklahoma, Seton Hall, and Georgetown—that were ranked in the Top 10 on the day of the game. Syracuse and Georgetown both were ranked No. 2 at the time, and Pitt beat Seton Hall twice. The February 11, 1989 win against the Hoyas at the Civic Arena was especially big for the Panthers, who had lost consecutive conference games beforehand.

Pitt, which had been ranked among the nation's elite teams throughout its first two seasons under Paul Evans, failed to crack the national rankings at all in 1988-89, but the younger players emerged as stars in their own right. Shorter led the team in both scoring (19.6) and rebounding (9.6), while Miller was the assists leader (6.0). The Panthers played especially well late in the season, winning five of their last six games. Pitt began Big East tournament play with a 96-88 win against Seton Hall, before losing to Syracuse 99-85 in the next round.

CHARLES SMITH GOES UP AGAINST SYRACUSE'S RONY SEIKALY.

Photo by George Gojkovich—Courtesy of University of Pittsburgh Athletics

PITT

FEBRUARY 11, 1989

Losers of back-to-back games to Syracuse and Providence, Pitt coach Paul Evans put his Panthers through an exhausting practice session two days before the Panthers were to meet second-ranked Georgetown at the Civic Arena. It must have worked: Pitt upset the Hoyas 79-74, giving their NCAA tournament hopes a boost.

"He [Evans] killed us in practice," Pitt's Rod Brookin said after the game. "I'm not going to say it helped, because I don't want to have to do it again."

The Hoyas brought an eight-game winning streak to town, and a boisterous crowd of 16,669 watched the Panthers knock off another Top 3 team (Pitt defeated No. 3 Oklahoma at Fitzgerald Field House 27 days earlier).

The head Panther explained the reasoning for the stern message to his players: "We've been down there with whale dung," Evans explained.

Several of Pitt's talented sophomores played crucial roles in the win.

Jason Matthews scored 24 points. Bobby Martin, who sang the national anthem before the game, held his ground inside against the Hoyas' Alonzo Mourning, scoring 16 points and grabbing 11 rebounds. Brian Shorter made only two of ten shots from the floor, but was 11 of 18 from the free throw line for 15 points, and point guard Sean Miller had 11 assists and zero turnovers.

"Sean had a terrific floor game," remarked Evans.

"Miller kept his composure a lot more than we wanted him to," noted Hoyas coach John Thompson. "He's the key to their offense. We weren't able to disrupt him."

The Hoyas appeared to be in control of the game in the second half, leading 66-59 with nine minutes remaining, but the Panthers outscored them 20-8 the rest of the way to register the key Big East win. The upset victory against another upper-echelon team left some observers baffled at the team's consistency, but its young point guard

summed it up quickly. "We're just young," said Sean Miller. "He [Evans] has shown more patience this year. He knows we're a younger team."

Including the win against the Hoyas, the 1988-89 Panthers won five of their last six games of the regular season, then defeated Villanova in the opening round of the Big East tournament. Much of the credit for a third straight trip to the NCAA's went to Evans.

"Evans revels in the role of tyrant," wrote *Pittsburgh Press* columnist Bob Smizik. "He enjoys building on his reputation as a taskmaster. If a reporter wasn't around for one of the many times he threw [former Panther] Jerome Lane out of practice, Evans was quick to inform him. But beneath the tough exterior is a man who isn't so tough, a man who cares about his players."

With a 17-12 record, Pitt received an at-large bid to play in the NCAA's for the third straight time—the first time Pitt had ever secured three consecutive invitations to participate in March Madness. This time, the Panthers were sent to the Hoosier Dome in Indianapolis, where they were paired with Rick Majerus's Ball State. Despite 23 points from Jason Matthews, Pitt was a first-round loser, 68-64.

Pitt's team balance was affected when Sean Miller underwent foot surgery prior to the 1989-90 season. With Miller having to take a redshirt, Darelle Porter assumed Miller's place in the lineup at point guard. Rod Brookin, entering his senior season, took Porter's spot at small forward. The Panthers' inside game was bolstered when six-foot-ten Darren Morningstar, a transfer from Navy who (contrary to popular belief) did not know Paul Evans when the coach was working there, joined the team as a sophomore.

With little depth, the Panthers dropped to 12-17 that year, 5-11 in the Big East. The Panthers avenged their loss to Siena the year before, winning the season opener 101-89 in the season opener at Fitzgerald Field House on November 28, 1989. Pitt also beat Oklahoma State twice in December, once at the Tournament of Champions in Charlotte, North Carolina—the other at the Kuppenheimer Classic in Atlanta, Georgia. A five-game losing streak in late December and early January, however, pointed the Panthers toward their first losing season under Paul Evans.

The season was not without one particularly noteworthy victory. Lute Olsen brought his Arizona Wildcats to Pittsburgh to meet the Panthers at the Civic Arena on January 27, 1990. Arizona featured six-foot-11 Brian Williams and six-foot-11 Sean Rooks up front. Pitt's Brian Shorter was up to the challenge, scoring 23 points and grabbing 11 rebounds in the Panthers' 100-92 victory. It was the

JANUARY 25, 1988

"Send it in, Jerome!" was how ESPN college basketball commentator Bill Raftery described it, and many years later, back home in Akron, Ohio, Jerome Lane still hears about it.

"It's about the only thing people around here remember me for," he said, laughing.

Pitt was leading Providence, 8-5, early in the first half on January 25, 1988, at Fitzgerald Field House when Lane took a pass from freshman point guard Sean Miller and shattered the backboard with a thunderous dunk. The game was delayed 32 minutes while workers with push brooms swept the glass away. Quick-thinking souvenir seekers scooped up shards and shoved them into purses and pockets.

"I was very surprised when it happened," Lane recalled in a 2005 interview. "I just thought the rim collapsed because the springs fell out. I didn't think the whole thing would come down."

A new backboard—estimated cost $800—was installed, and the fired-up Panthers made quick and easy work of the Friars, coasting to a 90-56 win that edged Pitt closer to an outright Big East Conference regular-season championship. Lane's monster slam, however, was the obvious storyline of the night.

"Man, it was unbelievable," he told the press after the game. "I was just going to try to slam it as hard as I could, make a good impression on the crowd, and get them fired up. I broke the glass, and it was like, 'Yeah!' I mean everyone was giving me high-fives. I could have broken three more after that."

"The emotion of the moment was a combination of awe and disbelief," wrote Bob Hertzel in the next day's *Pittsburgh Press*.

Lane's feat was captured in a photo on the front page of the January 26, 1988 *Press*. The headline on the front page of the sports section proclaimed, "Simply Smashing!"

Lane had never come close to causing such damage before, not even on a playground, where rims can be notoriously weak. The rim he brought down on that memorable night at the Field House is one that's never far away—it's his one souvenir from that night.

JEROME LANE'S DEFINING MOMENT. *Photo by Mike Drazdzinski—Courtesy of University of Pittsburgh Athletics*

first time any opponent had scored at least 100 points against an Olsen-coached Arizona team.

"Where he [Shorter] killed us was with second and third efforts," Olsen said after the game. "I can't imagine anybody his size being any tougher."

"When Shorter gets the ball in the paint, you're in trouble," remarked Sean Rooks.

Jason Matthews scored 26 points, and Brookin, recovering from a back injury, scored 21 to send the crowd of 14,127 away satisfied. "I was disappointed we didn't show them a little better Arizona team," Olsen said.

Pitt managed to defeat Boston College in its Big East tournament opener 88-70, but its season ended the following night in a 58-55 loss to Syracuse. Not since 1982-83—Pitt's first season in the Big East—had the Panthers not qualified for a postseason tournament.

With Miller, now a redshirt junior, set to rejoin his original recruiting class—now seniors—high hopes surrounded the 1990-91 Panthers. The starting lineup was back to what it had been two years earlier, and the roster was bolstered by Chris McNeal, a powerful six-foot-eight sophomore forward, and six-foot-seven forward Antoine Jones. Ahmad Shareef, a six-foot-three shooting guard from Chicago, also entered the program. Pitt was ranked No. 12 in the first AP poll. By the end of the season, they would be unranked.

The 1990-91 season started as expected, with Pitt winning four straight, and 11 of its first 12. The lone loss was an 84-80 setback to Virginia in the Big East/ACC Challenge on December 3, 1990, in Richmond, Virginia. Then, returning to Honolulu for the first time since winning the Rainbow Classic in 1986, the Panthers fell to the host Rainbows on December 30 in the title game, 84-82.

Pitt posted impressive home wins—both at the Civic Arena-against Villanova and Syracuse—and defeated Georgetown on the road for the first time in Big East play with a 78-65 win on February 20, 1991. The season, however, was disappointing for Brian Shorter, who entered his senior season as a legitimate candidate for Big East Player of the Year honors. Shorter contracted a strange virus that Pitt's medical people were challenged to diagnose. It attacked his muscles, sapping him of much of his strength.

"He went from being someone who could slam dunk a basketball with authority to a player who had trouble just getting off the ground," said Tony Salesi, the team's trainer, when asked about Shorter's situation in 2005. Despite the handicap, Shorter still managed to make second-team All-Big East, but his scoring (13.6) and rebounding (6.4) averages were down considerably.

If Pitt fans were puzzled by Shorter's unusual condition, they were angered when the team failed to make it past the first day of the 1991 Big East tournament in New York. Seton Hall's Oliver Taylor, taking a page from Barry Goheen three years earlier, made a length-of-the-court drive to the basket which ended with a game-winning layup to beat the buzzer. The Pirates won 70-69; but at 20-11 overall, Pitt was assured an NCAA bid.

Historic Freedom Hall in Louisville, Kentucky, was the site for the Panthers' first-round game against the Georgia Bulldogs on March 14, 1991. Trailing by 10 points in the second half, Pitt rallied to force overtime. A key second-half move was Evans insertion of seldom-used freshman guard Tim Glover for Jason Matthews with 15 minutes remaining in the game. Glover scored 12 points to spark a late rally. Matthews came back to force overtime as he hit an unobstructed three-point shot from the corner with 24 seconds left in regulation.

"A guy comes down and gets a shot out of the corner, and we weren't close enough to hit him with a whip," a disgusted Georgia coach Hugh Durham told the media after the game. Glover, one of Pitt's saviors that day, tried to remain unaffected by the surroundings.

"I didn't really think about it being in the NCAAs," he said. "If I had thought about it, it would bother me. In this tournament, you never know what can happen."

PAUL EVANS TOOK SIX OF HIS EIGHT PITT TEAMS TO POSTSEASON TOURNAMENTS. *Photo by Harry Bloomberg*

Georgia missed five straight free-throw opportunities to start overtime, and the Panthers outscored the Bulldogs 10-2 to win going away, 76-68. Matthews finished with 26 points, setting up a second-round meeting with the Kansas Jayhawks, coached by Larry Brown. The disappointing result, a 77-66 loss, ended Pitt's season at 21-12. It was the last game for Shorter, Matthews, Bobby Martin, and Darelle Porter. Shorter was held to just six points and three rebounds.

Sean Miller was back for his final season in 1991-92, but it was a different-looking cast of teammates.

Morningstar and McNeal played bigger roles inside, as did Eric Mobley, a six-foot-11 sophomore from New York City who had been ineligible as a freshman. Orlando Antigua, a six-foot-seven swingman, and five-foot-11 point guard Jerry McCullough also joined the program as freshmen in 1991, beginning a trend in Pitt basketball—bringing some of New York's Finest to Pittsburgh. Mobley, Antigua, and McCullough had been recruited primarily by assistant coach John Sarandrea, who had formerly been the head coach at St. Nicholas Tolentine High School in the Bronx. Sarandrea was working as a fireman for the New York City Fire Department when Evans hired hiim.

"Having a New York guy on the staff was a big plus," said Antigua. "He [Sarandrea] was able to communicate the similarities between the cities and make the players feel more at home in an urban campus."

In its earliest start of a season to date, Pitt opened the 1991-92 campaign with a 72-61 win against Manhattan in the first round of the Preseason NIT at Fitzgerald Field House on November 20, 1991. Two nights later, the Panthers shocked Kentucky 85-67 at Rupp Arena, before losing to Oklahoma State in the semifinals at Madison Square Garden.

Pitt was erratic throughout the season, winning three then losing four before winning three again. The Big East welcomed a new member that year, the Miami Hurricanes, and Pitt defeated the newcomer twice in the regular season. The Panthers slumped badly toward the end of the schedule, losing five of their last seven games to set up a third meeting with Miami on March 12, 1992 at Madison Square Garden. The Hurricanes surprised the Panthers, who shot a miserable 32 percent from the field, 83-71—sending Pitt away from New York City on yet another disappointing note. The season that had started on such a high, sparked by the win at Kentucky, had come apart at the seams.

"As the season has gone on, we've gotten worse," Sean Miller told reporters after the loss to Miami.

A PACKED FITZGERALD FIELD HOUSE DURING THE EVANS ERA. *Courtesy of University of Pittsburgh Athletics*

MARCH 6, 1988

Pitt's 85-84 win against Syracuse at the Carrier Dome on March 6, 1988 was a milestone win for Pitt's basketball program. Foremost, it gave the Panthers the 1987-88 Big East regular-season title, but it also firmly established Pitt's program on a national scale.

The Panthers and Syracuse both entered the game with 11-4 records in conference play tied for first place. Pitt, ranked seventh in the nation, was 21-5 overall, while SU (22-7)

Lane was one player the Panthers needed to come up big, and he was up to the challenge. He scored 29 points and collected 15 rebounds to help the Panthers avenge an earlier loss to Syracuse in the regular season.

"Pitt needed Lane, a six-foot-six junior forward, yesterday, and he was there with the life preserver, playing one of those games he always seems to play when the water is choppy and the ship has a

They led by as many as 14 points, 59-45, at one point in the second half. The win was even more impressive in light of Pitt's foul problems that day; Lane played most of the second half with four personals, as did freshman point guard Sean Miller. Two of Lane's most important points of the day came with about 1:30 to play. Freshman Darelle Porter blocked a shot by Sherman Douglas, leading to a driving dunk by Lane.

Syracuse put up a furious rally late in the game, and when Pitt's Charles Smith went to the foul line for a one-and-one opportunity with 17 seconds remaining, the Panthers were up by just a point, 83-82. Syracuse's Rony Seikaly tried to rattle Pitt's big man.

"I told him [Smith] he wasn't going to make them," Seikaly said to reporters after the game. "He gave me a nod like, 'We'll see.'"

"I just looked at him and smiled," Smith said, in response to questions about the incident. "I thought it was funny, more so than worrying about the pressure."

Smith calmly sank both free throws to give Pitt a three-point lead. Douglas and Earl Duncan both missed three-point shots at the other end, and the Panthers hung on for the huge victory.

"We were struggling the whole game," Boeheim said. "It wasn't as close as the score."

Pitt ended the season with a 24-7 record.

THE 1987-88 PANTHERS WERE RANKED AS HIGH AS No. 2 IN THE NATION.
Courtesy of University of Pittsburgh Athletics

was ranked No. 12. The final game of the regular season, played on a Sunday afternoon in front of 34,492, had all the trappings of a classic college basketball game.

"With that many people there, who needed any more incentive," Jerome Lane remembered, looking back at that game many years later.

few gaping holes," wrote Gerry Dulac for *The Pittsburgh Press*.

"The last two games we controlled him [Lane]," said Syracuse coach Jim Boeheim. "Today we had no control at all. He got what he wanted."

The Panthers opened a 10-2 lead to start the game, and never trailed.

"The last month or so, the intensity in our practices wasn't there. Every passing day seemed to mean less."

Pitt basketball beat writer Mike DeCourcy, then writing for the *Pittsburgh Press,* put the loss in a different perspective:

"They didn't used to put this on television, this Thursday night prelude to the heart of the Big East

Conference tournament. The league picked one heck of a time to start. It seems almost routine for Pitt to end a basketball season amid rancor."

The Panthers, who had been 11-4 at one point of the season, stood at 17-15 following the loss to Miami. Their only hope—if interested—was a bid to the NIT. Evans wasn't so sure.

NOVEMBER 22, 1991

A funny thing happened to the Kentucky Wildcats on their way to Madison Square Garden for the 1991 Preseason NIT Final Four. They were waylaid on their home turf by a determined group of Pitt Panthers.

Pitt had defeated Manhattan at the Field House in the first round, and Kentucky had easily dispatched of West Virginia at the same time, setting up the Pitt-UK quarterfinal-round game November 22, 1991—a Friday night—at Rupp Arena in Lexington. The Panthers were heavy underdogs and understood why. Darren Morningstar and Sean Miller, the team's two key seniors and team leaders, were roommates on the trip and were aware of Kentucky's strength, but also understood how it could be exploited.

"Kentucky was a real quick team," Miller recalled. "They liked to press, but they didn't have a whole lot inside. The key was being able to break the press, which we did."

Once that obstacle was down, it was Miller (time) to Morningstar.

"We got the ball to Darren a lot that night," said Miller, "and he really delivered. He was a lot better player than people realize, and that night he was very good."

So good, in fact, that the final stats sheet credited the six-foot-10 Morningstar with 27 points and 10 rebounds. He made 12 of 16 shots from the floor. Pitt won easily, 85-67.

"That game they played me man to man, and I thought the guys guarding me were a little soft compared to what we were used to seeing in the Big East," said Morningstar. "They were guarding me, but my shots weren't as contested as I was used to. Jamal Mashburn was a great player, but he wasn't a center."

Pitt received important contributions from many sources that night. Guard Ahmed Shareef scored 21 points, while freshman Orlando Antigua, a sophomore, added nine points, eight rebounds, and four blocked shots. The 18-point win had special significance for Antigua.

"Kentucky had recruited me, and I looked at them as one of the schools I wanted to go to," he said. "They offered me a scholarship, but then it was withdrawn and given to someone else. Plus, Jamal Mashburn was a guy I knew growing up and playing with on the Gauchos [an amateur team in New York City], so that was special."

Everything was directed by Miller, the fifth-year senior who was masterful from his point guard position.

"Sean, as usual, played a strong floor game and controlled the tempo," said Antigua.

"He [Miller] played a perfect floor game," said Kentucky coach Rick Pitino.

Winning at Rupp Hall was especially significant, for the Wildcats had entered the contest riding a 22-game winning streak. The crowd of 22,555 was ecstatic when the Wildcats opened an early 11-2 lead, but watched in disbelief as the Panthers roared back to take a 13-point lead, 43-30, into the locker room at halftime.

"That was a great environment and a great experience," said Antigua. "We came out for the warmups and there were already 10,000 or 11,000 people, mostly dressed in blue and white, and already screaming."

"The aura of being at Kentucky, with Rick Pitino on the sideline and Dick Vitale doing the game for ESPN made it extra special," added Morningstar. "It was a big deal. Pitino was from New York, and they already had their travel plans set to go to New York for the next rounds."

Pitt—not Kentucky—advanced to the Final Four, where it was defeated by Oklahoma State 74-63 in the semifinals. The Panthers were 91-87 winners against Texas in the consolation round.

"Not unless they [players] want to work and do what they're supposed to do," he told reporters.

The Pitt players held an impromptu meeting on a sidewalk in Manhattan, vowing to put their best effort forward if an NIT bid were in the offing. Pitt did receive a bid, and defeated Penn State at Rec Hall, 67-65, in overtime on March 18. The Panthers then played Florida in Pittsburgh five nights later, but their long season ended with a 77-74 loss to the Gators. Miller, in his final act as a Pitt player, missed a 40-foot desperation shot at the buzzer that would have sent the game into overtime.

Jerry McCullough replaced Miller at point guard in 1992-93, when the Panthers were 9-1 to start the season. The only loss was an 80-66 defeat at Georgetown on December 9 in the team's Big East opener. The Panthers recorded an impressive 91-79 victory against No. 12 UCLA at the Civic Arena on December 28.

The season continued on a forward path with four straight Big East wins in mid-January, including a last-second upset of Connecticut on January 12 when Antoine Jones scored on a tip-in with six-tenths of a second left on the clock. Four nights later, back at Fitzgerald Field House, Garrick Thomas hit a three-point jumper from beyond the top of the key with four seconds left to give Pitt a 76-73 upset of No. 7 Seton Hall. Thomas finished

DARREN MORNINGSTAR DROPS IN TWO POINTS.

Courtesy of University of Pittsburgh Athletics

SIGNIFICANT WINS: THE EVANS YEARS

1/26/87   PITT 84, AT SYRACUSE 70
• Pitts hadn't won at Syracuse since the 1961-62 season.

2/3/88   PITT 88, AT ST. JOHN'S 71
• Pitt's 1000th basketball victory.

2/20/88   PITT 70, GEORGETOWN 65
• Panthers avenge first loss of season by beating Hoyas.

3/6/88   PITT 85, AT SYRACUSE 84
• Regular-season finale produces Big East title for Panthers.

1/4/89   PITT 81, AT SYRACUSE 76
• No. 2 Orange shocked by Pitt team with losses to Siena and Duquesne earlier.

1/15/89   PITT 99, OKLAHOMA 91
• Brian Shorter's 37 points delight jammed, noisy Field House.

2/11/89   PITT 79, GEORGETOWN 74
• Second time this season Pitt beat a team ranked No. 2.

1/27/90   PITT 100, ARIZONA 92
• No other team had ever scored 100 against Lute Olsen-coached Wildcats.

11/22/91   PITT 85, AT KENTUCKY 67
(Preseason NIT)
• Pitt's first basketball win against UK stuns Rupp faithful.

2/13/93   PITT 95, AT ILLINOIS 79
• Quality win in Pitt's first trip to Big Ten country since 1971 loss at Wisconsin.

with 16 points, while Chris McNeal contributed 19 points and 11 rebounds. Road wins against Boston College and Miami followed, but the Panthers stumbled after that, losing six of their next eight games.

Pitt was 17-9 at the end of the regular season. After another opening-round loss in the Big East tournament—this time a 55-50 setback against Syracuse—the Panthers accepted an invitation to the NCAA's. In what became Paul Evans's last NCAA tournament appearance with the Panthers,

Continued on page 105

SMITH AND LANE

Most Pitt basketball fans can't say either name by itself. You don't think of one without the other. It's as if they were joined at the hip. Many of the Panthers' opponents might have felt that way during their two most productive seasons together, when they were the cornerstones of shared (1986-87) and outright (1987-88) Big East regular-season championships.

Charles Smith and Jerome Lane—Smith and Lane.

"Sounds like a recent model of some firearm finery that no proud member of the NRA would be without," wrote Kimball Smith, Pitt's basketball publicist during that era.

By any moniker, Smith and Lane—perhaps more than any other Pitt basketball players—did as much to put Pitt's basketball program on the national map during the 1980s. Smith, a six-foot-10 natural forward who played center for the Panthers, and Lane, an erstwhile six-foot-six point guard who led the nation in rebounding as a junior, were the best among the best as Pitt knocked down the Big East door during Paul Evans's first two seasons as coach. Smith arrived at Pitt in 1984 following a stellar scholastic career at Warren Harding High School in Bridgeport, Connecticut. Lane didn't have as far to come; he played his high school basketball at St. Vincent-St. Mary High School in Akron, Ohio.

And, yes: his position was point guard.

"I was still the tallest guy on the team," Lane recalled. With Smith, Curtis Aiken, and Demetreus Gore already Panthers, Lane saw an opportunity:

"With the players who were at Pitt then, I felt I could fit in and we could win," he said. "I was the final piece of the puzzle that they needed to win the Big East two times in a row."

The Panthers won 64 games during the three years that Smith and Lane played together. Basketball

people around the country took notice.

"I don't think there's a six-foot-10 player in the country more versatile than Charles Smith," ESPN's Dick Vitale said at the time.

"Jerome Lane is the most dominant player in the Big East," said Syracuse coach Jim Boeheim. "No one in the country, I don't care how big he is, can outrebound Jerome Lane one on one.

The people who knew the talented duo best—Pitt's players—continued to marvel at their combined talents long after their playing careers had ended.

"Jerome amazed me; he shocked me," said Curtis Aiken, who was a senior guard for the 1986-87 team. "He didn't do the things that he was able to do because of preparation. He did the things he was able to do because of willpower and God-given ability. But he was also a smart player. Most of his rebounds weren't because he could sky over you—which he could—but because of positioning. He had a knack for the ball."

Lane never overanalyzed what he did on the basketball court, particularly on the defensive end.

"You can't teach it [rebounding]," he said. "You just have to have a knack for the ball. I guess I just wanted the ball more than anybody else. When the ball goes up, you just attack the rebound. In my situation, I figured, 'If I can't get the rebound, then I can't get to the other end of the court and score.'"

Smith, a graceful big man who somehow looked and seemed much taller than his listed six-foot-ten, also left his teammates awestruck at times.

"The thing that stands out about Charles was how long he was, how he stretched out around the basket, blocking shots and the way he shot his jumper," said Sean Miller the freshman point guard who was named Big East Freshman of the Year in 1987-88, Smith's senior sea-

son. "He was just so smooth, the way he would move."

Miller became the starter as that season progressed, and was the primary feeder for Pitt's frontcourt scorers—namely Smith, Lane, and Demetreus Gore.

"I could make or break his [Smith's] senior year by coming through or not coming through," said Miller.

Smith and Lane set the tone for the team in 1987-88, creating a settled mood for the team's all-freshman backcourt, Miller and Jason Matthews.

"Charles was more the type who would take you under his wing," said Miller. "He had an intelligent air about himself."

"He worked hard, and he was a very bright guy," added Aiken. "He knew what he could do, and what he couldn't do he worked on. Charles Smith was the type of player who got better every practice and every game."

What made the pair even more impressive was their seeming lack of effort, at times, on the court.

"He [Smith] exerted very little effort on the court, because he always knew where to be," Aiken explained. "He knew how to box out. He didn't have to exert the same amount of energy that other guys had to in order to accomplish the same things. He progressed every year."

Critics weren't so sure about Lane.

"Jerome Lane wasn't a Chevy Troutman [Pitt's power forward from 2001-2005]," Aiken said. "Chevy works his tail off, and he goes out and it pays off. Jerome wasn't that type of guy. He practiced and worked at his own pace. He did what he had to do, and he wasn't going to do a whole lot of extra stuff. But when the lights went on and the ball was thrown up, he was there. He was ready."

"Jerome's one of my all-time favorite players," said Miller. "He

Continued from page 104

was a warrior on the court. The bigger the game, the bigger and better he played. He was fearless. To watch a guy rebound like that was amazing. He's the best rebounder I've ever seen."

"It was so much fun playing with him," said Matthews. "No matter what game we played, I knew he would show up. Any big game we had, he was ready. And he was a super-nice guy. He [Lane] would coach me in practice and during the games. He'd tell me where to go, how to be, where he was gonna set a pick, et cetera. He was a very cerebral player."

Smith and Lane both left Pitt after the 1987-88 season, Lane opting to turn pro after his junior year. Both were first-round selections in the NBA Draft. Smith went to the Philadelphia 76ers as the third overall pick, while Lane was chosen 23rd overall by the Denver Nuggets. They remain two of the school's most decorated basketball players. Smith was a two-

JEROME LANE (LEFT) AND CHARLES SMITH.
Courtesy of Universty of Pittsburgh Athletics

time first-team All-Big East honoree, and the 1987-88 Big East Player of the Year. Lane was first-team All-Big East and a second-team selection in 1987-88.

The Pitt record book also bears their imprints. Through Pitt's first 100 years of basketball, Smith was its all-time scorer with 1,914 points. Lane ranked 18th with 1,217. Lane collected 970 rebounds in three seasons, and would have easily become the second player—Sam Clancy is the only one—in school history to grab at least 1,000 rebounds in a career.

Sean Miller, who grew up the son of a basketball coach, was named head coach at Xavier [Ohio] University in 2004 and has a special appreciation for what it was like, as a freshman, to play with Charles Smith and Jerome Lane in 1987-88.

"The thing that people don't realize about both of those guys is that they could handle the ball and do a lot of other things very well," he said. "They were both inside players, but they could pass the ball. They were complete basketball players."

Pitt lost to Utah, 86-65, in Nashville, Tennessee. McNeal (15) and Mobley (14) were Pitt's leading scorers.

The 1993-94 season was Paul Evans's eighth—and final—season as coach of the Panthers. The recruitment of top-flight high school seniors had fallen off toward the end of his reign, and the Pitt coaches looked to the junior-college circuit to find new players. A pair of forwards entered the program that season: six-foot-seven Willie Cauley, from Dodge City (Kansas) Community College and six-foot-seven Jaime Peterson, from Champlaign (Vermont) Junior College. Cauley was impressive during Pitt's third game of the season, a 94-82 win against Providence in Pitt's Big East opener at

Fitzgerald Field House, but that was a rare bright spot in what was his only season as a Panther.

Pitt started the season 4-0, and was 13-5 after winning at Miami, 80-71, on February 1, 1994. Nobody could have imagined that night that Pitt would not win another game the rest of the season. With Evans in the final year of his contract, and the administration avoiding any commitment, rumors began to swirl that Evans's days as Pitt's coach were numbered.

"That was a difficult time," said Orlando Antigua. "His [Evans's] status was up in the air. I wasn't sure what to make of it. He wasn't getting any vote of confidence from the administration, and I think the older players recognized that. When you're

Eric Mobley (above left), Jerry McCullough (above right), and Orlando Antigua (opposite page) all came to Pitt from New York City in the early 1990s.

Photos by Harry Bloomberg—Courtesy of University of Pittsburgh Athletics

in the Big East, all the games are tough. You have to be together and on the same page. We didn't have that then."

"Those last two seasons, for some reason instead of pulling together after a few losses, those teams pulled apart," said Jason Maile.

A new administrative team, Chancellor J. Dennis O'Connor and A.D. L. Oval Jaynes, arrived at Pitt in 1991. Neither had any prior connection to Evans.

"The recruiting had dried up," said Larry Eldridge, Pitt's assistant athletics director for public relations. "Paul didn't like to recruit, and he had soured on it. With each passing year, the facility [Fitzgerald Field House] became more of an issue."

With the Field House aging considerably and New York City recruiter John Sarandrea having decided to leave Pitt, Evans's position became even more precarious.

"It wasn't a totally pretty picture, but if you looked at his record, and in terms of his kids not getting into trouble, you could make a strong case to keep him [Evans]," Eldridge said.

With Evans's contract situation hanging over the program, the Panthers fell apart on the court, losing

their final eight regular-season games. Before then, Pitt's longest losing streak under Evans had been five games in 1989-90, the season without Sean Miller. It was the first time since 1918 that Pitt had lost eight straight games to finish a regular season.

"A lot of local columnists and a lot of the national television commentators were lampooning the Pitt administration for letting Paul twist in the wind," said Eldridge.

Finally, on March 2, 1994—three days before the regular-season finale at Seton Hall—Pitt announced that Evans would not be back as basketball coach in 1994-95. After an 80-54 loss at Seton Hall in the regular-season finale on March 5, a prominent member of the coaching fraternity spoke up in defense of the fallen coach.

"It's a terrible situation," Seton Hall coach P.J. Carlesimo told reporters after his team defeated Pitt. "He's one of the most respected guys in our profession—not in our conference, in our profession. His numbers speak for themselves. There are a lot of talented people in this league who have not done what Paul Evans has done."

Eleven years later, when asked about the last days of Paul Evans's term as Pitt's basketball coach, Oval Jaynes remembered it this way:

"We had a contract on the table for him, and he did not agree to it. It was an extension of his contract, and there were some things with which he didn't agree. Finally, when he didn't sign it, we—the chancellor, myself, and some others—decided to go in another direction. It's not that I disliked Paul, or anything like that. I've recommended Paul for a couple of jobs since then. He just didn't agree to some of the conditions that were in the contract."

The Paul Evans Era, one of the most successful—and volatile—in Pitt basketball history, came to an end as St. John's beat the Panthers, 80-72, in the first round of the Big East tournament on March 10, 1994.

"He [Evans] told us, 'I'm not going to be around here, but still go out and play for Pitt, play for

pride,'" Eric Mobley recounted for the media after the final game in New York.

"The bewitching hour finally arrived for Paul Evans last night, and it came the way so many others have in Madison Square Garden—with a loss in the first round of the Big East Conference tournament," Gerry Dulac wrote in the *Pittsburgh Post-Gazette*.

Evans's aggressive approach to coaching won't be forgotten by some of the young men who played for Pitt during those years.

"He was very strict, very rough, and he didn't pull any punches," said Antigua. "He let you know how he felt. He shot from the hip. He was very demanding. His way of motivating was to be very hard and critical."

Miller, the point guard-turned coach, had maybe the most educated view of his coach.

"He didn't deviate a whole lot from his philosophies in how we played," he said. "That's why his teams generally had a high field-goal percentage and shot a lot of free throws. It was inside-oriented. It was consistent basketball."

"Coach Evans had a great system in place for big guys," said Darren Morningstar. "It was called the 'Power Offense,' and it was designed to get the ball inside. That was a huge advantage big guys had playing for Coach Evans.

And the in-your-face instructions?

"A lot of his coaching style was almost reverse psychology," said Morningstar.

Joe DeSantis, another New Yorker who replaced Sarandrea at Pitt, cherishes his time at Pitt.

"I have good memories of Pittsburgh," DeSantis said. "I would work again for Paul in a heartbeat. I think his record spoke for itself. Whether or not his time had run out was for other people to decide, which they did."

Unfulfilled Promise(s): 1994–1999

"**Ralph Willard was one of the best X and O coaches I ever had. I learned many things from him. . . . His practices were well organized, and he could come up with a play in a second at crunch time of a big game.... During the season he had basketball on his mind 110 percent of the time.... College basketball is definitely a big business, but you have to remember that you're dealing with college students, and people don't have basketball on their minds 110 percent of the time.**"

—Jason Maile

"**You know that guy from the movie, Groundhog Day? That's how I feel.**"

—Ralph Willard

By March 1994, a particularly harsh Pittsburgh winter finally was winding down, but inside Pitt's athletics administration offices at Pitt Stadium, AD Oval Jaynes was burning up his telephone line. Once again, the school was looking to hire a new basketball coach.

Among the people Jaynes talked to were University of Massachusetts coach John Calipari, Tulane's Perry Clark, Texas A&M's Tony Barone, Marquette's Kevin O'Neill, Pete Gillen from Xavier, and Ralph Willard, whose Western Kentucky Hilltoppers were coming off back-to-back NCAA

tournament appearances. Calipari was the first coach to speak with Jaynes.

"He [Calipari] made it pretty clear up front that the timing was not right," Jaynes recalled in an interview many years later. "He had a very good package at UMass. John and I talked two or three times, but I never could get him interested. But he was very helpful in recommending some people. John had a great feel for Pitt."

As the search progressed, Gillen and Willard appeared to emerge as the most likely candidates. Interestingly, Providence—a Big East rival—was courting the same two coaches. Willard ended up taking the Pitt job, and he was introduced at a press conference at Pitt Stadium on March 29, 1994—his 48th birthday. Providence hired Gillen.

"Had we not hired Ralph, we may have hired Pete Gillen," said Jaynes. "But Ralph was probably one of the hottest coaches in the country at the time when he was at Western Kentucky. They were coming off a Sweet 16 appearance the year before."

Ralph Willard certainly had an impressive coaching pedigree. Born in Brooklyn, New York, he played college basketball and baseball at Holy Cross. After coaching in the high school ranks, he joined Jim Boeheim at Syracuse, and later worked under Rick Pitino with both the NBA's New York Knicks and later at the University of Kentucky. His four-

year (1990-94) record at Western Kentucky had been 81-42, where his Hilltoppers played an aggressive full-court press and shot plenty of three-pointers, emulating the style of Pitino, his mentor. He promised the same type of basketball for Pitt.

"Basketball is going to be fun at the University of Pittsburgh," he noted at that introductory press conference. "We are going to have fun. We are going to put a team on the floor that is going to get after it for 40 minutes, and that is going to play with a great deal of enthusiasm and emotion.

"I believe that no basketball program anywhere in the country right now has greater potential than the University of Pittsburgh's."

Willard had reason to be optimistic. In 1993, then-Pennsylvania Governor Robert Casey and then-Pitt Chancellor J. Dennis O'Connor had agreed to build a new basketball facility on campus with $30 million in state funding. That arrangement, however, would be amended later.

When October arrived, Willard was forced to deal with his first major setback, but it wasn't his last. Senior point guard Jerry McCullough suffered a knee injury and was forced to miss the entire season. That meant seldom-used junior Andre Alridge had to replace McCullough in the lineup. Willard's first team was game, but undermanned. Nate Cochran, the punter on Pitt's football team, joined the basketball squad early in the season to provide additional support.

Pitt lost at North Carolina 90-67 in Willard's debut on November 29, 1994. He picked up his first victory four nights later in a 75-73 win against Buffalo State at Fitzgerald Field House, but the Panthers were 1-5 at one point, before winning three straight prior to the start of Big East play. An early-season game against undefeated and second-ranked Connecticut on January 11, 1995 gave Pitt fans a glimpse—they hoped—of Willard's future in Pittsburgh.

With the Field House jammed to capacity, Pitt jumped to a 25-point lead with 4:50 remaining in the first half, before wilting down the stretch. They finally relinquished the lead when UConn's Brian Fair made a three-pointer at 8:03 to put the Huskies ahead 63-62. UConn coach Jim Calhoun was impressed by Pitt's relentless style of play.

PITT CHANCELLOR J. DENNIS O'CONNOR (RIGHT) AND AD OVAL JAYNES (CENTER) NAMED RALPH WILLARD BASKETBALL COACH ON MARCH 29, 1994, HIS 48TH BIRTHDAY. *Courtesy of University of Pittsburgh Athletics*

PITT

"V" FOR VONTEEGO

Vonteego Cummings arrived at Pitt in the fall of 1995, just one member of a heralded recruiting class that coach Ralph Willard was confident would make Pitt basketball a national contender—with the help of a new playing facility. Cummings—and Willard—weren't around when ground was broken for the Petersen Events center in June 2000, but Cummings at least made it through to the proper end of his college career, unlike the other members of his recruiting class.

A third-team Parade All-American at Thomson (Georgia) High School, the six-foot-four Cummings was a natural second guard who ended up playing more at the point as his career progressed. He possessed all the physical attributes needed to excel in basketball-good hands, quickness, strength, ball-handling, shooting ability, and instincts.

"I don't know of anything that 'V' can't do on the basketball court," his teammate, Kelli Taylor, once said. "He's the whole package. I should know. I go up against him every day at practice."

"Very seldom is a point guard that explosive," remarked Miami coach Leonard Hamilton. "This guy is so explosive. He's outstanding."

Pitt fans during the Willard-Cummings years remember the rash of injuries and defections that plagued those teams, but Cummings endured and excelled. He was a four-year starter who led the Panthers in both scoring and assists during each of his last three seasons (1996-99). He scored 1,581 points as a collegian. His per-

sonal recognition took a hit from the fact that his teams weren't as successful. He made second-team All-Big East in his sophomore and junior years, and was third-team All-Big East as a senior. He was named the conference's Player of the Week three times. He had four 30-plus-point games as a Panther.

"I have three words to describe Vonteego," said Curtis Aiken, who starred for Pitt in the mid-1980s. "Excellent. Excellent. Excellent."

"Vonteego can break down a defense at will," said his coach, Ralph Willard. "Basically, Vonteego has no fear."

Because Pitt's teams were under-manned, Cummings was often forced to play for extended periods. He played all 50 minutes of the Panthers' double-overtime loss to Villanova in the 1998 Big East tournament, scoring 37 points in the process. He played all but one minute of another double-overtime contest, a 90-83 loss to St. John's on January 22, 1998. He averaged 40.1 minutes played per game that year, a Pitt single-season record for the first 100 years.

Unfortunately for Cummings—and his coach—Pitt's NIT team of 1996-97 was the only winning campaign either experienced in Pittsburgh. Following his career, Cummings was taken by the Indiana Pacers in the first round of the 1999 NBA Draft, but was traded immediately to the Golden State Warriors. He played for Golden State as a rookie in 1999-2000 before being traded to Philadelphia the following year. He later played professionally in Europe.

VONTEEGO CUMMINGS DRIVES PAST A DEFENDER.
Courtesy of University of Pittsburgh Athletics

"No team has attacked us like they attacked us in the first half," he said at the postgame press conference. "We weren't flat, they just attacked us. We sat back and took the blows. In the second half, we didn't do anything different but execute."

Pitt lost 10 of 11 Big East games in January and February, the lone win being a 94-87 win against St. John's at Madison Square Garden on January 22,

1995. The Panthers also defeated St. John's in the first round of the Big East tournament 74-71 before bowing out the following day to Connecticut, 81-78.

Willard's first team finished with an overall record of 10-18, but did win four of its last six games of the regular season. All five starters averaged in double-figures in scoring. It was a positive end to

FEBRUARY 12, 1997

Jason Maile, a fifth-year senior from Forest City, Pennsylvania—a small town not too far from Scranton—shot his way into Pitt basketball history with a 40-point game in a 95-89 victory against Villanova at Fitzgerald Field House. He became only the third player in the school's first 100 years of basketball—Don Hennon and Ed Pavlick were the others—to score at least 40 points in a game.

"If anybody ever had a better game at the Field House than Jason Maile [tonight], I want to see it," his coach, Ralph Willard, asked the media afterward.

"It was one of those nights when the ball was coming off my hand nice," Maile explained. "I wish there were more nights like that.

"When you release the ball, you know it's going in as soon as you shoot it. It's weird, but it feels good."

Maile scored 12 points in the first half, connecting on two of six three-point shot attempts, but caught fire for 28 more points after intermission, hitting all six of his trey attempts. The Panthers needed every one of them, too, having trailed the Wildcats 67-60 with 7:30 remaining before going on a 21-3 tear to take control of the game.

A sellout crowd of 6,798 crowded the Field House to witness Maile's historic performance.

"The way Maile shot the ball, he was great," a disappointed Villanova coach Steve Lappas said during postgame remarks.

Maile's performance went a long way toward validating former coach Paul Evans's decision to give Maile a scholarship in 1992.

"I got my scholarship late," Maile told *The Pittsburgh Post-Gazette*. "I come from a small town and no one thinks you can play. Some low Division I schools were interested. But I waited around. I figured there might be some openings."

Maile made 85 three-pointers in the 1996-97 season, and also led the Panthers in free-throw percentage (80 percent) that year.

JASON MAILE LETS FLY FROM BEYOND THE ARC. *Courtesy of University of Pittsburgh Athletics*

the careers of seniors Orlando Antigua, Chris Gant, and Jaime Peterson, and offered encouragement for the coming years, especially considering the recruiting class Willard was putting together during his first season.

Mark Blount, Vonteego Cummings, Michael Gill, Andre Howard, and Kellii Taylor were going to be the cornerstones for Pitt's basketball resurrection. Blount was a seven-foot center from Dobbs Ferry, New York. Cummings was a six-foot-four guard from Thomson, Georgia. Gill, a six-foot-five forward, came to Pittsburgh from Washington, D.C. Basketball hotbed Overbrook High School in Philadelphia produced the six-foot-six Howard, and Taylor, a six-foot guard, was from Forestville, Maryland. Two transfers also became eligible in 1995-96. The coach's son, Kevin Willard, was a six-foot guard who began his career at Western Kentucky when his father was the head coach. He

would have three years of eligibility at Pitt, but left after his junior year. Gerald Jordan, a six-foot-10 forward from Philadelphia, came to Pitt from Morgan State.

The Field House was packed for Midnight Madness festivities on the night of October 14, 1995. Success-starved Pitt fans were hoping Willard's basketball team could fill the void left by another disappointing football season. Earlier that evening, Pitt's football team lost at Temple, 29-27—the Owls' first ever win in the Big East. Willard stoked the flames of the enthusiastic crowd, urging the crowd to hold up cards bearing the message "3" after every Pitt try that season. There also was talk of an NCAA tournament bid.

The 1995-96 Panthers went 10-17, including a 5-13 mark in Big East play. The season started encouragingly enough, an 84-73 win against Duquesne at the Civic Arena. School officials had

ORLANDO ANTIGUA WAS PART OF A STRONG
SENIOR CLASS IN WILLARD'S FIRST SEASON.
Courtesy of University of Pittsburgh Athletics

JAIME PETERSON SCORES AGAINST DUQUESNE IN
A 1994 GAME. *Courtesy of University of Pittsburgh Athletics*

decided to play the annual game at the downtown arena rather than at either campus facility. It was billed as "The City Game," and evolved into an annual college basketball doubleheader, featuring a game between the schools' women's basketball teams in the opener, followed by the men's game.

The Duquesne game also was the debut for the celebrated newcomers, most notably Cummings, who led the Panthers with 18 points, eight rebounds, and four assists in 30 minutes. It also was Pitt's eighth win in a row against the Dukes, and 16th in the last 17 meetings.

"If this trend continues, the City Game will become the City Bore," wrote Bob Smizik in *The Pittsburgh Post-Gazette.*

Jerry McCullough returned from knee surgery and played the entire season at point guard, leading the team in scoring (13.4 ppg). Another key player that season was junior forward Chad Varga, a burly six-foot-six inside player who had transferred to Pitt from Vincennes (Indiana) the year before. He averaged 12. 5 (ppg) and 6.3 (rpg), but the Panthers lost 12 of 13 games in January and February after a five-game winning streak that concluded with successive victories against West Virginia, Georgetown (ranked No. 5 in the nation at the time), and Notre Dame.

Early in the losing streak, however, the Panthers almost knocked off unbeaten and No. 1-ranked Massachusetts, coached by John Calipari.

There was little room to turn inside Fitzgerald Field House when Calipari brought his Minutemen—minus star center Marcus Camby, who was ill—to Pittsburgh on January 23, 1996. The Panthers rallied from a 62-53 deficit in the last six minutes to force overtime. Pitt could have won the game, but Alridge's last-second 16-foot jumper was no good. Pitt scored the first basket in overtime on a layup by McCullough, but the Minutemen scored the next 10 points and won going away, 79-71. Pitt, which had led by 12 points in the first half, was piloted by McCullough's 20 points and a career-high 11 rebounds.

Willard's chances for a more successful second season were hindered substantially when Cummings missed nine straight games with a hand injury. Kellii

Taylor, one of the heralded recruits, missed the entire season with a back injury.

The 1995-96 season ended when Pitt lost to Boston College, 70-66, in the first round of the Big East tournament.

The 1996-97 campaign produced Willard's best team—and his only winning season at Pitt. The Panthers lost five of their first six games, but the first victory came at the Civic Arena against Connecticut on December 4, 1996. Varga and Jordan missed time because of leg injuries early in the season, and Blount had a hand infection after a teammate's tooth caught him during a practice session. Willard also had one less player available—Michael Gill had transferred to California.

"When we had everyone healthy and playing toward the end of that year, we were playing pretty well," Jason Maile recalled in a 2005 interview.

Pitt's inside game was bolstered that year by the presence of six-foot-eight forward Isaac Hawkins, who had been a member of the recruiting class the year before. He had spent the 1995-96 season at Hargrave (Virginia) Military Academy.

The Panthers defeated Northwestern and Michigan at the Rainbow Classic in Honolulu in late December. The Wolverines were ranked fourth in the nation at the time. Villanova was No. 18 when Jason Maile's 40 points led Pitt to a 95-89 win at home in February, but the injury bug left Pitt with a 13-13 record heading into the final three games of the regular season. The Panthers, finally together and healthy, won all three. Boston College fell 75-71 on Senior Day, then Pitt closed the regular season with back-to-back road victories at Connecticut (77-74) and Syracuse (66-63).

With a 16-13 overall record, an at-large berth in the NCAAs was remote at best, but the Big East tournament provided the Panthers with more opportunities. Pitt defeated UConn for the third time that season, 63-62, before falling to Boston College—the eventual tournament champion—76-68.

Pitt did receive an NIT bid and hosted a first-round game against New Orleans on March 12, 1997, winning easily, 82-63. The NIT committee sent the Panthers to Fayetteville for a second-round game against Arkansas five nights later.

CHAD VARGA WAS A KEY ADDITION FOR WILLARD.
Courtesy of University of Pittsburgh Athletics

NOVEMBER 26-27, 1998

Ralph Willard's final season as Pitt's basketball coach started promisingly enough. The Panthers defeated two ranked opponents, Xavier and Kentucky, on back-to-back days of the Puerto Rico Shootout in Bayamon. The games, played at tiny Guerra Fieldhouse in front of approximately 1,200 fans seated on wooden bleachers, propelled Pitt into the nation's Top 20 in early December.

Pitt forced 13 first-half turnovers on its way to a 94-76 defeat of Xavier on November 26, Thanksgiving Day. The Panthers made 10 of their first 12 shots against the Musketeers, yet trailed 23-22. Attila Cosby, playing on an injured right ankle, scored 12 points in the first half to turn the game in Pitt's favor. He finished with 23 points and 12 rebounds. Vonteego Cummings scored a game-high 24 for Pitt, which improved to 5-0 on the season. Pitt's defense limited Xavier to 35 percent shooting from the field.

The Panthers came back the next day and surprised Kentucky, the defending national champion, 68-56. It was the first time since the 1985-86 season (Villanova) that a Pitt team had beaten a reigning national champion.

Cummings scored 20 points to lead the Panthers, who were aided by their ability to limit UK's points in the transition game. Freshman guard Fred Primus made three of five three-pointers to keep the Wildcats from creeping back into the game.

"There's one thing Fred believes," Willard said after the game. "If he's outside the locker room, he can make that shot."

The victory lifted Pitt's season mark to 6-0, and placed the Panthers at No. 20 in the following week's AP rankings, even though Pitt was defeated by Steve Francis and Maryland, 87-52, in the Shootout title game the next night.

"This team has a lot of character," Willard told reporters after the Kentucky game. "That's showed the last two days. These kids won these two games with heart. They battled. They won with defense. And it's something they're going to continue to build on."

A little more than nine weeks later, Willard announced that he would be stepping down as Pitt's coach at the end of the 1998-1999 season.

A Bud Walton Arena crowd of 17,068 cheered the Razorbacks to a hard-fought 76-71 victory. Arkansas made four three-pointers in the last 7:29 to keep the Panthers at bay. Ralph Willard's third season ended with an 18-15 record, but a winning aura had finally emerged.

"It was a heck of a stretch to get to the postseason," Willard commented after the Arkansas game. "I'm proud of the effort and the growth of the kids. We became a better basketball team."

A year later, Willard remembered his 1996-97 team in another interview.

"It was rewarding in that the kids never quit, and we finished real strong," he said. "It was frustrating, because we never had Gerald Jordan or Chad Varga really playing at their level for any significant period of time during the season. With those two kids playing at their level, not only do I think we are an NCAA team, but an NCAA team that could do some damage."

Pitt was unable, however, to use the strong 1996-97 finish as a springboard to a successful 1997-98 season. Two more players left school. Andre Howard transferred back to his native Philadelphia, where he enrolled at St. Joseph's. An even bigger loss was

KEVIN WILLARD JOINED HIS FATHER AT PITT AFTER A SHORT STINT AT WESTERN KENTUCKY.
Courtesy of University of Pittsburgh Athletics

JANUARY 21, 1998

Much like the 1981 invitation to join the Big East Conference, another event that didn't take place on a basketball court had significant ramifications for Pitt's basketball program. At a news conference staged under a makeshift tent in a parking lot across from Pitt Stadium, Pennsylvania governor Tom Ridge told a gathering on January 21, 1998, that the state was releasing $138 million in capital funds for Pitt projects over the next five years. Included in that total was $38 millions toward construction of a new convocation center/basketball arena on campus.

"We celebrate today a new University of Pittsburgh," Ridge told the media and assorted Pitt officials, coaches, boosters and student-athletes. "A University of Pittsburgh that is looking toward the future with a goal of elevating its academic excellence and its place in the Pennsylvania community—not just in the city, the county and the region—but throughout the Commonwealth of Pennsylvania. And by helping the University of Pittsburgh achieve its potential I believe we help Pennsylvania achieve its potential."

Among those in attendance were chancellor Mark Nordenberg, athletics director Steve Pederson, and head men's basketball coach Ralph Willard.

THEN-PENNSYLVANIA GOVERNOR TOM RIDGE ADDRESSES THE GATHERING ON PITT'S UPPER CAMPUS.
Courtesy of University of Pittsburgh/CIDDE

"The news that you [Ridge] have brought 'over the mountain'—capital commitments totaling $138 million—is wonderful," said Nordenberg. And for the reason noted in my introduction, it is a source of real personal satisfaction for me that this good news was brought by you."

"To get great students and great athletes, they have to feel good about where they will go to school," added Pederson. "Students want nice facilities for education and recreation, and if you don't provide those things, you are not in step with other schools."

"It's an unbelievable day for the university," said Willard. "This will help our recruiting and will help recruiting on campus. No longer will we lose kids because of facilities."

Precisely where the new facility would be built became official 14 months later, when Pitt announced on March 18, 1999 that Pitt Stadium would be razed to make way for the new building. The Pitt football team played its games at Pitt Stadium for the final time during the 1999 season. The Panthers used Three Rivers Stadium during the 2000 season, at the same time a new football stadium [Heinz Field] was being constructed adjacent to it. The football Panthers moved into Heinz Field on a permanent basis in 2001.

Blount, who decided to give professional basketball a shot. Willard had seen it coming.

"About two weeks after the [1997] Big East tournament, Mark was taking the bus home to New York City on weekends," the coach said a year later. "An agent got involved with him, and Mark's financial situation was a little different from most kids. He had no financial support from anybody, and he struggled with that in his two years at Pitt. He came to me and explained that he just didn't feel like he could go on this way without having any money."

More bad news awaited Willard and the 1997-98 Panthers. Slowed by a stress fracture in his foot, Kellii Taylor underwent surgery in February 1998.

He missed most of the Big East season. With the key personnel losses, Willard was hoping for instant contributions from his recruiting class that included six-foot-six John Finneman (Fairfax, Virginia), six-foot-eight Stephen Flores (East Liverpool, Ohio), six-foot-five Ricardo Greer (New York City), six-foot-nine Kevin Leslie (Washington, D.C.), and six-foot-eight Michael Shin (Richmond, Virginia). Another freshman, six-foot-nine Attila Cosby, enrolled following a season at Oak Hill (Virginia) Academy. Only Greer played four seasons at Pitt.

Greer made a major impact as a freshman, averaging 12.4 points per game. Vonteego Cummings, in his junior season, led the Panthers with 19.5

RALPH WILLARD SHARES HIS STRATEGY.
Courtesy of University of Pittsburgh Athletics

SIGNIFICANT WINS: THE WILLARD YEARS

1/22/95   PITT 94, ST. JOHN'S 87
(Madison Square Garden)
• Ralph Willard's first Big East win at Pitt.

3/9/95   PITT 74, ST. JOHN'S 71
(Big East Tournament)
• Panthers defeat St. John's for second time at Garden in 1994-95.

1/10/96   PITT 75, GEORGETOWN 56
• Panthers' 31-6 run in second half keys upset of fifth-ranked Hoyas at Civic Arena.

12/30/96   PITT 85, MICHIGAN 78
(Rainbow Classic, Hawaii)
• Wolverines were ranked No. 4 at the time.

1/25/97   PITT 89, AT GEORGETOWN 71
• Kellii Taylor's 15 points, 10 rebounds, six assists and four steals spark Pitt's first road win of season.

2/12/97   PITT 95, VILLANOVA 89
• Jason Maile becomes third Pitt player to score 40 points in a game.

3/2/97   PITT 65, AT SYRACUSE 63
• Back-to-back road wins against Connecticut and Syracuse to end regular season.

11/26/98   PITT 94, XAVIER 76
(Puerto Rico Shootout)
• Panthers force No. 13 Musketeers into 13 first-half turnovers.

11/27/98   PITT 68, KENTUCKY 56
(Puerto Rico Shootout)
• Second win in two days against a ranked opponent.

1/30/99   PITT 60, MIAMI 54
• Pitt upsets No. 23 Hurricanes two days before Ralph Willard announces resignation.

(ppg). Hawkins, stepping in where Blount, Jordan, and Varga had contributed so much late in the season before, averaged 14.2 points per game as a sophomore, but the Panthers didn't get much help from their bench in 1997-98, and slipped to 11-16 overall, 6-12 in the Big East. Freshmen Finneman and Leslie both sustained knee injuries that year. Finneman didn't play at all; Leslie was used sparingly. Even the City Game went Duquesne's way. The Dukes beat the Panthers, 80-69. The disappointing season ended when the Panthers lost in double-overtime to Villanova, 96-93, in the opening round of the Big East tournament. Vonteego Cummings played the entire game, scoring 37 points in the loss.

Cummings's senior season (1998-99) was short-changed at the start when he suffered a broken left hand in a freakish accident during preseason practice. Steve Flores broke his thumb around the same time, and six-foot-nine, 220-pound freshman center

KELLII TAYLOR DRIVES TO THE BASKET.
Courtesy of Sean Brady

Chris Seabrooks was limited by a lingering knee injury.

Despite the setbacks, the Panthers started quickly, winning their first six games for the first time since the 1987-88 season. Pitt upset nationally ranked opponents in back-to-back games when it knocked off Xavier and Kentucky in the Puerto Rico Shootout over Thanksgiving weekend. But the 6-0 mark was the high-water point in what became Ralph Willard's final season as Pitt's basketball coach.

Pitt was ranked No. 20 by AP when top-ranked and undefeated Connecticut visited Fitzgerald Field House on December 12, 1998. A sold-out crowd, dressed mostly in white in response to an athletics department edict, roared throughout as the Panthers led during most of the game. But in the final seconds, UConn's Khalid El-Amin intercepted an inbounds pass in the

backcourt, drove the distance, and hit a last-second shot to stun the Panthers, 70-69.

The 1998-99 Panthers seemed unable to shake the effects of the numbing defeat. Pitt lost five of its next seven games, and what was happening off the court suddenly was more pertinent than what occurred on it. In late December, Kellii Taylor missed six games to undergo alcohol rehabilitation treatment. Then, on January 19, 1999, while the Panthers were in Philadelphia for a game against Villanova, freshman guard Fred Primus was arrested on charges of theft and receiving stolen property. He was dismissed from the team by AD Steve Pederson, who had replaced Oval Jaynes in late 1996. Primus eventually transferred to East Carolina, where he finished a productive career.

With the Panthers struggling to stay above .500, Willard wanted assurance from Pederson that his job was safe. When no assurance was given, Willard made his move first. At a February

ISAAC HAWKINS IS POISED TO SHOOT.
Photo by Image Point Pittsburgh

1, 1999 press conference, he announced that he would be resigning as Pitt's coach at the end of the season. He stated that media speculation about his job security and potential coaching replacements had damaged his ability to recruit for the next season. Willard told the gathering that he had made the decision to resign after Pitt's 60-54 win against No.23-ranked Miami two days earlier at Fitzgerald Field House. Pederson negotiated a settlement with Willard for the remaining three years on his contract.

Ralph Willard's last team limped—literally—into the 1999 Big East tournament with only seven players in uniform. Junior guard Jarrett Lockhart didn't dress for Pitt's game with Rutgers because of a hamstring pull. Attila Cosby had been suspended late in the season for fighting with assistant coach Oliver Antigua. Not surprisingly, the Panthers made a quick exit from New York,

RICARDO GREER AND ISAAC HAWKINS WERE WILLARD RECRUITS WHOSE CAREERS ENDED UNDER BEN HOWLAND.
Courtesy of University of Pittsburgh

MARK BLOUNT REBOUNDS DURING A 1997 WIN AGAINST NOTRE DAME AT THE CIVIC ARENA.
Photo by Image Point Pittsburgh

falling to Rutgers 64-51 on March 3, 1999. After a 6-0 start, Willard's last team finished 14-16. His five-year record at Pitt was 63-82. In an interview several years before his departure, he was philosophical about the problems he'd encountered but remained optimistic about the opportunity for success.

"I envisioned that this [Pitt] could be a Top 25 program on a consistent basis, with a new facility," he said in late 1997. "When I came here in 1994, I was told that we'd be breaking ground for a new building within two years, and the fact that that hasn't happened is a little frustrating, because I think we could have a great home-court advantage here, and we could have a great product to sell. But we have to get past facilities at this point to recruit."

Oval Jaynes, the man who brought Willard to Pitt in 1994, stood by his man during an interview many years after both men had left Pittsburgh.

"I thought we made a great hire and still do," said Jaynes. "You hire coaches who are used to winning. Everywhere he'd been, he'd been associated with outstanding teams and winning programs. But I don't think any coach experienced as many injuries in the course of two to three years that Ralph did."

Willard did leave an impressive legacy in terms of his staff. Tom Crean (Marquette), Sean Miller (Xavier), Bobby Jones (St. Francis, Pennsylvania), and Jim Christian (Kent State) all became head coaches after working for Willard at Pitt.

The outgoing coach, who then returned to become head coach at his alma mater, Holy Cross, also left a pair of signed recruits for his successor, players who had inked with Pitt during the early signing period the previous November. Their names were Brandin Knight and Jaron Brown, and their contributions to Pitt's basketball program would be significant.

Steve Pederson, meanwhile, began his search for Pitt's next basketball coach.

Renaissance: 1999–2004

> "Better jump on the bandwagon that is Pitt basketball, because it's going to get crowded the way the Panthers are going."

—Phil Axelrod, *Pittsburgh Post-Gazette*
January 5, 2002

> "What Ben Howland did in resurrecting the program, and the way Jamie Dixon has continued that is phenomenal. What's changed, obviously, is the facility. Basketball has grown so much in popularity on the collegiate level, and Pittsburgh certainly has been a major part of that. The excitement here is unreal."

—Dick Vitale at the Petersen Events Center
February 15, 2004

Steve Pederson, a man unafraid to make difficult decisions, had another one on his plate in February 1999. He was looking to hire a replacement for Ralph Willard.

Pederson, Pitt's Athletics Director, had arrived in Pittsburgh from the University of Nebraska in late 1996. Almost immediately, he oversaw a dramatic restructuring of the department, and jobs were eliminated. The following year, he announced a plan to make the name "Pittsburgh" more prominent—rather than "Pitt." He talked about creating more of a national identity. Henceforth, team uniforms would bear the name of the city instead of the familiar P-I-T-T. New marketing opportunities arose as well.

The biggest change, however, became official on March 19, 1999, when the University of Pittsburgh's Board of Trustees endorsed plans to move Pitt's home football games to a new football stadium on the city's North Shore. That stadium became Heinz Field. That spelled the end for 75-year-old Pitt Stadium. In its place would rise a new

Continued on page 123

MARCH 7-10, 2001

Nobody can pick the precise moment when Pitt's dramatic rise to basketball prominence began, but a good place to start would be the 2001 Big East tournament at Madison Square Garden. The 2000-2001 Pitt team did something that none of its predecessors had done—win more than one game at the conference's postseason event.

Pitt entered the Big East tournament with an overall record of 15-12, having won three of its last four regular-season games, but not even the most optimistic Pitt fan could have predicted what was about to happen, even if Pitt's coaches were quietly confident.

"I knew by the way we were preparing and buying in to what we were doing and moving Jaron [Brown] into a more significant role that we were getting there," said coach Ben Howland.

Barry Rohrssen, one of the team's assistant coaches, pointed to a late-season win, a 68-61 victory at Seton Hall just four days after a 20-point loss at Rutgers, as a turning point.

"That game was when we really started to come together," Rohrssen explained. "That was one of those games where things began to click. I had a real good feeling after that game."

In New York, Pitt met Miami in the first round on March 7. The Panthers had defeated the Hurricanes in their only meeting during the regular season, and quickly established control of the game. Pitt led by 16 points in the first half, and by 11 at halftime, 37-26. Miami closed the deficit to two points with 8:37 to play, but a 20-9 Pitt run clinched the 78-69 victory. Senior Ricardo Greer—who was named to the All-Tournament team—had 27 points and 11 rebounds. Brandin Knight had 16 points and six rebounds, and Donatas Zavackas scored 16 as well, including all six of his free-throw attempts.

That victory set up a quarterfinal-round game with Notre Dame, which had beaten Pitt twice in the regular season. This time, however,

Howland made a key strategic adjustment.

"We did something we hadn't done all year, which was to double [team] the post every time Troy Murphy got the ball," he said. "That was big for us."

Murphy, a six-foot-11 shooting forward who led the Big East in scoring that season, was held to eight points on just two-of-11 shooting. It was the first time in 78 games that Murphy did not score in double figures.

Pitt had plenty of stars against the Irish. Greer had 17 points and eight rebounds. Brown came off the bench to score a career-high 14 points, and Brandin Knight had 10 points and 11 assists. Pitt jumped to an early 15-2 lead, but ND rallied to take a 26-23 lead with 4:51 left in the first half. The Panthers ended the half with a 13-3 run to take a 36-29 lead at intermission.

In the second half, Notre Dame could get no closer than four points, 42-38, with 14:20 remaining, but Pitt scored the next six points and later stretched its lead to as many as 15 points. The Panthers won, 66-54.

Syracuse, another team Pitt had lost to twice in the regular season, was next in Pitt's first Big East semifinal appearance since 1988-89. A free throw by Isaac Hawkins with three seconds left in overtime lifted the Panthers to a 55-54 victory that had the crowd of 19,528 limp. Hawkins and Ricardo Greer, Pitt's seniors, were clutch for the Panthers. Greer hit a three-pointer with 2:48 left in overtime to tie the score at 54-54. Hawkins was a force inside, scoring 17 points and grabbing a game-high 12 rebounds. Brandin Knight handed out a game-high nine assists to lead Pitt into the Big East tournament title game—for

the first time—against Boston College.

The Panthers, trying to become the first team in conference history to win the tournament by playing on four consecutive days, started quickly against the Eagles, racing to an 11-point lead, 20-9, to start the game, but BC runs of 9-2 and 13-0 helped stake the Eagles to a 37-29 halftime lead.

A three-pointer by Zavackas with 12:11 remaining pulled the Panthers to within five points, but that was as close as Pitt could get. The Eagles won going away, 79-57, but the dramatic run was in stark contrast to most previous Big East tournaments in which the Panthers were usually early-round losers. "Remember the Run" became Pitt's battle cry heading into the 2001-2002 season, and was the perfect springboard for what Pitt's teams accomplished in the next few seasons.

"It [2001 Big East tournament success] was all over the world," said Howland. "I can't tell you how much the exposure meant to us. I've gotten so much positive feedback from people. We were on national

THE MADISON SQUARE GARDEN MARQUEE ON THE NIGHT OF PITT'S FIRST BIG EAST TITLE GAME APPEARANCE.
Courtesy of University of Pittsburgh

television, in its entirety, four nights in a row in prime time. We made huge gains in that, and the fact that we beat good teams—Miami, Notre Dame, and Syracuse—there were a lot of positive things for us to hang our hats on, trust me."

CHANCELLOR MARK NORDENBERG (FAR RIGHT) AND AD STEVE PEDERSON (FAR LEFT) WITH JOHN AND GERTRUDE PETERSEN, FOR WHOM PITT'S BASKETBALL FACILITY WAS NAMED. *Photo by Mike Drazdzinski/CIDDE*

convocation center, a student recreation center, and a student-housing complex. Finally, Pitt would have a modern home basketball facility. Critics of Pederson—and there were many—charged that he had spearheaded the effort to eliminate important elements of the school's history and tradition.

The decision to raze Pitt Stadium—even with the construction of a spectacular new home for the basketball program—touched the nerves among longtime Pitt people, many of whom thought they should have been a part of the decision process. In any event, Pederson was able to tell coaching candidates that a terrific basketball facility was going to be constructed.

One day in the late 1990s, Pederson found himself watching the NCAA basketball tournament. He was struck by the play of Northern Arizona, a member of the Big Sky Conference.

"You watch them [Northern Arizona] play, and there was something special about them," Pederson later told the *Pittsburgh Post-Gazette*. "They took the right shots, they rebounded, they were disciplined. When they showed [head coach] Ben [Howland], I liked his presence.

"It's one of those deals where you file something in the back of your head: 'That's a neat guy.'"

Ben Howland visited Pittsburgh in late February 1999 and met with Pederson. No other coach made such a trip. Steve Pederson had found his man.

"I had a very short list," Pederson recalled.

Pitt officials sealed the deal with their new basketball coach via long-distance telephone calls from New York City and the Big East tournament. Howland was introduced as Pitt's 13th basketball coach at a press conference inside Pitt Stadium on March 8, 1999.

Continued on page 125

TIGER PAUL, FANATICS, AND THE OAKLAND ZOO

It's doubtful that any members of Pitt's famed student cheering section, the Oakland Zoo, are aware that once there were Field House Fanatics. And, two decades before that, a singular, uninhibited gentleman known as Tiger Paul stormed the sideline in front of the student section leading the crowd in the popular "Let's go Pitt!" cheer. But the three shared one important characteristic—each made attending a Pitt home basketball game more fun and enjoyable.

Through the 1960s, Pitt students were more or less left to their own devices when it came to supporting the basketball teams. Indeed, during one bleak period in the late 1960s, there were instances when the

TIGER PAUL AUSLANDER WAS A REGULAR AT PITT BASKETBALL GAMES THROUGHOUT THE 1970S.
Courtesy of University of Pittsburgh Athletics

school's cheerleaders wouldn't bother to show up for the games. As cheerleading itself developed more into dance and entertainment, opportunities arose for enterprising souls to step forward to lead and inspire the younger folks during the games.

Tiger Paul, whose real name was Paul Auslander, was a Pittsburgh original, a graduate of Peabody High School who loved sports but, at five-foot-four and 181 pounds, wasn't cut out for serious competition. He tried out for football one year, where

he was joined by a classmate, Bob Smizik, who later became a sports columnist in Pittsburgh.

Tiger earned his nickname at practice one day when the coach urged him to be more aggressive in attacking the blocking sled. "C'mon, Paul, hit that thing! Be a tiger!"

The name stuck, and Tiger Paul eventually took his love for sports to the Jewish Y in Pittsburgh, located right behind Heinz Chapel on Pitt's campus. There he coached amateur basketball teams in the Maccabiad Games. In the early 1970s, Pitt assistant coach Tim Grgurich and two boosters, former Panther basketball players Bill Baierl and Frank Gustine, Jr., observed Tiger Paul's enthusiasm on the sideline. They discussed the idea of bringing the aspiring coach to Pitt's home games, where he might liven things up as an unofficial cheerleader. Tiger accepted and was a regular at Fitzgerald Field House from 1973-1982.

His end-to-end sprints, jumping jacks, push-ups, and flailing arms came to be Tiger Paul's trademarks, along with his outlandish outfits. He normally wore a blue varsity Pitt letter sweater over a long-sleeved white shirt, but for special occasions—big games against Duquesne and West Virginia, and a 1980 home date with Duke—he would do

THE FIELD HOUSE FANATICS WERE AROUND FOR MUCH OF THE 1990S.
Photo by Image Point Pittsburgh

something more outrageous. He once cheered in his pajamas. Another time he wore a tuxedo. He came dressed as Santa Claus for one mid-December home game.

"He was a reasonably bright guy," said Smizik.

"People made fun of 'Tiger,' but he did a lot that people don't realize," said Tim Grgurich. "He brought enthusiasm to the Field House. Now, it's all about enthusiasm. Before, some folks looked down on that kind of stuff."

Tiger Paul also was a heavy gambler, and there was a concern that his personal life, not to mention his behavior on the court, was embarrassing the university. Tiger would sometimes make bus trips to road games with the Panthers. In a 1973 game at Notre Dame, where Pitt blew a seven-point lead in the final minute of a game and lost in overtime, Tiger Paul had the Notre Dame student section howling when he stripped off his Pitt sweater, flung it up in the air, then had it land over his head. Two years later, during a Pitt win against Temple in Philadelphia, he was ejected for taking issue with an official's call—he normally sat at the end of the team bench at away games.

Feeling unwanted and unappreciated, and not wanting to cause any friction with school officials, Tiger Paul drifted away from the Field House in the early 1980s, and later moved to Nevada. He died there in 1992.

Around that same time, an organized band of Pitt students pooled their efforts and enthusiasm and formed the Field House Fanatics, a group that sat in one section of the end zone. They had special T-shirts made up with their name, and specialized in providing an even greater home-court advantage for Pitt.

"It was started by a few guys who had grown up following Pitt basketball," said Jeff Kamis, a Fanatic who, in his professional life, later picked

MEMBERS OF THE OAKLAND ZOO AT THE PETERSEN EVENTS CENTER.
Courtesy of University of Pittsburgh Athletics

Continued from page 124

up a Super Bowl ring as a member of the Tampa Bay Buccaneers' front office. "The main thing was that we wanted to be as loud as we could be, and get the students fired up."

Unlike other notorious student bodies, this one chose only to accentuate the positive, and not make sport of Pitt's opponent.

"There was nothing ignorant or obscene about it," said Kamis. "It was all good, clean fun."

In terms of membership, the Field House Fanatics never came close to

approaching the membership of the more prominent Oakland Zoo. For one thing, logistics were against them.

"We only had that one small section of the one end zone, which was actually general admission seating," explained Kamis. "We had to have one or two guys get to the games real early and then hold some seats for the rest of us."

When the Petersen Events Center was opened in 2002, Pitt officials made sure that those students who were privileged to attend the games would have some of the best seats in the house. Student-body seating encompasses one side of the court and an area in one end zone. They're easily recognized by their gold T-shirts as residents and members of the Oakland Zoo.

The Oakland Zoo was the brainstorm of a Pitt student, Matt Cohen, who was put off by the lack of enthusiasm at home games when he first started going to games at the Field House as a freshman in 2000. A Philadelphian who had grown up enjoying the fervor of that city's Big Five rivalries, he wanted to bring the same type of excitement to Pittsburgh. He noticed, and recruited, a pair of fellow basketball junkies, Zach Hale and Jon St. George, and a new institution was started. During the 2004-05 season,

estimates of Oakland Zoo membership had topped 6,000.

And the name? How did it evolve?

"Matt [Cohen] and I were just talking about it, and we came up with the zoo because there are a lot of crazy animals," Hale told *The Pitt News.* "We thought students would respond more to Oakland."

Zoo members have even taken their show on the road—and drawn the wrath of opposing student sections.

"At Notre Dame, we had their entire student section turning and yelling us," Cohen explained in the same *Pitt News* article. "The student section focused its attention on us."

Pitt coach Jamie Dixon was an assistant coach to Ben Howland in 2000 when he first met with Cohen to discuss the possibility of forming The Zoo. After seeing the impact of the group—Pitt won its first 34 games at the Petersen Events Center—Dixon embraced the group, and hosted a special meeting on the basketball court in early 2005.

"They are the best," Dixon told *The Pitt News.*

"It's taken off," Cohen said in a *Beaver County-Allegheny Times* article. "Schools like North Carolina, UConn, UCLA, they don't have anything as good as this. I really believe we've become one of the Top 10 student sections in the country."

"He [Howland] is a guy who would be good at almost anything he does," said Pitt Chancellor Mark Nordenberg. "He's a guy, I'm sure, who has the ability to manage and work with people and get them to effectively work with each other. Those are qualities you want in anyone you work with."

"He is intelligent, enthusiastic, and demanding, and he will be a great addition to a great university," said Pederson.

Howland—whose Northern Arizona teams had registered three successive 21-win seasons while also leading the nation in three-point field goal percentage—was asked about his philosophy of basketball.

"I try to recruit good shooters," Pitt's new coach explained. "You don't try to teach them to be good

shooters. This is something they have to hone since they were young. We want good shooters, and we take good shots."

Not too long after accepting the job, Howland laid out his intentions for rebuilding Pitt's program.

"I'm in this for the long haul," he said. "I'm not looking to be here three years and get out. I'm looking to be here a long time. How you start off and how you do things—initially—really have a lot to do with your ultimate success. I feel very lucky to be here. I'm very happy and fortunate to be here. Timing is everything, and the timing is perfect right now."

Born in Oregon, Howland spent his developing years in Cerritos, California. He played basketball

THE VIEW UP DESOTO STREET (ABOVE), ALSO KNOWN AS CARDIAC HILL, SO FAMILIAR FOR 75 YEARS, CHANGED DRAMATICALLY WHEN PITT STADIUM WAS RAZED IN EARLY 2000, AND CONSTRUCTION BEGAN ON THE PETERSEN EVENTS CENTER. *Courtesy of Sean Brady*

and graduated from Weber State in 1979. His roots and connection were primarily West Coast. He brought two members of his NAU staff—Jamie Dixon and Chris Carlson—with him to Pittsburgh. Barry Rohrssen, a New Yorker who had played his scholastic ball at Xaverian High School in Brooklyn, joined the program as director of basketball operations. He later became a full-fledged assistant coach.

The coach was new, but at least one remnant of the Ralph Willard period—misfortune—remained. Forward Isaac Hawkins fractured his tibia before Howland's first season and redshirted in 1999-2000. Ricardo Greer was back for his junior campaign, along with rugged six-foot-nine Chris Seabrooks, a coveted Willard recruit from Macon, Georgia. Seabrooks's freshman season was limited to brief spurts in 21 games. He had chronic knee problems and developed asthma.

Howland had inherited a pair of recruits—Brandin Knight and Jaron Brown—from Willard.

He also brought in six-foot-eight shooting forward Donatas Zavackas, a Lithuanian who played his junior year of high school basketball at St. Benedict's Prep in Newark, New Jersey before moving to Ohio for his senior year. A transfer rule caused Zavackas to miss his senior season at St. Vincent-St. Mary. Howland was impressed with Brandin Knight especially, the coach's son from New Jersey whose brother, Brevin, had played at Stanford and later in the NBA.

"A kid like Brandin Knight," he said. "He epitomizes the type of kid I want to coach, and I haven't even coached him yet. Here's a kid who's a 3.6 student, comes from a solid family, is a real good player. He's everything."

Pitt defeated Wright State, 69-52, on November 19, 1999 to kick off the Ben Howland Era. The Panthers won their next three games—all at home—before losing to Tennessee, 76-50, on December 4 at the Field House. Howland's first Pitt team finished

GOODBYE FITZGERALD, HELLO PETERSEN

People in the Pittsburgh area needed a scorecard to keep up with the comings and goings of major sporting venues around the city before and after the turn of the new millennium. Pitt Stadium closed following the 1999 football season, and was demolished during the subsequent winter months. Three Rivers Stadium, home since 1970 to the Pittsburgh Pirates and Pittsburgh Steelers—and Pitt's football team in 2000—was imploded in February 2001. Adjacent to it, and not too far from it, Heinz Field and PNC Park were constructed—both opened in 2001.

The removal of Pitt Stadium, an edifice that stood for 75 years on Pitt's upper campus, made way for the construction of the John M. and Gertrude E. Petersen Events Center. The facility was named in honor of the Petersens, who donated $10 million toward the construction of the facility. Ground was broken on June 14, 2000, at a special ceremony involving the couple.

"John and Gertrude Petersen have been among the University of Pittsburgh's most active, loyal, and generous friends," remarked Pitt Chancellor Mark Nordenberg at the time of the Petersen's gift. "Now they have made a commitment to the University that is historic in both size and its impact."

The contribution was the largest individual contribution in the University of Pittsburgh's history.

THE SCOREBOARD TELLS THE STORY AS PITT ENDS A 51-YEAR RUN AT FITZGERALD FIELD HOUSE WITH A WIN AGAINST WEST VIRGINIA.
Photo by Image Point Pittsburgh

Before Pitt's basketball team could move into its new home, it had two more seasons of basketball to play at old Fitzgerald Field House. The 2001-02 season was Pitt's final year at the Field House, and the Panthers made it special, losing only one game, a 56-53 setback against Notre Dame on January 12, 2002. The final college basketball game played at Fitzgerald was March 2, 2002, when Pitt easily defeated West Virginia, 92-65. School officials invit-

ed back all former basketball players, who were honored by decade during a special ceremony at half-time. Panther greats Don Hennon, Billy Knight, Brian Generalovich, and Charles Smith were among the former Panthers in attendance that night and at a special dinner on campus the night before.

"It was a great ending for a storied building," Pitt coach Ben Howland told the media after the final game. "I think the players who came back feel good about their alma mater. I think they feel good about the program."

Pitt's final record at Fitzgerald Field House was 414-176.

Eight months later, on November 23, 2002, John and Gertrude Petersen were among the crowd of 12,508 who watched Pitt defeat city rival Duquesne, 82-67, in the first game played in the facility bearing their names. It also marked the first time since the 1989-90 season, when Pitt beat Duquesne at Fitzgerald Field House, that the game was played at either school's on-campus facility. The next 12 Pitt-Duquesne games were played at Civic Arena—later renamed Mellon Arena.

with a 13-15 record, including a 5-11 mark in Big East play. Pitt won three of its last four games, including road victories at Boston College and Providence. Greer led the 1999-2000 Panthers in scoring with 18.1 points per game.

The renaissance started during the 2001-2002 season. The Panthers won their first five games before an 88-74 loss at Penn State on December 6, 2001. Greer suffered an ankle injury during an overtime loss at Virginia Commonwealth on December 17, four days before the Panthers were scheduled to play Duquesne at Mellon Arena. On game day, Howland dismissed Chris Seabrooks from the team

for "behavioral conduct detrimental to the program." The Panthers lost to the Dukes, 71-70.

The 8-3 Panthers began Big East play with a 62-51 home victory against Miami before losing to Syracuse and Connecticut. A home win against Seton Hall was followed by a road loss at Notre Dame, setting up a conference game against undefeated and ninth-ranked Georgetown in the nation's capital on January 20, 2001, Inauguration Day for George W. Bush.

The Panthers surprised the Hoyas, 70-66.

Continued on page 129

KNIGHT AND KRAUSER: AT THE POINT

Ben Howland inherited Brandin Knight as a freshman point guard when he became Pitt's head coach in 1999. That didn't mean he was content with the situation at that position. Howland set his sights on another rising star at that position, Carl Krauser, who entered Pitt as a 20-year-old freshman in 2001. Krauser redshirted that first season, but made a significant contribution to the Panthers' rising status.

"One of the keys to us becoming a dominant team in my third year [2001-2002] there was the fact that Brandin had an unbelievable level of competition every day in practice from Carl," said Howland. "Carl was redshirted because of the partial qualifier rules, and he pushed Brandin every day. Carl is an unbelievable competitor, and I think he really helped Brandin improve. They went at it, and it was physical."

Krauser, who grew up in the Bronx, reached 25th place on Pitt's all-time scoring list during the 2005 Big East tournament in New York, but he and Knight—who scored 1,440 points from 1999-2003—will forever be remembered as the men who made the Panthers go during their basketball revival at the beginning of this century.

Knight was named to the 2002-2003 Wooden All-America team, one of only 10 players nationwide selected to that squad. He also was named second-team All-America by *The Sporting News* in 2001-2002. Krauser was named the Big East's Most Improved Player for 2003-2004, and was selected second-team All-Conference the following year.

"They [Knight and Krauser] are both winners," said former Notre Dame point guard, Chris Thomas, in a 2004 interview. "They give their teams a chance to win. They both step up and make plays."

Knight first gained the college basketball spotlight late in the 2000-2001 season when, as a sophomore, he directed Pitt's surprising run that ended with a loss to Boston College in the Big East finals. His play at the point set the tone for the team's back-to-back Sweet 16 appearances.

"As Brandin went, that's how we went," said Howland. "He was the consummate point guard. He was our All-American. His leadership was outstanding. He was the player

CARL KRAUSER ON THE MOVE.
Photo by Image Point Pittsburgh

BRANDIN KNIGHT AGAINST GEORGETOWN.
Courtesy of University of Pittsburgh Athletics

who really believed that we could win everything. That kind of confidence exuded amongst all the other players, and it all started with him. He was so unselfish. All he cared about was winning. Winning was the only thing that mattered to Brandin Knight."

Krauser's pushing and prodding also helped.

"By doing that with Brandin, it raised Brandin's level with everybody else," remarked Howland. "If Brandin was playing and practicing as hard as he could, that was just infectious on everybody else. Jaron [Brown] was like that every day. It helped Julius [Page]. It helped everybody. It was huge."

Brown, whose stellar career also had its genesis at the 2001 Big East tournament, attended several Pitt

home games in 2004-2005, one year after his final season as a player. He was asked to compare Knight and Krauser.

"Both of them were great leaders," he said. "Brandin was probably a little better student of the game, and Carl learned a lot from Brandin."

Thomas, who saw both of them many times in some memorable Pitt-Notre Dame clashes, was more specific about his two counterparts.

"Brandin was more of an 'I'll get into you defensively' type," he said. "Carl Krauser is more laid-back, older, a flashy kind of guy who really knows how to play. I really respect Krauser's game, though, because he had to come out from Brandin's shadow, and he's played very well. Brandin Knight had quite a reputation. Brandin's success fueled Carl, and helped make him the player that he is. I liked playing against both guys."

Krauser has fond memories of his practice battles with Knight.

"We both helped each other at the same time," he noted. "We both got after it. We're a couple of passionate players, a couple of passionate point guards going at it. He's from Jersey; I'm from New York."

Krauser's development as an understudy was consistent with the development and growth of key players in Pitt's program who sat out their first year on campus before becoming eligible players. Jaron Brown was redshirted in 1999-2000—Howland's first season—forward Chevon Troutman sat out the 2000-2001 season, then Krauser did not play in 2001-2002.

"All of those guys got better as their redshirt year progressed," said Howland. "They all improved by being in the program. The same thing's going to happen for players like Aaron Gray and Levon Kendall."

JULIUS PAGE WAS THE PRIZE OF BEN HOWLAND'S 2000 RECRUITING CLASS.
Courtesy of University of Pittsburgh Athletics

BRANDIN KNIGHT DRIBBLES UNDER THE WATCHFUL EYES OF JAMIE DIXON (BACKGROUND LEFT) AND BEN HOWLAND (RIGHT). *Courtesy of Sean Brady*

"In a city turned upside down by the inauguration of a president who didn't receive a mandate from the people, Pitt turned the world of college basketball upside down," wrote Phil Axelrod in *The Pittsburgh Post-Gazette*.

Six-foot-three freshman guard Julius Page set the tone with a tomahawk dunk over Georgetown's Ruben Boumjte-Boumjte six minutes into the contest.

"Julius is probably the best athlete I've ever coached," Howland admitted in 2005. "That dunk against Georgetown has to be the greatest single play that I've ever witnessed. I don't care about Jerome Lane knocking down the backboard. That dunk against Georgetown was phenomenal."

A crowd of 12,109 at the MCI Center couldn't believe its eyes.

"We knew they [Georgetown] overlooked us," said Ricardo Greer. "They were passive, ripe for the beating. This was a prefect opportunity for us."

The big win failed to spark the Panthers, who lost five of their next six games. The only win was a 63-46 defeat of West Virginia on January 31 at Fitzgerald Field House. On the same day that Three Rivers Stadium was being imploded in Pittsburgh— February 11, 2001—the Pitt basketball team was an 84-64 loser in a Sunday afternoon game at Rutgers. The Panthers took a 12-11 overall record to Continental Airlines Arena to meet Seton Hall four nights later. Freshman center Toree Morris was a surprise starter, replacing the injured Isaac Hawkins, and his play helped the Panthers to an important 68-61 victory. Pitt's defense limited the Pirates to only one basket—by Eddie Griffin—in the final 14:57.

"We wanted it more than they did," the six-foot-ten Morris told the media after the game. "We played a team game better than they did. That's why we won."

"That win at Seton Hall was a big win, and some of that good play was just about fighting through adversity," said Howland. "We had had several tough losses in a row. Our guys never quit working hard and they never quit playing hard."

The Panthers returned home and beat Rutgers 70-60 to avenge the earlier loss, then lost at Syracuse before finishing the regular season with a 70-51 victory against Virginia Tech, which was playing its first season as a member of the newly configured Big East Conference. Pitt finished 7-9 in the Big East's West Division, ahead of Seton Hall (5-11) and Rutgers (3-13).

Pitt captured the attention of college basketball followers by winning three straight games in the Big East tournament before bowing to Boston College in the championship game. The Panthers received an invitation to the National Invitation Tournament (NIT), where they were awarded a first-round home game against St. Bonaventure on March 14, 2001. The Panthers rallied to defeat the Bonnies 84-75, but were defeated by Mississippi State 66-61 in a second-round home game. Pitt finished the season 19-14—its highest win total since Ralph Willard's 1996-97 NIT club went 18-15. It also marked the career finales for seniors Ricardo Greer, Isaac Hawkins, and Griffin Abel.

Pitt's late-season surge failed to impress most of the Big East's coaches. When the preseason polls were announced for the 2001-2002 campaign, the Panthers were picked sixth in the seven-team West Division. It also was Pitt's final season at Fitzgerald Field House. There had been talk of the basketball team moving into the Petersen Events Center in time for Big East play in January 2002, but that didn't materialize. That would have to wait until the following November.

For the second straight season, Pitt won its first five games. The Panthers' first loss in 2001-2002

JARON BROWN WAS THE GLUE TO PITT'S GREAT TEAMS. *Courtesy of University of Pittsburgh Athletics*

came in the championship game of the University Hoops Invitational at Robert Morris College. Pitt lost to South Florida 69-63, a team coached by former Panthers' assistant coach Seth Greenberg. The Panthers wouldn't lose another game until almost seven weeks later.

Following the loss to USF, the Panthers won 10 in a row, including an impressive 62-55 win at Ohio State on December 19, 2001. The Panthers were 9-1—and unranked—heading into the contest. It was the first time Pitt and Ohio State had met in basketball since they played the first college basketball game at the new Civic Arena in Pittsburgh in December 1961. Ohio State won that game, but Pitt was the winner 40 years later. The Panthers scored 15 straight points in the second half to take a 59-50 lead and never looked back. Ontario Lett—a burly six-foot-six junior-college transfer forward from Pensacola, Florida, was a late-summer recruit

Continued on page 134

PITT-UCONN: BIG EAST TITLE TRILOGY

The Pitt-Connecticut basketball rivalry evolved into one of college basketball's fiercest during the early years of the 21st Century. For three consecutive seasons (2002-04), New York City's Madison Square Garden was the setting when the Panthers and Huskies fought for top bragging rights in the Big East Conference. The Huskies won the first and third championships, while Pitt claimed the middle game for its first ever Big East tournament title.

Pitt and Connecticut did not meet during the 2001-2002 regular season, but staged a memorable Big East championship game on March 9, 2002. The Huskies prevailed, 74-65, in double overtime, but not before Pitt junior point guard Brandin Knight almost pulled off a Kirk Gibson-like miracle shot that would have given the Panthers the win at the end of the first overtime.

With 31 seconds remaining in regulation, Knight crumpled to the ground, clutching his right knee. He left the court and went to the locker room, but emerged with 1.7 seconds remaining in the first overtime. Pitt coach Ben Howland inserted Knight, who took the inbounds pass and fired a desperation shot from just inside mid-court that hit the front of the rim. He did not play during the second extra period, and UConn won, 74-65.

"When you lose your best player, your point guard, your quarterback, you lose Michael Jordan, Magic Johnson . . . that's who [Knight] is to our team," Howland told reporters after the game. "I was so proud of the effort, the way our guys kept fighting without him."

"That was one of the most physical basketball games we've been involved in, and we think we're a pretty tough basketball team," said Huskies' coach Jim Calhoun.

Pitt would exact its revenge in 2002-03, defeating Connecticut not once, but twice. The Panthers were 71-67 winners against UConn in the

Huskies' first visit to the Petersen Events Center on March 2, 2003. Both teams then breezed to the Big East finals for the second straight year, but this time Pitt claimed the trophy as the Big East's best. Again, Knight was not at full strength, having injured his right ankle the night before in Pitt's 61-48 win against

BIG EAST COMMISSIONER MIKE TRANGHESE (RIGHT) PRESENTS BEN HOWLAND WITH HIS AWARD FOLLOWING PITT'S 2003 BIG EAST TOURNAMENT TITLE GAME WIN AGAINST CONNECTICUT. *Photo by Harry Bloomberg*

Boston College in the semifinals. Knight did play against Connecticut, and responded with 16 points, six assists, and two steals in leading the Panthers to a 74-56 victory.

"I wasn't going to miss this game for anything," Knight explained afterward. "The only way I wouldn't have played was if I couldn't walk."

"I've never seen another one like him, and I've been in this game for quite awhile," remarked Ben Howland. "He's absolutely the toughest, best winner I've ever been fortunate to play with or coach."

As a testament to the Panthers' balance throughout the 2002-03 season, and at the Big East tournament, Julius Page was awarded the Dave Gavitt Trophy as the tournament's outstanding player.

Pitt and Connecticut played two regular-season games in 2003-04, Jamie Dixon's first season as the Panthers' head coach. Dixon didn't experience defeat until Pitt lost to the Huskies, 68-65, on January 19 at the Hartford Civic Center. The loss

only made the anticipation for the rematch in Pittsburgh that much greater. The February 15 return engagement at the Petersen Events Center was probably the most highly anticipated college basketball game ever in the city of Pittsburgh.

"There were about 120 requests for media credentials, and we had to turn away 10 to 15 people," said Greg Hotchkiss, Pitt's associate director of media relations. "There were some bogus requests, as well. There were a few media people who had never been here before—some people from Ohio—who tried to get in."

On the online auction website Ebay, tickets to the game were going for as much as $600. A single parking pass sold for $75. Several radio outlets had to cancel their planned broadcasts because of a lack of space, but when the game finally started, Pitt was a 75-68 winner, and almost everybody in the building sensed that the two teams hadn't seen the last of each other.

True to the script, Pitt and UConn both advanced to the finals of the 2004 Big East tournament. The Huskies had a more difficult road, playing the first two games without their injured star center, Emeka Okafor. Both teams had their full complement of stars, however, when they met in Round 3 of the Big East Title Trilogy on March 13, 2004.

Pitt led by nine at halftime and by as many as 11 points in the second half, but Connecticut rallied for a 61-58 victory. Ben Gordon, who won the Dave Gavitt Trophy, hit a jumper in the lane with 30 seconds to play to give the Huskies a 59-58 lead and the victory. Despite the loss, Pitt placed three players—Chris Taft, Jaron Brown, and Carl Krauser—on the All-Tournament team.

"I thought we played with tremendous heart and desire, as always," a disappointed Jamie Dixon said after the title game. "We responded and did everything we wanted to do. We just came up short."

HILLGROVE AND GROAT

Bill Hillgrove made his debut as radio Voice of the Panthers on December 1, 1969, when Pitt lost at Rutgers, 91-79. Dick Groat didn't join the team on a permanent basis until 10 years later, but by 2005, the duo had the longest-running tenure of anyone directly involved with the school's basketball program.

DICK GROAT (LEFT) AND BILL HILLGROVE IN 2005.
Photo by Mike Drazdzinski/CIDDE

Hillgrove grew up playing on the streets of Garfield. He snuck in to football games at Pitt Stadium, where an uncle was an usher at Gate 3. Groat, a product of Swissvale who turns 75 on November 4, 2005, had two older brothers—Charles and Martin—who went to Pitt on basketball scholarships. A sister, Elsie, was engaged to Pete Noon, captain of one of Pitt's teams, who lettered from 1934-36. The first basketball Groat ever owned was the game ball from Pitt's 1935 victory against Temple.

A baseball and basketball standout, Groat enrolled at Duke, where he led the nation in both scoring and assists—the only player ever to do so—and was College basketball's Player of the Year in 1952. He also was the first Blue Devil to have his jersey number retired. After one year in the NBA, Groat signed a major-league baseball contract with the hometown Pirates, and was the National League's batting champion and Most Valuable Player in 1960.

"I've been a Pitt fan all my life," Groat said during a 2005 interview. "When I came home from Duke after my sophomore year, I must have played 30 to 40 games with George McCrossin, who was captain of the Pitt team the following year. George Belich was another. I knew all those Pitt guys. I knew DoDo [Canterna] and Sam David."

Hillgrove, Groat's broadcast partner, enrolled at Duquesne University in the late 1950s, where he broadcast Dukes' basketball games on the student radio station. He took a part-time job at Pittsburgh radio station WKJF—now B94-FM—during his sophomore year.

"In my seven years there, full-time and part-time, they didn't do any sports," Hillgrove remembered. "That was at a time when FM radio was in its infancy."

Hillgrove's career received a boost in 1967, when he was hired by WTAE-TV.

"In late '67, the station boss came to me and said, 'Would you like to do radio?'" he remembered. "WTAE was changing its format. They wanted to go more middle of the road. They wanted disc jockeys. They wanted to try to cut into KDKA baseball broadcasts by giving a lot of scores. They wanted to attract baseball fans and gamblers."

Del Taylor, who became familiar to a generation of Pittsburghers as the host of the daytime movie *Dialing for Dollars*, moved to TV. Hillgrove became a nighttime disc jockey, where his slot was known as the "Hillgrove Happening." In late 1968, WTAE's program director approached Hillgrove with an offer:

"They told me that the station was talking to Pitt about getting the [football] games away from WWSW, which had Red Donley doing the games," said Hillgrove. "Pitt

had just hired Buzz Ridl as its basketball coach, and the school wanted the station to cover basketball, too. Pitt games hadn't been broadcast regularly since Don Hennon played there in the late '50s. WWSW broadcast some of the games then. Pitt wanted WTAE to commit to basketball if it wanted the contract to do football."

Ed Conway, WTAE TV's sports director at the time, was given the assignment to do Pitt's football games, which he did through the 1973 season. (Author's note: Conway died after the 1973 football season. Hillgrove, who had been color analyst for Pitt football games, became play-by-play man starting in 1974.) The station, however, didn't want Conway on the road during the lengthier, more irregular basketball season, so the program director asked Hillgrove if he would be interested in becoming Pitt's basketball play-by-play man.

"I said, 'Darn right,'" said Hillgrove.

The 1969-70 season, Buzz Ridl's second at Pitt, was the first year that WTAE broadcast Panthers basketball. Hillgrove, broadcasting without a color analyst, recalled that first game at Rutgers.

"It was a bear," he said. "It was in the old gym they had there. It was loud. Early on [that season], it was just me."

THROUGHOUT THE 1970s, SPORTS INFORMATION DIRECTOR DEAN BILLICK (IN OPEN COLLAR) WAS THE COLOR ANALYST NEXT TO BILL HILLGROVE.
Courtesy of University of Pittsburgh Athletics

Continued from page 132

Ron Rininger, a WTAE radio news anchor—and a basketball fan—provided color commentary for some home games. Dean Billick, Pitt's sports information director who traveled with the team, became Hillgrove's sidekick for road broadcasts. Billick eventually did the commentary for all the games, an arrangement that ultimately caused some problems.

"In the Tim Grgurich years, Timmy didn't like the fact that Dean would bend over backwards to criticize the team," explained Hillgrove. "Dean would become pretty negative, and that bothered Tim, who said, 'We have to get somebody else in there.'"

"That was a tough position for me to be put in, as SID," Billick explained many years later. "I always considered myself a positive person. Our teams weren't perfect those years. If they had been, we never would have lost. I had to be the eyes for the people who were listening at home."

Dick Groat had done some Pitt basketball games on radio, filling in as color man when Billick traveled with Pitt's football teams to bowl games in December. He got the assignment after the 1978-79 season.

"It was because of Bill and Gurg [Grgurich], that I got the job," he said.

The 2004-2005 season was their 26th year together. Hillgrove recalled how it was in the beginning.

"Dick was never a professional broadcaster, and he'd be the first one to admit that," said Hillgrove. "He kind of, in that regard, felt like a fish out of water. But he knows the game, and he knows what's right and wrong."

Pitt fans who listen to Groat are aware of his passion for the game and for the Panthers. He has a couple signature words, though not entirely by design. "Excellent" is a word he uses to describe something positive done by the Panthers. "Wow" usually means an opposing player has just made a backbreaking three-point shot, or some other misfortune has befallen Pitt.

Hillgrove and Groat are asked the same questions many times. For example, which teams were better, the Charles Smith-Jerome Lane teams from 1985-1988 or the powerhouse clubs coached by Ben Howland and Jamie Dixon 25 years later?

"These [later] guys are better defensively," said Hillgrove. "I also think these teams are more fundamentally sound than those past teams were."

Groat is more blunt when asked his assessment of the former clubs, teams that won back-to-back Big East regular-season titles in 1987 and 1988.

"They never achieved what they should have achieved," he said.

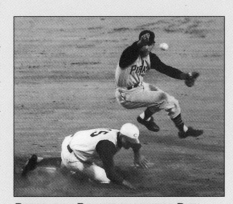

PITTSBURGH PIRATES SHORTSTOP DICK GROAT COMPLETES A DOUBLE PLAY IN A 1959 GAME. *Courtesy of Pittsburgh Pirates*

When asked to remember a particularly galling defeat, Hillgrove has little difficulty producing an answer.

"The Barry Goheen game was a sad thing," said Hillgrove, harkening back to Pitt's overtime loss to Vanderbilt in the second round of the 1988 NCAA tournament. "And a lot of those close losses to West Virginia over the years were hard to swallow."

Pitt's announcers have come to know all of Pitt's players and coaches during their long association with the program. Hillgrove counts Billy Knight, Tom Richards, Cleve Edwards, Sam Clancy, Charles Smith, Clyde Vaughan, and Chevon Troutman as some of his favorite players over the years. Groat, as fate would have it, has become particularly close to the Panthers of the 21st century. He underwent neck surgery several years ago, making him a regular in Pitt's training facilities inside the Petersen Events Center.

"They see me in there a lot, and we have a great time just talking and joking around," said Groat.

Groat is particularly impressed by Chevon Troutman, who was a senior in 2004-2005.

"Chevon Troutman has been such a special kid," said Groat. "He worked his butt off to graduate, and when you consider where he came from, it makes his story so special. I'm very close to saying that he's the greatest college player I've seen since I've been broadcasting, at both ends of the court."

As for their relationships with the grownups—i.e., Pitt's basketball coaches—some have been better than others.

"Buzz Ridl was my basketball dad," said Hillgrove. "Timmy [Grgurich]—I'm still a good friend of Tim's. I got close to him when he was Buzz's assistant and did the recruiting. I would go to high school and [Pittsburgh] City League games with him.

"I was never real close to Roy Chipman, but I liked him because he was a very honest man. Paul Evans was brutally honest, and I came to know Paul well. Ralph Willard? No. He kept everybody at arm's length. He was different. Ben Howland, Jamie Dixon? Good guys, but they never went out of their way to socialize with you."

The two broadcasters room together on road trips and, on the air, have developed a good sense of timing.

"He and I have developed a chemistry," said Hillgrove. "He knows when I have my head down to write something, so he'll jump in when there's a steal or something."

"He [Hillgrove] has taught me everything and anything that I know about broadcasting," added Groat. "It's been a great experience. Bill's the ultimate pro. It's been so much fun working with him."

STEVE PEDERSON (LEFT) AND BEN HOWLAND VISIT DURING THE 2002 NCAA TOURNAMENT AT MELLON ARENA IN PITTSBURGH. *Photo by Chaz Palla—Courtesy of* Pittsburgh Tribune-Review

who contributed 15 points and eight rebounds against the Buckeyes.

"We got lucky," said Howland, when asked about Lett, who signed with Pitt in August that year. "Sometimes you have to get lucky. He has the ability to score. That's nothing we've taught him."

Pitt opened Big East play with a 77-54 thrashing of St. John's on January 2, 2002 at the Field House. That set up a road game at defending Big East champion Boston College, which had defeated Pitt in the Big East finals 10 months earlier. The Eagles were riding a 25-game winning streak at Conte Forum. The winning streak was erased—as were doubts about Pitt's legitimacy. The Panthers won 77-74—their ninth consecutive victory.

"The Panthers look like a team that can play with every Big East opponent," opined Bob Smizik in the *Post-Gazette*. "They also look like a team

capable of gaining an invitation to the NCAA tournament."

Junior point guard Brandin Knight played a masterful all-around game, scoring 20 points, grabbing seven rebounds, and handing out seven assists. Julius Page, who customarily guarded the opponent's top scorer, limited BC's Troy Bell to six-of-21 shooting. Bell was scoreless in the first half.

Two weeks later, the Panthers won another crucial conference game on the road. Jaron Brown's offensive rebound and lay-up with eight seconds left gave Pitt a 68-67 win at Georgetown on January 19, 2002. GU's Drew Hall missed a wide-open three-point attempt with three seconds remaining. The game also marked a debut of sorts for Pitt's six-foot-seven freshman forward Chevon Troutman, who had red-shirted the year before. Troutman played a career-high 19 minutes against the Hoyas, and contributed eight points and four rebounds.

PANORAMIC VIEW OF MELLON ARENA DURING 2002 NCAAs. *Photo by Mike Drazdzinski/CIDDE*

The Panthers followed that victory with a 72-57 home win against Syracuse three nights later, then beat Georgetown (67-56) again—this time at Fitzgerald Field House. Notre Dame snapped Pitt's winning streak at three with a come-from-behind 79-76 victory at the Field House on January 30. The loss turned out to be Pitt's only home loss that season—and last ever at Fitzgerald Field House. In fact, Pitt teams went on a 40-game home winning streak following the loss to the Irish.

Pitt won its last seven games of the 2001-2002 regular season. One memorable victory came at the Carrier Dome on February 10, 2002. Sporting a 21-4 record—and still unranked—the Panthers rallied from a 14-point second-half deficit to upend Syracuse, 75-63.

"I can never remember being speechless," Howland told the press later. "What could I say? This might be the biggest win I've had at Pitt."

Syracuse had been ahead 47-33, but a 22-3 Pitt run put the Panthers ahead 55-50 with 5:30 remaining. Knight had 16 points, nine assists, and four steals while playing all 40 minutes.

"It all starts with Brandin," observed Howland. "I can't say enough about Knight. He looked like the best point guard in the Big East."

Needing a win to clinch the Big East's West Division, the Panthers traveled to Continental Airlines Arena to meet Seton Hall on February 26, 2002. Donatas Zavackas hit a three-pointer from the top of the key with 3.4 seconds left in regulation to tie the game at 61, sending it into overtime. The Panthers scored the final 12 points of the extra period and won, 73-66. The pollsters finally noticed, and Pitt was ranked as high as seventh by the Associated Press that season.

Pitt ended its 51-year run at Fitzgerald Field House with an easy 92-65 thrashing of West

Virginia on March 2, 2002. The Panthers finished 16-1 at the Field House that season, the highest single-season home-win total in school history. The Big East tournament in New York City was next, and the Panthers dispatched Boston College (76-62) and Miami (76-71) to return to the championship game, this time against the Connecticut Huskies. In one of the most memorable Big East title matchups, UConn defeated Pitt in double overtime, 74-65.

The 2001-2002 Pitt team benefited from the NCAA's plan to assign high-seeded teams to venues close to home. The Panthers were assigned to the Pittsburgh sub-regional at Mellon Arena. Pittsburgh had also hosted the first two rounds in 1997.

In its first-round game, Pitt utilized a second-half rally to defeat the champion of the Northeast Conference, Central Connecticut State, 71-54. Pitt outrebounded CCSU 44-22. Brandin Knight had 17 points to lead the Panthers, while Julius Page added 16.

Chevon Troutman was in the starting lineup in Pitt's second-round game against California. The Panthers advanced to the Sweet 16 for the first time since 1974 with a 63-50 win against the Golden Bears. A 16-0 second-half run was the catalyst. Page scored 17 points, including a trio of three-pointers.

The Panthers' magical season ended in Lexington, Kentucky, where Kent State defeated Pitt in overtime, 78-73. Pitt had trailed by four points in the final two minutes, but baskets by Page and Knight forged a tie. Each finished the game with 18 points, but Kent State made all six of its free-throw attempts in the final minute to seal the win. Pitt's final record was 29-6; the 29 wins were the most in school history, and the Panthers received their due. Howland was the consensus National Coach of the Year, and Knight was a *Sporting News* second-team All-American, first-team Big East All-Conference, and co-Big East Player of the Year along with Connecticut's Caron Butler.

The 2002-2003 season had a dreamlike feel for Ben Howland, his players, and Pitt administrators. Not only were all five starters returning to a team that had gone 29-6 the year before, but the team would begin play in its new facility—the Petersen Events Center. The season sold out before it even started. The Panthers attracted 174,017 fans to their

ONATRIO LETT SCORES AGAINST CENTRAL CONNECTICUT STATE IN NCAA ACTION.
Photo by Mike Drazdzinski/CIDDE

16 regular-season home games. The fans went home happy; Pitt was 16-0 at home. Overall, the Panthers were 28-5, and finished 13-3 in the Big East, tied for first place with Syracuse in the West Division.

November 23, 2002 was Opening Night at the Petersen Events Center, and Pitt defeated Duquesne, 82-67. The Panthers began the season 9-0 before dropping an afternoon decision at Georgia, 79-67. Pitt bounced back from that defeat to win its next six games, including an 80-61 victory at West Virginia on January 14, 2003. The win was the Panthers' second straight in Morgantown, and Ben Howland became Pitt's first coach to register more than one victory against WVU at the Coliseum.

FRESHMAN CHRIS TAFT IN ACTION AGAINST BOSTON COLLEGE DURING THE 2003-2004 SEASON. *Photo by Image Point Pittsburgh*

Pitt's three seniors—Knight, Lett, and Zavackas—became the school's all-time winningest senior class with 89 victories. That mark would be topped by each of the next two groups of seniors. Unlike the year before, when Pitt didn't make the national rankings until later in the season, the 2002-2003 Panthers were ranked in the Top 10 throughout the season, and were second in eight polls throughout the campaign.

Connecticut came to Pittsburgh on March 2, 2003, and a boisterous gathering of 12,508 seemed more prepared than Pitt's players did at the outset. The Huskies started quickly, converting 11 of their first 14 shots to take leads of 24-11 and 28-15

before star center Emeka Okafor went to the bench with his second personal foul with 8:41 left in the first half. UConn coach Jim Calhoun wasn't happy with the officiating to that point.

"If they [officials] are going to allow [Ontario] Lett to be physical, they have to allow Emeka [Okafor] to be physical," he told reporters after the game.

The Huskies maintained a 39-35 lead at halftime, but the Panthers, sparked by Julius Page's 11 straight points during the second half, came back to win, 71-67. Sophomore Chevon Troutman added 13 points and 10 rebounds. Howland credited Pitt's fans for their role in the victory.

"You saw the effect of our crowd today," he said. "We need to have a decibel reader up there. It was absolutely awesome."

There were more fireworks in the postgame press conferences. Jim Calhoun paid Pitt what some interpreted as a backhanded compliment.

"I don't think they [Pitt] are the most talented team in the league," said Calhoun. "But I do think they're the best team in the league. They know what they are. That's how they play."

Howland, who was not present to hear Calhoun's remarks, met with the media a few minutes later. He was told of Calhoun's comments.

"That's his opinion," responded Howland. "I don't think you can win unless you're very talented. Talent is toughness. Talent is unselfishness. We are very talented. You can't be 50 and 10 [the past two seasons] without having pretty darn good talent."

Pitt and UConn would meet one final time that season, but the Panthers still had to close the regular season. They cruised past Seton Hall (86-54) on Senior Night, then won at Villanova (56-54) in the final game of the regular season.

At the Big East tournament, Pitt defeated Providence (67-59) in the quarterfinals, then topped Boston College (61-48) in the semifinals. That set up a rematch with Connecticut in the title game. This time Pitt prevailed, 74-56, in one of the most significant victories in school history.

Entering NCAA tournament play as a No. 2 seed, Pitt was sent to Boston's Fleet Center, where Northeast Conference champion Wagner was its first-round opponent. The Panthers had little trou-

ble with the Seahawks and cruised to an 87-61 victory. Zavackas had 16 points and seven rebounds—one of seven Pitt players who scored at least eight points.

The Indiana Hoosiers were Pitt's second-round opponent, but the Panthers won with stunning ease, 74-52. Pitt dominated inside, and its stifling defense limited Indiana to one basket during a stretch of 12 minutes and 24 seconds.

"We played some really good basketball teams, but we hadn't played a team like that all year," said IU coach Mike Davis. "They were under control the whole game, never wasted any motion."

The overpowering defense—a staple of Pitt's teams during its renaissance—was keyed by the outside play of Knight, Page, and Brown. Brown, who originally had entertained thoughts of attending Kentucky in his hometown Lexington, had 20 points and eight rebounds against Indiana. His all-around play drew praise from at least one teammate.

"I call him [Brown] 'Glue' because he keeps us together," said Julius Page. "He does whatever he has to do to win. He doesn't get recognized, but I don't think he's bothered by that. He makes the big plays in big games."

Brown, who was in Pittsburgh to watch the Panthers defeat Notre Dame during the 2004-2005 season, was asked about his career at Pitt.

"I'm glad I came to Pittsburgh and was able to help put the program back on the map," he said. "It's one of the elite programs now. It was a fun experience playing here, getting to be in another part of the country. I met many good people and made many good friends. I just love it here in Pittsburgh."

Brown and his teammates returned to the Sweet 16 in March 2003. Winners of 11 straight, Pitt met Marquette, coached by a former Pitt assistant, Tom Crean. Marquette, which ended its season in the Final Four that year, took control of the game early and held off the Panthers' rally in the second half. Pitt got to within one point, 75-74, but Marquette's Dwayne Wade hit several crucial shots as part of his 22-point performance. Knight scored 16 points and had 11 assists in his final game in a Pitt uniform.

Another key member of the Pitt program had also made his last appearance with the team. Steve

Lavin had been dismissed as UCLA's basketball coach, and Ben Howland's name was being rumored as a possible replacement. Despite public pronouncements that he wasn't interested, the prospect of returning to his home area—and to UCLA, one of the biggest names in college basketball—appealed to Howland. He admitted as much when he was presented as the Bruins' new coach at a press conference in Los Angeles.

"I am honored to be the head basketball coach at UCLA, and I am grateful to [director of athletics] Dan Guerrero for giving me this opportunity," said Howland. "Having grown up in southern California as a Bruin fan, watching the televised replays of the games was special for me. To now be the head coach of this program is something I dreamed about but never thought possible."

Two years after leaving Pittsburgh, Howland reflected on the difficult time.

"It was so difficult for me to leave that [Pitt] team behind," he admitted. "I didn't appreciate the timing of when my dream job came open, but that was that."

Howland left Pitt with a four-year record of 89-40, and he wasn't the only prominent figure to leave Pitt's athletic department around that time. Three months earlier, Steve Pederson also responded to a call from home, leaving Pitt to become director of athletics at Nebraska, his alma mater. Pederson's top aide at Pitt, Marc Boehm, was named interim A.D., and he led the search to find Howland's replacement. Several names were kicked around, most notably Wake Forest's Skip Prosser and Memphis's John Calipari, both from western Pennsylvania. Closer to campus, Pitt's players made a strong push for assistant coach Jamie Dixon.

"We wanted a coach who could build upon the success that the program was already going through," Boehm remarked in a 2005 interview. "Jaron Brown came and met with me for about an hour. At one point, there were tears running down his face. The emotions of changing coaches can be difficult for players. You could tell the affection that the players had for Jamie [Dixon], but the decision was not based only on that. It was just one element. You could tell the importance of what Jamie Dixon meant to him [Brown] and to the team."

CHANCELLOR MARK NORDENBERG (CENTER) PRESIDES AT A GROUNDBREAKING CEREMONY FOR THE PETERSEN EVENTS CENTER ON THE FORMER PITT STADIUM SITE IN JUNE 2000. FROM LEFT TO RIGHT ARE: PITT BASKETBALL COACH BEN HOWLAND, JOHN CONOMIKES, PITTSBURGH MAYOR TOM MURPHY, MARK NORDENBERG, JOHN PETERSEN (SON), JOHN PETERSEN (FATHER) AND GERTRUDE PETERSEN.

Photo courtesy of University of Pittsburgh

Point guard Carl Krauser, a redshirt freshman during Howland's final season, also made a plea to elevate Dixon—he spotted Chancellor Mark Nordenberg walking across campus one day, and he ran after Pitt's top official to make his plea for the assistant coach. Prosser turned out to be the first serious candidate.

"We did meet with Skip Prosser at just about the same time that we talked with Jamie Dixon," said Boehm.

Prosser considered his options. At the same time, Dixon remained calm. He had options of his own.

"Either way, I knew that I was going to be in a good situation," Dixon recalled about a year after the search, pointing out that Howland had left a spot open for him at UCLA. "I felt very comfortable about my situation in that regard, so that probably had a lot to do with it."

Boehm eventually met with the team as a group. He told the story of how the University of Miami had hired one of its assistant coaches, Larry Coker, to replace football coach Butch Davis, and he had won the national championship in his first season. Dixon got the job, and he was officially introduced on April 15, 2003.

"We felt very good about Jamie Dixon," remembered Boehm. "He has a great demeanor, and a great way with kids, and that is important. That struck me."

The team Dixon inherited for 2003-2004 wasn't as experienced as Pitt's previous team was, but the cupboard was hardly bare. Three starters—Knight, Lett, and Zavackas—were gone, but Page and Brown were back, along with Troutman, who had started at times. Krauser moved into Knight's point guard position, and everybody was looking forward to the collegiate debut of six-foot-ten freshman cen-

SIGNIFICANT WINS: THE RENAISSANCE YEARS

1/20/01   PITT 70-GEORGETOWN 66
• Julius Page's spectacular dunk highlights win against unbeaten Hoyas.

3/9/01   PITT 55, SYRACUSE 54
(Big East Tournament)
• Free throw by Isaac Hawkins puts Pitt in Big East title game for first time.

1/5/02   PITT 77, AT BOSTON COLLEGE 74
• Panthers pass crucial early-season Big East road test against defending conference champs.

2/10/02   PITT 75, AT SYRACUSE 63
• Unranked Pitt buries Orange under 22-3 run during second half

3/2/02   PITT 92, WEST VIRGINIA 65
• Panthers close Fitzgerald Field House with easy win.

3/2/03   PITT 71, CONNECTICUT 67
• First of two wins against UConn for 2002-2003 Panthers.

3/15/03   PITT 74, CONNECTICUT 56
(Big East Tournament)
• Julius Page named MVP as Panthers win their first Big East tourney title.

1/24/04   PITT 66, AT SYRACUSE 45
• Pitt limits Syracuse to its lowest scoring output at Carrier Dome.

2/15/04   PITT 75, CONNECTICUT 68
• First-ever game between two Top 5 teams on Pitt campus.

3/21/04   PITT 59, WISCONSIN 55
(NCAA Tournament)
• NCAA second-round win earns Panthersthird straight Sweet 16 trip.

York City area. His father was an actor, and young Jamie Dixon played a role or two in television commercials during his childhood. He ultimately was hired by Howland at Northern Arizona, then made the transition to head coach following Howland's move to Westwood.

Most of the concerns about Pitt's personnel losses were quickly quieted. Taft was named Big East Rookie of the Year, and Krauser became second-team All-Big East.

"Krauser has done a phenomenal job," said ESPN commentator Dick Vitale, in Pittsburgh for the February 15, 2004 Pitt-Connecticut game. "I thought the problem they would have would be replacing Brandin Knight, but Krauser has been great. In fact, it gives them another dimension, because it gives them a scorer as well. He's a guy who can penetrate and break defenses down. The arrival of [Chris] Taft has been a big plus for them, too."

Taft averaged 10.9 points and 9.5 rebounds per game. He and Troutman gave the Panthers a powerful one-two inside combination. Six-foot-ten senior center Toree Morris was in reserve.

Pitt defeated Alabama 71-62 in Jamie Dixon's debut on November 14, 2003, at Madison Square Garden in the Coaches vs. Cancer Classic. The Panthers won their first 18 games under Dixon. They kept the streak going in dramatic fashion with an 84-80 double-overtime win at Miami on January 10, 2004. Trailing by two points with 3.9 seconds left, Krauser took an inbounds feed from Jaron Brown and went the length of the floor to hit a game-tying lay-up at the buzzer. Krauser was impressed by the coach's calm during the timeout before the big play.

"He [Dixon] smiled and said, 'Everybody calm down, it's okay; We're going to win this game,'" Krauser related.

Dixon and the Panthers suffered their first loss on January 19, 2005, a 68-65 loss to Connecticut at the Hartford Civic Center. Facing a road game at Syracuse five nights later, Dixon was facing his first test in adversity, but the Panthers passed it remarkably well, blowing away the Orange, 66-45. It was Syracuse's lowest-scoring output to date in the 24-year history of the Carrier Dome, and its lowest

ter Chris Taft, who had been a *Parade* All-American at Xaverian High School in Brooklyn—Barry Rohrssen's alma mater.

Dixon, the rookie head coach, was a 1987 graduate of Texas Christian University. Born in southern California, he spent part of his youth in the New

score ever under coach Jim Boeheim. Pitt dominated the boards, holding a 50-36 edge in rebounds.

Junior Mark McCarroll, who had once committed to Syracuse but changed his mind while attending Milford (Connecticut) Academy, had 15 points for Pitt. Taft had 15 points and eight rebounds, while Troutman added 12 points and 11 rebounds.

The Panthers scored another major win by defeating Connecticut 75-68 on February 15 at the Petersen Events Center. Dick Vitale was in town to provide color commentary for the telecast and was asked his assessment of Pitt's team.

"Physically and mentally, they're very tough," he said. "They know how to win. They don't do it in a flashy way. They do it in a fundamental way. They beat you up."

Seton Hall and Syracuse—in the rematch in Pittsburgh—were Pitt's only other two regular-season losses during Dixon's first season as head coach. The 49-46 loss to the Orange was Pitt's first at the Petersen Events Center and stopped its overall home winning streak at 40 games.

The Panthers entered the Big East tournament with an overall record of 27-3. Pitt earned the Big East's regular-season title and No. 1 seed in the tournament by virtue of its 88-61 win at Providence on March 2. With another first-round bye in New York, the Panthers were well rested for their first game against Virginia Tech. The Panthers defeated the Hokies, 74-61, in what turned out to be Virginia Tech's final game as a member of the Big East. The game also was another meeting between the Panthers and Seth Greenberg, their one-time assistant coach who had most recently been the head coach at South Florida.

Playing Boston College in the Big East tournament semifinals for the second time in a row, Carl Krauser made a shot in the lane, then hit a three-pointer to thwart the Eagles' comeback bid in the final minutes. Pitt had trailed 26-22 at halftime but shot 53.6 percent from the floor in the second half to take command of the game. Krauser was Pitt's top scorer with 18 points.

The third consecutive Big East title game with Connecticut looked promising for the Panthers. Pitt led by nine (34-25) at halftime and by 11 as Antonio Graves made a three-point basket with

8:23 remaining. But the Huskies fought back to take the crown, 61-58.

A No. 3 seed in 2004, the Panthers were sent to Madison, Wisconsin, where they played Central Florida in the first round. Pitt's 53-44 win was its 30th victory of the season, another single-season record. The Panthers shot only 29.5 percent from the floor, but rallied from a 36-33 deficit with 10:05 remaining. Pitt outscored UCF 13-2 over the next seven minutes. In that game, Julius Page established a Pitt record for career minutes played. Page, Brown, and Toree Morris were playing in their seventh NCAA tournament game, also a Pitt record.

The second-round opponent, Wisconsin, had a decided advantage, playing in front of a largely partisan crowd. The Panthers proved their mettle, winning 59-55 to advance to the Sweet 16 for the third straight season.

"Every time they [Wisconsin fans] got loud, we got better," Jaron Brown told reporters after the game. "We loved seeing all that red. It had a positive effect."

"I fed off their fans," added Carl Krauser. "I was glad we got to play in a hostile environment like this."

The lead changed hands 11 times. In a classic defensive struggle, Pitt shot only 35.6 percent from the floor while holding the Badgers to 35.4 percent. Pitt flexed its inside strength, scoring 32 points in the paint to Wisconsin's 12. Troutman had 14 rebounds.

A crucial sequence in the game occurred late when Brown fought through and rebounded a missed free throw to score with 45 seconds left.

"He [Brown] just knows how to get possession and has the will to get the ball," said Jamie Dixon.

The same could be said for the 2004-2005 Panthers.

"I thought our guys were pretty tough, but we just weren't tough enough," remarked Wisconsin coach Bo Ryan.

"I don't know a tougher group," said Dixon.

Pitt's third trip to the Sweet 16 ended the same way the previous two had—with a loss in the regional semifinals. Oklahoma State's March 25, 2004 63-51 victory at Continental Airlines Arena was Pitt's largest loss of the season. The Panthers held a 28-26 halftime lead, due largely to a 20-15 edge in rebounding, but the Cowboys fought back and utilized a 21-9 run in the second half to put the game away. Krauser had 15 points for the Panthers, who finished Dixon's first season as coach with a 31-5 record.

Record-setting teams, crowds, and players. Three straight trips to the Sweet 16. Unprecedented fan interest and media attention for Pitt basketball.

Chancellor Mark Nordenberg was asked what it all meant, not only to Pitt, but also to the city of Pittsburgh.

"The resurgence of Pitt basketball has been great for the University community and for the entire region," he said. "It really fills those winter months, and I'm not sure I've seen a team so quickly capture the hearts of the people.

"Whether you're in the Petersen Center on game day—which is electrifying—or you're walking the streets between games, everybody's interested, everybody's committed, and everybody's cheering for Pitt basketball. Again, it's a great feeling."

1,000-POINT CLUB (THROUGH 2004-05)

Charles Smith (1984-88) 2,045

Clyde Vaughan (1980-84) 2,033

Larry Harris (1974-78) 1,914

Don Hennon (1956-59) 1,841

Jason Matthews (1987-91) 1,840

Ricardo Greer (1997-01) 1,753

Billy Knight (1971-74) 1,731

Sam Clancy (1977-81) 1,671

Brian Shorter (1988-91) 1,633

Vonteego Cummings (1995-99) 1,581

Demetreus Gore (1984-88) 1,555

Julius Page (2000-2004) 1,512

Brandin Knight (1999-03) 1,444

Jerry McCullough (1991-96) 1,342

Sean Miller (1987-91) 1,282

Bobby Martin (1987-91) 1,282

Chevon Troutman (2001-05) 1,274

Jaron Brown (2000-04) 1,258

Jerome Lane (1985-88) 1,217

Curtis Aiken (1983-87) 1,200

Bob Lazor (1954-57) 1,175

John Riser (1954-57) 1,164

Carl Krauser (2002-05) 1,148

Kent Scott (1969-72) 1,143

Isaac Hawkins (1996-01) 1,127

Calvin Sheffield (1961-64) 1,115

Brian Generalovich (1961-64) 1,114

Donatas Zavackas (1999-03) 1,099

Chris McNeal (1990-93) 1,067

Carlton Neverson (1978-81) 1,057

Julius Pegues (1955-58) 1,050

Rod Brookin (1986-90) 1,047

Darelle Porter (1987-91) 1,007

PITT

PITT ALL-TIME COACHING RECORDS

Coach	Years	W-L	Pct.
Benjamin F. Printz	1905-07	8-14	.364
Harry Hough	1907-08	10-6	.625
Wohlparth Wegner	1910-11	6-6	.500
Dr. George M. Flint	1911-21	105-68	.607
Andrew Kerr	1921-22	12-8	.600
Dr. H.C. "Doc" Carlson	1922-53	367-247	.598
Bob Timmons	1953-68	174-189	.479
Charles "Buzz" Ridl	1968-75	97-83	.539
Tim Grgurich	1975-80	69-70	.496
Dr. Roy Chipman	1980-86	102-76	.573
Paul Evans	1986-94	147-98	.600
Ralph Willard	1994-99	63-82	.434
Ben Howland	1999-2003	89-40	.690
Jamie Dixon	2003-present	51-14	.785

Pitt's All-Time Field House Team

Source: *Pittsburgh Post-Gazette*
Don Hennon (1956-59)
Brian Generalovich (1961-64)
Bill Knight (1971-74)
Sam Clancy (1977-81)
Charles Smith (1984-88)

Fitzgerald Field House "Lasts"

Game: March 2, 2002 • Pitt 92, West Virginia 65
Pitt's Lineup: Donatas Zavackas, Chad Johnson, Toree Morris, Julius Page, Brandin Knight
Last Basket: Yuri Demetris (Pitt)
Last Free Throw: Yuri Demetris (Pitt)
Last Three-Point Basket: Julius Page (Pitt)
Last Assist: Gino Federico (Pitt)
Last Steal: Ontario Lett (Pitt)
Attendance: 6,798 (sellout)

Petersen Events Center "Firsts"

Game: November 23, 2002 • Pitt 82, Duquesne 67
Pitt's Lineup: Jaron Brown, Donatas Zavackas, Ontario Lett, Julius Page, Brandin Knight
First Basket: Jimmy Tricco (Duquesne)
First Free Throw: Jimmy Tricco (Duquesne)
First Three-Point Basket: Julius Page (Pitt)
First Assist: Simplice Njoya (Duquesne)
First Steal: Ontario Lett (Pitt)
Attendance: 12,508 (sellout)

NCAA TOURNAMENT HISTORY

100

Y
E
A
R
S

O
F

B
A
S
K
E
T
B
A
L
L

Date	Opponent (Location)	W/L	Score
1941			
3/21	North Carolina (Madison, Wisconsin)	W	26-20
3/22	Wisconsin (Madison, Wisconsin)	L	36-30
1957			
3/11	Morehead State (Columbus, Ohio)	W	86-85
3/15	Kentucky (Lexington, Kentucky)	L	98-92
3/16	Notre Dame (Lexington, Kentucky)	L	86-85
1958			
3/11	Miami of Ohio (Evanston, Illinois)	L	82-77
1963			
3/11	New York University (Philadelphia, Pennsylvania)	L	93-83
1974			
3/9	St. Joseph's (Morgantown, West Virginia)	W	54-42
3/14	Furman (Raleigh, North Carolina)	W	81-78
3/16	North Carolina State (Raleigh, North Carolina)	L	100-72
1981			
3/13	Idaho (El Paso, Texas)	W	70-69
3/15	North Carolina (El Paso, Texas)	L	74-57
1982			
3/12	Pepperdine (Pullman, Washashington)	L	99-88
1985			
3/14	Louisiana Tech (Tulsa, Oklahoma)	L	78-54
1987			
3/13	Marist (Tucson, Arizona)	W	93-68
3/15	Oklahoma (Tucson, Arizona)	L	96-93

Date	Opponent (Location)	W/L	Score
1988			
3/18	Eastern Michigan (Lincoln, Nebraska)	W	108-90
3/20	Vanderbilt (Lincoln, Nebebraska)	L	80-74 (OT)
1989			
3/10	Ball State (Indianapolis, Indiana)	L	68-64
1991			
3/14	Georgia (Louisville, Kentucky)	W	76-68 (OT)
3/16	Kansas (Louisville, Kentucky)	L	77-66
1993			
3/19	Utah (Nashville, Tennessee)	L	86-65
2002			
3/15	Central Connecticut State (Pittsburgh, Pennsylvania)	W	71-54
3/17	California (Pittsburgh, Pennsylvania)	W	63-50
3/21	Kent State (Lexington, Kentucky)	L	78-73 (OT)
2003			
3/21	Wagner (Boston, Massachusetts)	W	87-61
3/23	Indiana (Boston, Massachusetts)	W	74-52
3/27	Marquette (Minneapolis, Minnesota)	L	77-74
2004			
3/19	Central Florida (Madison, Wisconsin)	W	53-44
3/21	Wisconsin (Madison, Wisconsin)	W	59-55
3/25	Oklahoma State (East Rutherford, New Jersey)	L	63-51
2005			
3/17	Pacific (Boise, Idaho)	L	79-71

NIT HISTORY

Date	Opponent (Location)	W/L	Score
1964			
3/14	Drake (New York, New York)	L	82-67
1975			
3/15	Southern Illinois (New York, New York)	W	70-65
3/18	Providence (New York, New York)	L	101-80
1980			
3/6	Duquesne (Pittsburgh, Pennsylvania)	L	65-63
1984			
3/16	LaSalle (Philadelphia, Pennsylvania)	W	95-91
3/18	Florida State (Greensboro, North Carolina)	W	66-63
3/23	Notre Dame (Pittsburgh, Pennsylvania)	L	72-64
1986			
3/12	SW Missouri State (Springfield, Missouri)	L	59-52
1992			
3/18	Penn State (University Park, Pennsylvania)	W	67-65
3/23	Florida (Pittsburgh, Pennsylvania)	L	77-74
1997			
3/12	New Orleans (Pittsburgh, Pennsylvania)	W	82-63
3/17	Arkansas (Fayetteville, Arkansas)	L	76-71
2001			
3/14	St. Bonaventure (Pittsburgh, Pennsylvania)	W	84-75
3/19	Mississippi State (Pittsburgh, Pennsylvania)	L	66-61

PITT RECORD YEAR BY YEAR

Year	Overall W-L	Conf. W-L	Head Coach	NCAA/NIT
1905-1906	2-9		Benjamin F. Printz	
1906-1907	6-5		Benjamin F. Printz	
1907-1908	10-6		Harry Hough	
1908-1909	No Team			
1909-1910	No Team			
1910-1911	6-6		Wohlparth Wegner	
1911-1912	10-9		Dr. George M. Flint	
1912-1913	15-7		Dr. George M. Flint	
1913-1914	7-8		Dr. George M. Flint	
1914-1915	13-5		Dr. George M. Flint	
1915-1916	15-2		Dr. George M. Flint	
1916-1917	12-6		Dr. George M. Flint	
1917-1918	5-9		Dr. George M. Flint	
1918-1919	7-7		Dr. George M. Flint	
1919-1920	9-6		Dr. George M. Flint	
1920-1921	12-9		Dr. George M. Flint	
1921-1922	12-8		Andrew Kerr	
1922-1923	10-5		Doc Carlson	
1923-1924	10-7		Doc Carlson	
1924-1925	4-10		Doc Carlson	
1925-1926	12-5		Doc Carlson	
1926-1927	10-7		Doc Carlson	
1927-1928	21-0		Doc Carlson	
1928-1929	16-5		Doc Carlson	
1929-1930	23-2		Doc Carlson	
1930-1931	20-4		Doc Carlson	
1931-1932	14-16		Doc Carlson	
1932-1933	17-5		Doc Carlson	
1933-1934	18-4		Doc Carlson	
1934-1935	18-5		Doc Carlson	
1935-1936	18-9		Doc Carlson	
1936-1937	14-7		Doc Carlson	
1937-1938	9-12		Doc Carlson	

Year	Overall W-L	Conf. W-L	Head Coach	NCAA/NIT
1938-1939	10-8		Doc Carlson	
1939-1940	8-9		Doc Carlson	
1940-1941	13-6		Doc Carlson	NCAA
1941-1942	5-10		Doc Carlson	
1942-1943	10-5		Doc Carlson	
1943-1944	7-7		Doc Carlson	
1944-1945	8-4		Doc Carlson	
1945-1946	7-7		Doc Carlson	
1946-1947	8-10		Doc Carlson	
1947-1948	10-11		Doc Carlson	
1948-1949	12-13		Doc Carlson	
1949-1950	4-14		Doc Carlson	
1950-1951	9-17		Doc Carlson	

FITZGERALD FIELD HOUSE ERA BEGINS

Year	Overall W-L	Conf. W-L	Head Coach	NCAA/NIT
1951-1952	10-12		Doc Carlson	
1952-1953	12-11		Doc Carlson	
1953-1954	9-14		Bob Timmons	
1954-1955	10-16		Bob Timmons	
1955-1956	15-10		Bob Timmons	
1956-1957	16-11		Bob Timmons	NCAA
1957-1958	18-7		Bob Timmons	NCAA
1958-1959	10-14		Bob Timmons	
1959-1960	11-14		Bob Timmons	
1960-1961	12-11		Bob Timmons	
1961-1962	12-11		Bob Timmons	
1962-1963	19-6		Bob Timmons	NCAA
1963-1964	17-8		Bob Timmons	NIT
1964-1965	7-16		Bob Timmons	
1965-1966	5-17		Bob Timmons	
1966-1967	6-19		Bob Timmons	
1967-1968	7-15		Bob Timmons	
1968-1969	4-20		Buzz Ridl	
1969-1970	12-12		Buzz Ridl	
1970-1971	14-10		Buzz Ridl	
1971-1972	12-12		Buzz Ridl	
1972-1973	12-14		Buzz Ridl	

150

100

Y E A R S O F B A S K E T B A L L

PITT

Year	Overall W-L	Conf. W-L	Head Coach	NCAA/NIT
1973-1974	25-4		Buzz Ridl	NCAA
1974-1975	18-11		Buzz Ridl	NIT
1975-1976	12-15		Tim Grgurich	

EASTERN EIGHT CONFERENCE

Year	Overall W-L	Conf. W-L	Head Coach	NCAA/NIT
1976-1977	6-21	1-9	Tim Grgurich	
1977-1978	16-11	5-5	Tim Grgurich	
1978-1979	18-11	6-4	Tim Grgurich	
1979-1980	17-12	5-5	Tim Grgurich	NIT
1980-1981	19-12	8-5	Dr. Roy Chipman	NCAA
1981-1982	20-10	8-6	Dr. Roy Chipman	NCAA

BIG EAST CONFERENCE

Year	Overall W-L	Conf. W-L	Head Coach	NCAA/NIT
1982-1983	13-15	6-10	Dr. Roy Chipman	
1983-1984	18-13	6-10	Dr. Roy Chipman	NIT
1984-1985	17-12	8-8	Dr. Roy Chipman	NCAA
1985-1986	15-14	6-10	Dr. Roy Chipman	NIT
1986-1987	25-8	12-4	Paul Evans	NCAA
1987-1988	24-7	12-4	Paul Evans	NCAA
1988-1989	17-13	9-7	Paul Evans	NCAA
1989-1990	12-17	5-11	Paul Evans	
1990-1991	21-12	9-7	Paul Evans	NCAA
1991-1992	18-16	9-9	Paul Evans	NIT
1992-1993	17-11	9-9	Paul Evans	NCAA
1993-1994	13-14	7-11	Paul Evans	
1994-1995	10-18	5-13	Ralph Willard	
1995-1996	10-17	5-13	Ralph Willard	
1996-1997	18-15	10-8	Ralph Willard	NIT
1998-1999	14-16	5-13	Ralph Willard	
1999-2000	13-15	5-11	Ben Howland	
2000-2001	19-14	7-9	Ben Howland	NIT
2001-2002	29-6	13-3	Ben Howland	NCAA

PETERSEN EVENTS CENTER ERA BEGINS

Year	Overall W-L	Conf. W-L	Head Coach	NCAA/NIT
2002-2003	28-5	13-3	Ben Howland	NCAA
2003-2004	31-5	13-3	Jamie Dixon	NCAA
2004-2005	20-9	10-6	Jamie Dixon	NCAA

RETIRED JERSEYS

#10
Don Hennon

#32
Charles Smith

#34
Billy Knight

PITT–WEST VIRGINIA GRAND FINALES

Pitt and West Virginia have played each other in the final collegiate game at five different sporting venues. The Panthers have won all five contests.

Date	Facility	Sport	Score
February 26, 1951	Pitt Pavilion	Basketball	Pitt, 74-72
March 3, 1970	WVU Field House	Basketball	Pitt, 92-87
November 10, 1979	Mountaineer Field	Football	Pitt, 24-17
November 24, 2000	Three Rivers Stadium	Football	Pitt, 38-28
March 2, 2002	Fitzgerald Field House	Basketball	Pitt, 92-65

Individual Career Statistics

(Players listed have played in at least 10 career games, 1937-current)

Player, Years	GP	GS	Min.	Avg.	FG	FGA	Pct.	3FG	3FGA	Pct.	FT	FTA	Pct.	Off.	Def.	Tot.	Avg.	PF	FO	Ast.	TO	Blk.	Stl.	Pts.	Avg.
Abel, Griffin, 1998-01	29	4	209	7.2	15	42	.357	1	8	.125	6	14	.429	13	31	44	1.5	25	0	11	16	1	1	37	1.3
Abrams, Marvin, 1970-74	43	0	0	0.0	60	167	.359	0	0	.000	25	36	.694	0	39	39	0.9	45	0	26	0	0	0	145	3.4
Aggelou, Sotiris, 1993-95	47	12	758	16.1	84	236	.356	48	152	.316	45	64	.703	22	49	71	1.5	75	2	45	69	1	38	261	5.6
Aiken, Curtis, 1983-87	120	82	3216	26.8	489	1028	.476	46	117	.393	176	296	.595	26	159	185	1.5	245	5	378	247	12	155	1200	10.0
Allen, George, 1981-84	77	0	1913	24.8	276	645	.428	0	0	.000	150	200	.750	0	118	118	1.5	177	6	187	165	12	120	702	9.1
Alridge, Andre, 1992-96	77	46	1839	23.9	156	447	.349	110	307	.358	138	187	.738	42	115	157	2.0	127	2	258	186	0	63	560	7.3
Antigua, Orlando, 1991-95	116	78	2648	22.8	332	790	.420	117	303	.386	149	218	.683	147	262	409	3.5	253	9	195	216	78	77	930	8.0
Apple, Nate, 1943-47	58	0	0	0.0	179	0	.000	0	0	.000	116	179	.648	0	0	0	0.0	134	0	0	0	0	0	474	8.2
Armstrong, Keith, 1982-86	112	40	2383	21.3	230	452	.509	0	0	.000	113	219	.516	0	422	422	3.8	328	25	69	177	108	65	573	5.1
Artman, Bernard, 1951-54	50	0	0	0.0	86	272	.316	0	0	.000	70	136	.515	0	146	146	2.9	93	3	5	0	0	0	242	4.8
Artman, 1940-43	35	0	0	0.0	97	0	.000	0	0	.000	54	86	.628	0	0	0	0.0	66	0	0	0	0	0	248	7.1
Bailey, Nate, 1987-89	39	2	252	6.5	12	45	.267	0	4	.000	27	36	.750	13	21	34	0.9	42	1	21	31	1	4	51	1.3
Barnhart, Ray, 1968-69	10	0	0	0.0	0	3	.000	0	0	.000	3	8	.375	0	3	3	0.3	5	0	0	0	0	0	3	0.3
Beatty, Steve, 1980-84	81	0	1205	14.9	86	193	.446	0	0	.000	40	64	.625	0	185	185	2.3	153	4	20	71	24	35	212	2.6
Belich, Michael, 1948-51	67	0	0	0.0	234	701	.334	0	0	.000	127	196	.648	0	0	0	0.0	161	4	0	0	0	0	595	8.9
Benjamin, Keith, 2004-05	18	0	182	10.1	17	47	.362	4	15	.267	2	5	.400	8	25	33	1.8	14	0	9	16	1	7	40	2.2
Bennett, Bill, 1965-66	12	0	0	0.0	6	16	.375	0	0	.000	7	13	.538	0	32	32	2.7	13	0	0	0	0	0	19	1.6
Bennett, Mel, 1974-75	29	0	0	0.0	109	264	.413	0	0	.000	75	110	.682	0	295	295	10.2	95	7	29	0	70	0	293	10.1
Blanton, John, 1982-86	20	0	46	2.3	6	18	.333	0	0	.000	5	13	.385	0	6	6	0.3	4	0	5	5	0	0	17	0.9
Blount, Mark, 1995-97	56	36	1149	20.5	136	292	.466	1	2	.500	87	168	.518	91	187	278	5.0	173	10	39	129	105	28	360	6.4
Blyshak, Dave, 1962-65	34	0	0	0.0	64	195	.328	0	0	.000	9	19	.474	0	75	75	2.2	29	0	0	0	0	0	137	4.0
Bolla, Jim, 1971-75	82	0	0	0.0	107	244	.439	0	0	.000	56	101	.554	0	290	290	3.5	188	5	68	0	8	0	270	3.3
Bollens, Ken, 1965-68	61	0	0	0.0	213	481	.443	0	0	.000	133	183	.727	0	370	370	6.1	180	0	0	0	0	0	559	9.2
Boose, 1946-47	11	0	0	0.0	19	0	.000	0	0	.000	15	28	.536	0	0	0	0.0	29	0	0	0	0	0	53	4.8
Boyd, Arthur, 1950-53	49	0	0	0.0	84	273	.308	0	0	.000	77	130	.592	0	279	279	5.7	117	6	20	0	0	0	245	5.0
Boyd, Frank, 1973-77	32	0	0	0.0	10	40	.250	0	0	.000	5	16	.313	0	36	36	1.1	23	0	17	0	2	0	25	0.8
Bowman, Marcus, 2003-05	12	0	13	1.1	0	4	.000	0	2	.000	1	2	.500	0	4	4	0.3	1	0	0	0	0	0	1	0.1
Braumbeck, R., 1948-50	26	0	0	0.0	6	21	.286	0	0	.000	7	19	.368	0	0	0	0.0	37	0	0	0	0	0	19	0.7
Brautigam, Barry, 1954-57	56	0	0	0.0	57	140	.407	0	0	.000	31	49	.633	0	112	112	2.0	77	4	0	0	0	0	145	2.6
Brehm, William, 1946-50	15	0	0	0.0	16	29	.552	0	0	.000	18	40	.450	0	0	0	0.0	59	0	0	0	0	0	50	3.3
Brookin, Rod, 1986-90	94	25	2234	23.8	370	747	.495	94	230	.409	213	296	.720	113	239	352	3.7	145	6	113	157	19	88	1047	11.1
Brown, Jaron, 2000-04	137	109	3777	27.6	501	997	.503	36	153	.235	220	346	.636	272	379	651	4.8	269	1	295	279	59	192	1258	9.2
Brozovich, Paul, 1979-81	54	0	661	12.2	62	144	.431	0	0	.000	17	47	.362	0	123	123	2.3	131	4	16	59	10	20	141	2.6
Bruce, Kirk, 1972-75	83	0	0	0.0	400	847	.472	0	0	.000	102	136	.750	0	334	334	4.0	206	7	200	0	13	0	902	10.9
Brush, Brian, 1989-93	66	5	540	8.2	55	111	.495	1	2	.500	67	94	.713	63	86	149	2.3	73	1	18	37	3	11	178	2.7
Buck, Bill, 1965-67	25	0	0	0.0	25	68	.368	0	0	.000	8	13	.615	0	38	38	1.5	31	0	0	0	0	0	58	2.3
Buck, Rudy, 1943-44	12	0	0	0.0	9	0	.000	0	0	.000	2	6	.333	0	0	0	0.0	25	0	0	0	0	0	20	1.7
Burch, Clarence, 1951-54	45	0	0	0.0	196	548	.358	0	0	.000	196	282	.695	0	214	214	4.8	121	1	131	0	0	0	588	13.1
Caldwell, Bob, 1964-67	27	0	0	0.0	15	53	.283	0	0	.000	10	18	.556	0	15	15	0.6	47	0	0	0	0	0	40	1.5
Caldwell, Mike, 1968-71	59	0	0	0.0	158	383	.413	0	0	.000	72	83	.867	0	67	67	1.1	67	0	18	0	0	0	388	6.6
Canterna, Oland, 1944-49	71	0	0	0.0	286	278	1.029	0	0	.000	285	469	.608	0	0	0	0.0	209	0	0	0	0	0	857	12.1
Cardot, Willis, 1972-73	15	0	0	0.0	12	35	.343	0	0	.000	8	8	1.000	0	15	15	1.0	11	1	14	0	0	0	32	2.1
Carlson, Lloyd, 1941-43	25	0	0	0.0	16	0	.000	0	0	.000	11	24	.458	0	0	0	0.0	23	0	0	0	0	0	43	1.7
Carnahan, Milroy, 1950-53	29	0	0	0.0	6	33	.182	0	0	.000	5	8	.625	0	14	14	0.5	32	0	0	0	0	0	17	0.6
Carrigan, Rich, 1984-87	16	0	55	3.4	1	9	.111	0	0	.000	8	12	.667	1	15	16	1.0	11	0	2	8	0	0	10	0.6
Cauley, Willie, 1993-94	27	9	480	17.8	78	170	.459	6	19	.316	24	49	.490	33	63	96	3.6	64	2	23	35	11	24	186	6.9
Causer, Jerry, 1968-70	43	0	0	0.0	94	211	.445	0	0	.000	26	57	.456	0	183	183	4.3	87	0	0	0	0	0	214	5.0
Cavanaugh, Pat, 1986-90	109	5	990	9.1	74	177	.418	18	56	.321	64	99	.646	14	63	77	0.7	85	0	143	96	0	40	230	2.1
Cecconi, Louis, 1946-50	75	0	0	0.0	134	302	.444	0	0	.000	122	220	.555	0	0	0	0.0	201	0	0	0	0	0	390	5.2
Cercone, Eugene, 1953-57	19	0	0	0.0	7	21	.333	0	0	.000	7	10	.700	0	8	8	0.4	5	0	0	0	0	0	21	1.1
Christopher, Frank, 1950-51	15	0	0	0.0	0	22	.000	0	0	.000	4	11	.364	0	0	0	0.0	23	1	0	0	0	0	4	0.3
Cieply, William, 1943-48	53	0	0	0.0	143	0	.000	0	0	.000	67	120	.558	0	0	0	0.0	180	0	0	0	0	0	353	6.7
Cizmarik, Bob, 1969-71	33	0	0	0.0	30	68	.441	0	0	.000	26	39	.667	0	54	54	1.6	36	0	6	0	0	0	86	2.6
Clancy, Sam, 1977-81	116	0	3273	28.2	656	1362	.482	0	0	.000	359	538	.667	0	1342	1342	11.6	410	25	186	278	170	161	1671	14.4
Colombo, Scott, 1986-89	21	0	38	1.8	3	10	.300	2	3	.667	2	4	.500	0	4	4	0.2	5	0	3	8	0	3	10	0.5
Cooper, Tico, 1985-87	56	3	634	11.3	50	96	.521	0	0	.000	73	103	.709	28	146	174	3.1	104	5	10	31	12	24	173	3.1
Cosby, Attila, 1997-99	55	55	1552	28.2	206	430	.479	0	0	.000	74	107	.692	135	140	275	5.0	160	9	34	123	96	56	486	8.8
Cosentino, Sam, 1944-46	25	0	0	0.0	31	0	.000	0	0	.000	9	18	.500	0	0	0	0.0	39	0	0	0	0	0	71	2.8
Cost, Charley, 1954-55	14	0	0	0.0	15	49	.306	0	0	.000	13	26	.500	0	33	33	2.4	30	1	0	0	0	0	43	3.1
Cratsley, Mel, 1966-67	11	0	0	0.0	2	11	.182	0	0	.000	0	1	.000	0	4	4	0.4	0	0	0	0	0	0	4	0.4
Culbertson, Billy, 1981-84	78	0	1934	24.8	156	376	.415	0	0	.000	115	162	.710	0	135	135	1.7	151	2	343	182	4	113	427	5.5
Cummings, Vonteego, 1995-99	103	97	3532	34.3	554	1309	.423	134	401	.334	339	485	.699	134	278	412	4.0	285	13	458	364	35	235	1581	15.3
David, Joey, 1982-86	113	31	1909	16.9	186	435	.428	0	0	.000	95	132	.720	0	160	160	1.4	127	5	187	153	6	55	467	4.1
David, Samuel, 1946-49	76	0	0	0.0	317	0	.000	0	0	.000	287	456	.629	0	0	0	0.0	185	0	0	0	0	0	921	12.1
DeGroat, John, 2004-05	23	0	158	6.9	18	36	.500	4	13	.308	3	8	.375	15	20	35	1.5	13	0	11	14	2	2	43	1.9
DeLisio, Tony, 1966-69	50	0	0	0.0	141	404	.349	0	0	.000	89	137	.650	0	128	128	2.6	102	0	0	0	0	0	371	7.4
Demetris, Yuri, 2001-05	85	14	866	10.2	48	120	.400	25	75	.333	26	41	.634	21	81	102	1.2	82	1	74	47	2	36	147	1.7
Dietrick, Dick, 1951-54	59	0	0	0.0	165	478	.345	0	0	.000	141	270	.522	0	437	437	7.4	213	20	8	0	0	0	471	8.0
DiFrischia, Al, 1966-67	25	0	0	0.0	65	179	.363	0	0	.000	41	65	.631	0	59	59	2.4	45	0	0	0	0	0	171	6.8
Disco, Mark, 1973-75	10	0	0	0.0	4	8	.500	0	0	.000	3	4	.750	0	11	11	1.1	9	0	2	0	0	0	11	1.1
Ditka, Mike, 1958-60	32	0	0	0.0	36	109	.330	0	0	.000	16	27	.593	0	82	82	2.6	43	0	0	0	0	0	88	2.8
Dorazio, Carlo, 2001-03	13	0	25	1.9	3	6	.500	1	3	.333	1	2	.500	1	1	2	0.2	2	0	3	3	0	1	8	0.6
Dorman, Dennis, 1955-58	33	0	0	0.0	23	58	.397	0	0	.000	19	43	.442	0	103	103	3.1	41	2	0	0	0	0	65	2.0
Downes, Bill, 1968-71	72	0	0	0.0	149	295	.505	0	0	.000	91	157	.580	0	159	159	2.2	175	3	85	0	0	0	389	5.4
Doyle, Ray, 1964-65	13	0	0	0.0	1	9	.111	0	0	.000	6	11	.545	0	23	23	1.8	13	0	0	0	0	0	8	0.6
Duessel, David, 1952-55	56	0	0	0.0	79	257	.307	0	0	.000	62	110	.564	0	264	264	4.7	126	5	0	0	0	0	220	3.9
Dumancic, Dominik, 1990-92	10	0	44	4.4	5	18	.278	2	11	.182	1	2	.500	2	6	8	0.8	6	0	0	3	1	1	13	1.3
Edwards, Cleveland, 1969-73	41	0	0	0.0	93	236	.394	0	0	.000	57	91	.626	0	193	193	4.7	144	4	108	0	0	0	243	5.9
Egan, James, 1939-42	31	0	0	0.0	19	0	.000	0	0	.000	19	31	.613	0	0	0	0.0	37	0	0	0	0	0	57	1.8
Ellis, Sammie, 1978-80	55	0	1883	34.2	324	658	.492	0	0	.000	257	361	.712	0	414	414	7.5	198	13	55	104	33	63	905	16.5
Everett, Robert, 1948-51	15	0	0	0.0	4	14	.286	0	0	.000	7	10	.700	0	0	0	0.0	13	0	0	0	0	0	15	1.0

Player, Years	GP	GS	Min.	Avg.	FG	FGA	Pct.	3FG	3FGA	Pct.	FT	FTA	Pct.	Off.	Def.	Tot.	Avg.	PF	FO	Ast.	TO	Blk.	Stl.	Pts.	Avg.
Falenski, Dick, 1958-61	67	0	0	0.0	236	603	.391	0	0	.000	169	249	.679	0	206	206	3.1	158	2	0	0	0	0	641	9.6
Falenski, Stan, 1964-67	43	0	0	0.0	167	413	.404	0	0	.000	83	118	.703	0	163	163	3.8	111	0	0	0	0	0	417	9.7
Famularo, Frank, 1965-67	12	0	0	0.0	9	27	.333	0	0	.000	4	9	.444	0	11	11	0.9	11	0	0	0	0	0	22	1.8
Federico, Gino, 2001-03	16	0	25	1.6	3	4	.750	1	1	1.000	0	4	.000	2	4	6	0.4	1	0	3	1	0	1	7	0.4
Fenwick, Joe, 1953-56	74	0	0	0.0	253	729	.347	0	0	.000	119	191	.623	0	221	221	3.0	169	5	0	0	0	0	625	8.4
Ferguson, Marlon, 1983-87	38	0	188	4.9	26	51	.510	0	0	.000	7	16	.438	1	46	47	1.2	27	0	8	13	9	2	59	1.6
Finneman, John, 1999-00	15	1	78	5.2	13	26	.500	9	16	.563	7	7	1.000	2	9	11	0.7	6	0	4	4	2	2	42	2.8
Fisher, Brian, 1963-65	24	0	0	0.0	52	165	.315	0	0	.000	47	68	.691	0	73	73	3.0	51	0	0	0	0	0	151	6.3
Fleming, Sam, 1971-74	52	0	0	0.0	33	96	.344	0	0	.000	21	34	.618	0	37	37	0.7	43	0	28	0	0	0	87	1.7
Flores, Stephen, 1997-99	44	3	495	11.3	47	132	.356	15	67	.224	32	36	.889	21	22	43	1.0	52	0	13	22	12	18	141	3.2
Foley, James, 1959-61	25	0	0	0.0	7	26	.269	0	0	.000	5	9	.556	0	17	17	0.7	15	0	0	0	0	0	19	0.8
Forquer, 1946-47	16	0	0	0.0	5	0	.000	0	0	.000	1	7	.143	0	0	0	0.0	24	0	0	0	0	0	11	0.7
Fridley, John, 1958-61	72	0	0	0.0	337	807	.418	0	0	.000	176	261	.674	0	800	800	11.1	229	6	0	0	0	0	850	11.8
Frontone, Jack, 1951-55	27	0	0	0.0	16	75	.213	0	0	.000	2	13	.154	0	15	15	0.6	23	0	8	0	0	0	34	1.3
Gant, Chris, 1991-95	103	40	1923	18.7	234	514	.455	5	19	.263	187	295	.634	218	256	474	4.6	288	12	63	130	14	66	660	6.4
Garcia, Joseph, 1937-38	21	0	0	0.0	50	0	.000	0	0	.000	24	33	.727	0	0	0	0.0	31	0	0	0	0	0	124	5.9
Gardella, Chris, 1994-98	12	0	17	1.4	0	8	.000	0	3	.000	2	8	.250	0	3	3	0.3	3	0	8	4	0	1	2	0.2
Garnham, 1944-46	10	0	0	0.0	2	0	.000	0	0	.000	3	7	.429	0	0	0	0.0	8	0	0	0	0	0	7	0.7
Generalovich, Brian, 1961-64	72	0	0	0.0	420	983	.427	0	0	.000	274	360	.761	0	622	622	8.6	203	11	0	0	0	0	1114	15.5
Generalovich, Brock, 1989-93	33	0	134	4.1	14	33	.424	7	18	.389	5	11	.455	4	8	12	0.4	14	0	10	5	2	2	40	1.2
Generalovich, Nick, 1964-66	29	0	0	0.0	13	52	.250	0	0	.000	12	20	.600	17	18	35	1.2	38	0	0	0	0	0	38	1.3
Gerensky, Thaddeus, 1948-49	12	0	0	0.0	8	10	.800	0	0	.000	8	23	.348	0	0	0	0.0	31	0	0	0	0	0	24	2.0
Gill, Michael, 1995-96	21	2	252	12.0	31	84	.369	6	24	.250	18	28	.643	19	24	43	2.0	27	0	14	16	2	10	86	4.1
Gissendanner, Darrell, 1978-82	94	0	1197	12.7	177	401	.441	0	0	.000	126	165	.764	0	73	73	0.8	158	7	100	128	6	85	480	5.1
Glenn, 1943-44	12	0	0	0.0	10	0	.000	0	0	.000	7	13	.538	0	0	0	0.0	18	0	0	0	0	0	27	2.3
Glover,Tim, 1990-92	20	0	65	3.3	11	27	.407	10	22	.455	0	0	.000	0	4	4	0.2	5	0	2	0	1	0	32	1.6
Goodson, Mike, 1985-87	48	33	1169	24.4	102	223	.457	37	100	.370	39	56	.696	14	52	66	1.4	98	2	169	85	0	13	280	5.8
Gore, Demetreus, 1984-88	122	112	3122	25.6	645	1347	.479	24	73	.329	241	305	.790	72	322	394	3.2	295	7	300	336	20	126	1555	12.7
Graves, Antonio, 2003-05	60	29	1081	18.0	98	247	.397	49	115	.426	33	51	.647	12	63	75	1.3	87	1	83	63	8	24	278	4.6
Gray, Aaron, 2003-05	44	0	424	9.6	60	105	.571	0	0	.000	32	53	.604	45	59	104	2.4	61	0	26	33	19	5	152	3.5
Greer, Ricardo, 1997-01	117	115	4026	34.4	672	1468	.458	96	348	.276	313	460	.680	365	523	888	7.6	302	2	373	364	32	196	1753	15.0
Grevey, Scott, 1978-82	57	0	263	4.6	21	68	.309	0	0	.000	39	62	.629	0	24	24	0.4	51	0	12	33	3	6	81	1.4
Grgurich, Tim, 1961-64	61	0	0	0.0	52	139	.374	0	0	.000	46	73	.630	0	100	100	1.6	147	5	0	0	0	0	150	2.5
Gustine, Frank, 1967-68	13	0	0	0.0	5	32	.156	0	0	.000	3	7	.429	0	10	10	0.8	18	0	0	0	0	0	13	1.0
Harris, Larry, 1974-78	107	0	0	0.0	803	1584	.507	0	0	.000	308	396	.778	0	569	569	5.3	284	13	123	0	63	0	1914	17.9
Harrison, Ed, 1970-71	24	0	0	0.0	77	167	.461	0	0	.000	84	111	.757	0	121	121	5.0	59	2	63	0	0	0	238	9.9
Hartman, 1937-38	5	0	0	0.0	0	0	.000	0	0	.000	1	1	1.000	0	0	0	0.0	0	0	0	0	0	0	1	0.2
Hawkins, Isaac, 1996-01	118	90	3388	28.7	462	895	.516	3	13	.231	200	314	.637	343	491	834	7.1	280	4	100	225	143	96	1127	9.6
Haygood, Bob, 1974-76	19	0	0	0.0	20	49	.408	0	0	.000	13	14	.929	0	16	16	0.8	8	0	8	0	0	0	53	2.8
Hennon, Don, 1956-58	76	0	0	0.0	723	1827	.396	0	0	.000	395	480	.823	0	318	318	4.2	210	3	0	0	0	0	1841	24.2
Hill, Lew, 1973-75	56	0	0	0.0	226	528	.428	0	0	.000	70	123	.569	0	258	258	4.6	102	0	55	0	4	0	522	9.3
Holmes, Jeremy, 1998-00	58	20	1409	24.3	83	229	.362	40	119	.336	39	60	.650	19	91	110	1.9	96	1	192	115	1	50	245	4.2
Holstein, Floyd, 1949-51	12	0	0	0.0	1	5	.200	0	0	.000	1	3	.333	0	0	0	0.0	8	0	0	0	0	0	3	0.3
Howard, Andre, 1995-97	51	9	721	14.1	69	177	.390	1	7	.143	26	49	.531	86	86	172	3.4	67	1	18	59	17	28	165	3.2
Hromanik, George, 1948-51	69	0	0	0.0	174	501	.347	0	0	.000	139	207	.671	0	0	0	0.0	141	0	0	0	0	0	487	7.1
Hunt, Charles, 1967-69	36	0	0	0.0	34	114	.298	0	0	.000	37	77	.481	0	143	143	4.0	118	0	0	0	0	0	105	2.9
Hursh, Chuck, 1955-58	77	0	0	0.0	227	551	.412	0	0	.000	243	387	.628	0	742	742	9.6	282	27	0	0	0	0	697	9.1
Jacobsen, Morris, 1945-46	11	0	0	0.0	5	0	.000	0	0	.000	4	10	.400	0	0	0	0.0	29	0	0	0	0	0	14	1.3
Jinks, Ben, 1960-63	70	0	0	0.0	316	814	.388	0	0	.000	218	305	.715	0	384	384	5.5	209	8	0	0	0	0	850	12.1
Johnson, Chad, 2000-02	67	3	1105	16.5	103	275	.375	22	82	.268	63	107	.589	71	105	176	2.6	83	0	80	83	30	32	291	4.3
Johnson, Gilbert, 1988-90	35	0	157	4.5	14	36	.389	0	0	.000	11	16	.688	12	17	29	0.8	26	0	3	5	1	1	39	1.1
Johnson, II, 1937-38	20	0	0	0.0	6	0	.000	0	0	.000	3	10	.300	0	0	0	0.0	35	0	0	0	0	0	15	0.8
Johnson, Robert, 1936-39	38	0	0	0.0	60	0	.000	0	0	.000	46	70	.657	0	0	0	0.0	62	0	0	0	0	0	166	4.4
Johnson, Trent, 1981-83	52	0	1047	20.1	126	259	.486	0	0	.000	60	89	.674	0	246	246	4.7	139	7	24	60	7	20	312	6.0
Jones, Antoine, 1990-93	59	34	883	15.0	139	239	.582	2	8	.250	81	141	.574	75	111	186	3.2	93	1	56	91	15	26	361	6.1
Jones, Chris, 1970-72	31	0	0	0.0	34	94	.362	0	0	.000	35	74	.473	0	119	119	3.8	44	1	12	0	0	0	103	3.3
Jones, Walter, 1941-44	37	0	0	0.0	52	0	.000	0	0	.000	52	79	.658	0	0	0	0.0	74	0	0	0	0	0	156	4.2
Jordan, Gandhi, 1990-92	55	10	651	11.8	69	206	.335	29	105	.276	27	46	.587	34	82	116	2.1	92	1	38	38	6	25	194	3.5
Jordan, Gerald, 1995-97	55	25	1147	20.9	174	351	.496	1	1	1.000	107	168	.637	152	190	342	6.2	175	10	29	108	28	37	456	8.3
Kalata, Len, 1966-69	50	0	0	0.0	166	411	.404	0	0	.000	105	156	.673	0	195	195	3.9	98	0	0	0	0	0	437	8.7
Keese, Lucius, 1972-75	36	0	0	0.0	37	81	.457	0	0	.000	10	21	.476	0	105	105	2.9	39	1	8	0	6	0	84	2.3
Keller, Don, 1958-60	18	0	0	0.0	5	19	.263	0	0	.000	6	11	.545	0	31	31	1.7	22	0	0	0	0	0	16	0.9
Kelly, Willie, 1973-76	75	0	0	0.0	153	313	.489	0	0	.000	43	78	.551	0	259	259	3.5	118	5	42	34	3	0	349	4.7
Kendall, Levon, 2003-05	36	8	384	10.7	33	81	.407	11	36	.306	14	22	.636	31	37	68	1.9	50	1	16	21	12	11	91	2.5
Kendrick, John, 1949-52	56	0	0	0.0	114	372	.306	0	0	.000	66	114	.579	0	95	95	1.7	189	19	29	0	0	0	294	5.3
Kirby, Roosevelt, 1981-82	30	0	937	31.2	119	227	.524	0	0	.000	36	61	.590	0	154	154	5.1	101	8	36	52	10	25	274	9.1
Kleiman, Phil, 1955-56	20	0	0	0.0	24	71	.338	0	0	.000	13	24	.542	0	82	82	4.1	31	0	0	0	0	0	61	3.1
Klein, James, 1938-40	30	0	0	0.0	27	0	.000	0	0	.000	9	21	.429	0	0	0	0.0	26	0	0	0	0	0	63	2.1
Knight, Billy, 1971-74	78	0	0	0.0	750	1436	.522	0	0	.000	231	309	.748	0	938	938	12.0	189	4	206	0	0	0	1731	22.2
Knight, Brandin, 1999-03	127	119	4307	33.9	492	1233	.399	209	654	.320	247	460	.537	92	400	492	3.9	327	3	785	406	55	298	1440	11.3
Knight, Terry, 1974-79	86	0	966	11.2	351	754	.466	0	0	.000	177	226	.783	0	414	414	4.8	263	17	101	60	15	21	879	10.2
Kocheran, George, 1938-41	52	0	0	0.0	109	0	.000	0	0	.000	48	123	.390	0	0	0	0.0	94	0	0	0	0	0	266	5.1
Krauser, Carl, 2002-05	93	62	2783	29.9	347	839	.414	123	335	.367	331	437	.757	65	320	385	4.1	215	3	408	282	4	137	1148	12.3
Krieger, Paul, 1961-64	72	0	0	0.0	246	567	.434	0	0	.000	135	194	.696	0	666	666	9.3	254	20	0	0	0	0	627	8.7
Lane, Jerome, 1985-88	93	81	2970	31.9	436	831	.525	4	15	.267	341	543	.628	339	631	970	10.4	257	12	206	216	34	105	1217	13.1
Laneve, John, 1954-57	27	0	0	0.0	15	54	.278	0	0	.000	16	26	.615	0	21	21	0.8	32	0	0	0	0	0	46	1.7
Larkin, John, 1961-64	28	0	0	0.0	14	29	.483	0	0	.000	9	15	.600	0	12	12	0.4	14	0	0	0	0	0	37	1.3
Latagliata, Ed, 1942-48	53	0	0	0.0	68	0	.000	0	0	.000	39	66	.591	0	0	0	0.0	95	0	0	0	0	0	175	3.3
LaValley, James, 1964-67	70	0	0	0.0	218	525	.415	0	0	.000	209	327	.639	0	663	663	9.5	186	0	0	0	0	0	645	9.2
Layton, Derrick, 1988-90	15	0	22	1.5	3	5	.600	1	1	1.000	1	2	.500	2	1	3	0.2	2	0	0	1	0	0	8	0.5
Lazor, Bob, 1954-57	76	0	0	0.0	466	1167	.399	0	0	.000	243	353	.688	0	841	841	11.1	220	12	0	0	0	0	1175	15.5
Lazor, Paul, 1958-61	44	0	0	0.0	67	174	.385	0	0	.000	36	65	.554	0	110	110	2.5	62	3	0	0	0	0	170	3.9
Lepkowski, Richard, 1952-55	40	0	0	0.0	19	94	.202	0	0	.000	29	45	.644	0	71	71	1.8	46	0	0	0	0	0	67	1.7
Lerner, Morton, 1947-49	46	0	0	0.0	50	67	.746	0	0	.000	55	89	.618	0	0	0	0.0	113	0	0	0	0	0	155	3.4
Leslie, Kevin, 1997-98	20	0	158	7.9	7	17	.412	0	0	.000	1	9	.111	8	23	31	1.6	33	1	2	6	2	2	15	0.8
Lester, Howard, 1955-58	28	0	0	0.0	12	37	.324	0	0	.000	3	7	.429	0	35	35	1.3	21	0	0	0	0	0	27	1.0
Lett, Ontario, 2001-03	68	26	1299	19.1	245	416	.589	0	0	.000	129	216	.597	144	181	325	4.8	231	14	66	118	76	58	619	9.1
Levin, Solomon, 1939-40	10	0	0	0.0	16	0	.000	0	0	.000	3	10	.300	0	0	0	0.0	9	0	0	0	0	0	35	3.5
Lewis, Junie, 1984-85	24	1	174	7.3	43	95	.453	0	0	.000	18	25	.720	0	10	10	0.4	29	0	12	14	1	8	104	4.3
Player, Years	GP	GS	Min.	Avg.	FG	FGA	Pct.	3FG	3FGA	Pct.	FT	FTA	Pct.	Off.	Def.	Tot.	Avg.	PF	FO	Ast.	TO	Blk.	Stl.	Pts.	Avg.

Player, Years	GP	GS	Min.	Avg.	FG	FGA	Pct.	3FG	3FGA	Pct.	FT	FTA	Pct.	Off.	Def.	Tot.	Avg.	PF	FO	Ast.	TO	Blk.	Stl.	Pts.	Avg.
Lewis, Sonny, 1976-78	37	0	0	0.0	165	334	.494	0	0	.000	68	95	.716	0	103	103	2.8	90	2	99	0	7	0	398	10.8
Lewis, Steve, 1969-71	32	0	0	0.0	37	93	.398	0	0	.000	14	23	.609	0	22	22	0.7	23	0	7	0	0	0	88	2.8
Lockhart, Howard, 1958-61	30	0	0	0.0	34	98	.347	0	0	.000	55	81	.679	0	59	59	2.0	56	1	0	0	0	0	123	4.1
Lockhart, Jarrett, 1996-00	103	65	2439	23.7	314	833	.377	167	504	.331	105	139	.755	88	245	333	3.2	168	3	96	133	14	112	900	8.7
Lohmeyer, Paul, 1940-43	32	0	0	0.0	32	0	.000	0	0	.000	41	56	.732	0	0	0	0.0	62	0	0	0	0	0	105	3.3
Lovett, Bob, 1963-66	64	0	0	0.0	266	620	.429	0	0	.000	183	227	.806	0	393	393	6.1	198	3	0	0	0	0	715	11.2
Maczuzak, John, 1960-63	49	0	0	0.0	59	142	.415	0	0	.000	29	47	.617	0	159	159	3.2	73	1	0	0	0	0	147	3.0
Maile, Jason, 1992-97	111	51	2247	20.2	321	796	.403	196	500	.392	121	157	.771	79	126	205	1.8	194	8	148	151	10	72	959	8.6
Malarkey, Clare, 1941-46	56	0	0	0.0	151	0	.000	0	0	.000	115	218	.528	0	0	0	0.0	115	0	0	0	0	0	417	7.4
Malmberg, Arthur, 1948-51	32	0	0	0.0	14	67	.209	0	0	.000	7	13	.538	0	0	0	0.0	29	0	0	0	0	0	35	1.1
Maloney, Tom, 1957-62	58	0	0	0.0	138	373	.370	0	0	.000	150	205	.732	0	137	137	2.4	140	8	0	0	0	0	426	7.3
Marder, Philip, 1944-45	11	0	0	0.0	24	0	.000	0	0	.000	7	12	.583	0	0	0	0.0	36	0	0	0	0	0	55	5.0
Markovich, Milan, 1954-57	51	0	0	0.0	25	84	.298	0	0	.000	15	38	.395	0	90	90	1.8	41	0	0	0	0	0	65	1.3
Martin, Bobby, 1987-91	117	81	3161	27.0	416	829	.502	2	9	.222	448	641	.699	303	472	775	6.6	382	14	80	251	109	73	1282	11.0
Martin, Mickey, 1971-74	66	0	0	0.0	304	613	.496	0	0	.000	97	144	.674	0	288	288	4.4	169	4	50	0	0	0	705	10.7
Maruczewski, Edward, 1945-46	13	0	0	0.0	28	0	.000	0	0	.000	23	42	.548	0	0	0	0.0	34	0	0	0	0	0	79	6.1
Maslek, Steve, 1986-89	41	0	151	3.7	13	34	.382	0	0	.000	14	25	.560	13	16	29	0.7	37	0	6	14	2	1	40	1.0
Matthews, Jason, 1987-91	123	112	3552	28.9	550	1212	.454	259	567	.457	481	548	.878	93	195	288	2.3	325	5	225	224	20	109	1840	15.0
Matthews, Ted, 1953-54	17	0	0	0.0	13	43	.302	0	0	.000	10	31	.323	0	17	17	1.0	24	1	0	0	0	0	36	2.1
Mauro, Bill, 1957-60	51	0	0	0.0	123	294	.418	0	0	.000	78	97	.804	0	104	104	2.0	72	2	0	0	0	0	324	6.4
McBride, Greg, 1973-75	28	0	0	0.0	19	37	.514	0	0	.000	24	31	.774	0	31	31	1.1	7	0	8	0	0	0	62	2.2
McCarroll, Mark, 2000-05	116	10	1362	11.7	148	338	.438	23	76	.303	64	129	.496	81	165	246	2.1	124	0	61	69	45	13	383	3.3
McClelland, Ralph, 1974-76	51	0	0	0.0	63	141	.447	0	0	.000	20	37	.541	0	207	207	4.1	83	0	33	0	9	0	146	2.9
McClure, James, 1951-53	19	0	0	0.0	8	37	.216	0	0	.000	10	21	.476	0	37	37	1.9	23	1	1	0	0	0	26	1.4
McCrossin, George, 1946-50	73	0	0	0.0	147	407	.361	0	0	.000	80	126	.635	0	0	0	0.0	163	0	0	0	0	0	374	5.1
McCullough, Jerry, 1991-96	111	79	3337	30.1	378	1008	.375	152	477	.319	434	597	.727	105	255	360	3.2	300	7	552	307	37	257	1342	12.1
McFarland, Bob, 1967-70	56	0	0	0.0	196	514	.381	0	0	.000	127	185	.686	0	240	240	4.3	137	0	0	0	0	0	519	9.3
McIntyre, Bill, 1962-64	18	0	0	0.0	6	14	.429	0	0	.000	5	8	.625	0	12	12	0.7	7	0	0	0	0	0	17	0.9
McMillian, Lennie, 1979-81	59	0	1409	23.9	189	422	.448	0	0	.000	82	130	.631	0	228	228	3.9	176	9	117	112	25	115	460	7.8
McNally, Roth, 1964-65	19	0	0	0.0	25	67	.373	0	0	.000	12	15	.800	0	17	17	0.9	20	0	0	0	0	0	62	3.3
McNeal, Chris, 1990-93	95	62	2462	25.9	416	874	.476	11	43	.256	224	323	.693	279	416	695	7.3	204	2	92	145	42	80	1067	11.2
Medich, 1945-46	13	0	0	0.0	19	0	.000	0	0	.000	17	26	.654	0	0	0	0.0	34	0	0	0	0	0	55	4.2
Mesher, John, 1957-59	28	0	0	0.0	64	178	.360	0	0	.000	22	49	.449	0	93	93	3.3	51	2	0	0	0	0	150	5.4
Michalik, Karl, 1944-45	11	0	0	0.0	4	0	.000	0	0	.000	11	14	.786	0	0	0	0.0	16	0	0	0	0	0	19	1.7
Miklasevich, Matt, 1982-86	93	2	597	6.4	38	106	.358	0	0	.000	58	78	.744	0	108	108	1.2	106	2	23	45	2	17	134	1.4
Milanovich, Samuel, 1938-41	49	0	0	0.0	98	0	.000	0	0	.000	34	79	.430	0	0	0	0.0	93	0	0	0	0	0	230	4.7
Miller, Sean, 1987-92	128	124	4146	32.4	363	845	.430	239	574	.416	317	358	.885	38	223	261	2.0	321	2	744	321	7	102	1282	10.0
Mills, John, 1957-60	66	0	0	0.0	195	483	.404	0	0	.000	245	373	.657	0	472	472	7.2	255	15	0	0	0	0	635	9.6
Mitchell, Bryan, 1982-84	19	0	66	3.5	16	26	.615	0	0	.000	3	8	.375	0	11	11	0.6	15	0	3	5	0	4	35	1.8
Mobley, Eric, 1991-94	88	50	2091	23.8	371	666	.557	0	0	.000	158	325	.486	211	388	599	6.8	243	9	124	175	184	40	900	10.2
Morgan,Jermaine, 1990-94	57	9	478	8.4	47	109	.431	11	33	.333	26	42	.619	23	37	60	1.1	58	0	29	30	11	16	131	2.3
Morningstar, Darren, 1989-92	96	56	1787	18.6	287	590	.486	0	0	.000	181	310	.584	179	247	426	4.4	297	5	77	139	10	46	755	7.9
Morris, Carl, 1970-73	69	0	0	0.0	199	479	.415	0	0	.000	57	95	.600	0	372	372	5.4	177	9	65	0	0	0	455	6.6
Morris, Frank, 1944-47	13	0	0	0.0	16	0	.000	0	0	.000	9	19	.474	0	0	0	0.0	28	0	0	0	0	0	41	3.2
Morris, Toree, 2000-04	131	52	1546	11.8	158	294	.537	0	0	.000	68	159	.428	119	220	339	2.6	194	0	25	106	79	16	384	2.9
Moses, Omo, 1990-91	26	0	178	6.8	8	18	.444	2	3	.667	12	21	.571	2	10	12	0.5	20	0	16	22	1	6	30	1.2
Murray, Leon, 1996-97	10	0	44	4.4	7	14	.500	1	4	.250	4	10	.400	8	2	10	1.0	2	0	3	5	1	3	19	1.9
Naponik, Paul, 1967-68	15	0	0	0.0	27	75	.360	0	0	.000	24	38	.632	0	63	63	4.2	23	0	0	0	0	0	78	5.2
Navokovich, Alex, 1952-54	16	0	0	0.0	12	47	.255	0	0	.000	12	18	.667	0	34	34	2.1	20	1	0	0	0	0	36	2.3
Nedrow, Scott, 1973-74	71	0	0	0.0	195	440	.443	0	0	.000	46	71	.648	0	90	90	1.3	165	6	76	0	2	0	436	6.1
Neverson, Carlton, 1978-81	89	0	2748	30.9	447	905	.494	0	0	.000	163	217	.751	0	313	313	3.5	269	10	202	219	52	194	1057	11.9
O'Gorek, Paul, 1969-72	70	0	0	0.0	286	611	.468	0	0	.000	121	174	.695	0	544	544	7.8	164	0	68	0	0	0	693	9.9
Olinger, David, 1977-81	90	0	936	10.4	178	437	.407	0	0	.000	67	92	.728	0	154	154	1.7	150	2	56	95	15	20	423	4.7
Paffrath, Lawrence, 1938-42	52	0	0	0.0	184	0	.000	0	0	.000	78	139	.561	0	0	0	0.0	85	0	0	0	0	0	446	8.6
Page, Julius, 2000-04	136	128	4398	32.3	544	1250	.435	210	624	.337	214	301	.711	52	350	402	3.0	208	1	244	197	44	87	1512	11.1
Palesko, Chester, 1950-53	48	0	0	0.0	104	334	.311	0	0	.000	107	185	.578	0	125	125	2.6	89	4	2	0	0	0	315	6.6
Pandak, William, 1943-44	12	0	0	0.0	28	0	.000	0	0	.000	3	11	.273	0	0	0	0.0	14	0	0	0	0	0	59	4.9
Pataky, 1939-40	15	0	0	0.0	16	0	.000	0	0	.000	10	30	.333	0	0	0	0.0	23	0	0	0	0	0	42	2.8
Patcher, Mike, 1967-70	70	0	0	0.0	203	532	.382	0	0	.000	136	186	.731	0	509	509	7.3	251	0	0	0	0	0	542	7.7
Paul, Mike, 1969-72	68	0	0	0.0	294	707	.416	0	0	.000	198	245	.808	0	294	294	4.3	210	4	115	0	0	0	786	11.6
Pavlick, Ed, 1952-55	51	0	0	0.0	314	812	.387	0	0	.000	302	444	.680	0	604	604	11.8	136	2	0	0	0	0	930	18.2
Pegues, Julius, 1955-58	77	0	0	0.0	355	792	.448	0	0	.000	340	480	.708	0	377	377	4.9	293	29	0	0	0	0	1050	13.6
Peterson, Jaime, 1993-95	54	29	1352	25.0	191	369	.518	0	0	.000	134	197	.680	148	206	354	6.6	123	7	37	113	89	57	516	9.6
Petrini, Bob, 1967-70	45	0	0	0.0	142	358	.397	0	0	.000	54	73	.740	0	78	78	1.7	49	0	0	0	0	0	338	7.5
Phillips, Scott, 1950-53	48	0	0	0.0	20	77	.260	0	0	.000	13	37	.351	0	11	11	0.2	73	3	6	0	0	0	53	1.1
Port, Mel, 1938-41	53	0	0	0.0	125	0	.000	0	0	.000	73	158	.462	0	0	0	0.0	127	0	0	0	0	0	323	6.1
Porter, Darelle, 1987-91	123	86	3369	27.4	369	820	.450	48	141	.340	226	303	.746	146	320	466	3.8	273	4	617	317	40	170	1012	8.2
Primus, Fred, 1998-99	14	0	159	11.4	20	60	.333	16	49	.327	6	7	.857	4	13	17	1.2	14	0	12	11	1	4	62	4.4
Ptacek, Charles, 1942-43	16	0	0	0.0	16	0	.000	0	0	.000	12	24	.500	0	0	0	0.0	11	0	0	0	0	0	44	2.8
Radosevich, George, 1949-51	26	0	0	0.0	33	111	.297	0	0	.000	29	56	.518	0	0	0	0.0	60	1	0	0	0	0	95	3.7
Radvansky, Michael, 1936-38	21	0	0	0.0	33	0	.000	0	0	.000	24	33	.727	0	0	0	0.0	54	0	0	0	0	0	90	4.3
Ragan, Thomas, 1944-47	14	0	0	0.0	20	0	.000	0	0	.000	17	36	.472	0	0	0	0.0	41	0	0	0	0	0	57	4.1
Rasp, John, 1986-90	15	2	56	3.7	5	9	.556	0	0	.000	2	4	.500	5	9	14	0.9	5	0	5	6	1	2	12	0.8
Ramon, Ronald, 2004-05	28	4	732	26.1	62	171	.363	43	128	.336	24	31	.774	11	36	47	1.7	58	1	52	23	0	24	191	6.8
Resutek, Joseph, 1952-55	36	0	0	0.0	64	175	.366	0	0	.000	42	62	.677	0	66	66	1.8	40	1	0	0	0	0	170	4.7
Reuschel, Bill, 1951-53	32	0	0	0.0	17	73	.233	0	0	.000	18	33	.545	0	35	35	1.1	22	1	2	0	0	0	52	1.6
Rhymes, Marlon, 1992-93	24	3	387	16.1	52	129	.403	21	70	.300	22	33	.667	7	17	24	1.0	22	0	33	46	2	9	147	6.1
Rice, Michael, 1976-77	24	0	0	0.0	118	240	.492	0	0	.000	18	39	.462	0	193	193	8.0	75	6	20	0	16	0	254	10.6
Richards, Tom, 1972-76	101	0	0	0.0	390	870	.448	0	0	.000	93	130	.715	0	161	161	1.6	181	2	307	0	4	0	873	8.6
Riggle, Mike, 1968-71	67	0	0	0.0	63	165	.382	0	0	.000	110	146	.753	0	209	209	3.1	116	1	18	0	0	0	236	3.5
Riser, John, 1954-57	78	0	0	0.0	394	1046	.377	0	0	.000	376	566	.664	0	775	775	9.9	282	25	0	0	0	0	1164	14.9
Roantree, Tom, 1962-65	12	0	0	0.0	5	14	.357	0	0	.000	11	15	.733	0	18	18	1.5	10	0	0	0	0	0	21	1.8
Roman, Dave, 1962-64	50	0	0	0.0	266	545	.488	0	0	.000	97	130	.746	0	140	140	2.8	112	2	0	0	0	0	629	12.6
Ruby, Daryle, 1962-65	67	0	0	0.0	198	454	.436	0	0	.000	117	151	.775	0	274	274	4.1	155	1	0	0	0	0	513	7.7
Ryan, John, 1979-81	33	0	275	8.3	21	54	.389	0	0	.000	14	21	.667	0	17	17	0.5	20	0	37	24	0	7	56	1.7
Sankey, Bob, 1959-62	68	0	0	0.0	142	392	.362	0	0	.000	100	139	.719	0	202	202	3.0	124	2	0	0	0	0	384	5.6
Sauer, Dave, 1961-64	73	0	0	0.0	278	637	.436	0	0	.000	87	135	.644	0	313	313	4.3	162	5	0	0	0	0	643	8.8
Sawyer, Dave, 1956-59	66	0	0	0.0	157	372	.422	0	0	.000	115	170	.676	0	374	374	5.7	200	14	0	0	0	0	429	6.5
Scherer, John, 1937-40	40	0	0	0.0	30	0	.000	0	0	.000	24	70	.343	0	0	0	0.0	48	0	0	0	0	0	84	2.1
Scheuermann, Ed, 1976-81	98	0	510	5.2	205	454	.452	0	0	.000	118	185	.638	0	401	401	4.1	203	8	37	37	45	0	528	5.4

Player, Years	GP	GS	Min.	Avg.	FG	FGA	Pct.	3FG	3FGA	Pct.	FT	FTA	Pct.	Off.	Def.	Tot.	Avg.	PF	FO	Ast.	TO	Blk.	Stl.	Pts.	Avg.
Schoon, Rodney, 1970-71	10	0	0	0.0	1	10	.100	0	0	.000	3	4	.750	0	11	11	1.1	4	0	0	0	0	0	5	0.5
Scott, Jack, 1937-39	25	0	0	0.0	19	0	.000	0	0	.000	15	31	.484	0	0	0	0.0	22	0	0	0	0	0	53	2.1
Scott, Kent, 1969-72	72	0	0	0.0	502	1006	.499	0	0	.000	139	171	.813	0	174	174	2.4	115	0	161	0	0	0	1143	15.9
Seabrooks, Chris, 1998-01	56	33	1055	18.8	149	285	.523	0	1	.000	53	101	.525	98	154	252	4.5	148	7	20	91	40	19	351	6.3
Shareef, Ahmad, 1990-94	118	71	1983	16.8	271	645	.420	38	129	.295	142	235	.604	60	108	168	1.4	178	6	109	126	28	79	722	6.1
Shay, Bill, 1957-61	33	0	0	0.0	11	47	.234	0	0	.000	10	30	.333	0	26	26	0.8	37	0	0	0	0	0	32	1.0
Sheffield, Calvin, 1961-64	73	0	0	0.0	372	869	.428	0	0	.000	371	505	.735	0	289	289	4.0	191	6	0	0	0	0	1115	15.3
Shepherd, Darryl, 1984-86	58	7	954	16.4	182	346	.526	0	0	.000	73	112	.652	0	175	175	3.0	115	5	44	68	23	30	437	7.5
Shin, Michael, 1997-98	13	0	130	10.0	5	17	.294	0	1	.000	6	19	.316	5	9	14	1.1	27	1	1	13	2	4	16	1.2
Shorter, Brian, 1988-91	92	91	2949	32.1	540	1004	.538	1	10	.100	552	778	.710	283	489	772	8.4	282	5	123	267	45	61	1633	17.8
Shrewsbury, Bob, 1973-76	61	0	0	0.0	63	173	.364	0	0	.000	42	63	.667	0	54	54	0.9	76	1	177	0	2	0	168	2.8
Shuber, Stephen, 1941-47	30	0	0	0.0	26	0	.000	0	0	.000	20	30	.667	0	0	0	0.0	54	0	0	0	0	0	72	2.4
Simpson, Lloyd, 1957-60	15	0	0	0.0	11	35	.314	0	0	.000	5	12	.417	0	23	23	1.5	11	0	0	0	0	0	27	1.8
Small, Charles, 2003-05	10	0	9	0.9	0	4	.000	0	0	.000	1	2	.500	0	0	0	0.0	0	0	0	2	0	1	1	0.1
Smith, Charles, 1984-88	122	122	4103	33.6	707	1324	.534	3	11	.273	628	834	.753	173	814	987	8.1	392	22	171	249	346	114	2045	16.8
Smith, Darwin, 1958-61	48	0	0	0.0	28	103	.272	0	1	.000	40	70	.571	0	101	101	2.1	83	0	0	0	0	0	96	2.0
Smith, Kelvin, 1976-77	15	0	0	0.0	9	29	.310	0	0	.000	1	3	.333	0	19	19	1.3	18	0	4	0	1	0	19	1.3
Smith, Pete, 1965-68	68	0	0	0.0	156	438	.356	0	0	.000	135	160	.844	0	174	174	2.6	148	0	0	0	0	0	447	6.6
Spartz, 1940-42	16	0	0	0.0	1	0	.000	0	0	.000	1	4	.250	0	0	0	0.0	7	0	0	0	0	0	3	0.2
Spotovich, Ed, 1935-38	21	0	0	0.0	60	0	.000	0	0	.000	35	62	.565	0	0	0	0.0	46	0	0	0	0	0	155	7.4
Starr, Keith, 1972-75	78	0	0	0.0	281	630	.446	0	0	.000	126	179	.704	0	340	340	4.4	146	4	329	0	19	0	688	8.8
Steinhart, Don, 1959-61	40	0	0	0.0	92	234	.393	0	0	.000	74	109	.679	0	267	267	6.7	63	1	0	0	0	0	258	6.5
Stevanovic, Zelimir, 2000-01	27	10	433	16.0	45	114	.395	25	58	.431	13	27	.481	10	32	42	1.6	26	0	21	32	5	8	128	4.7
Stevenson, Steve, 1966-68	37	0	0	0.0	77	187	.412	0	0	.000	55	105	.524	0	118	118	3.2	97	0	0	0	0	0	209	5.6
Stewart, E., 1945-46	10	0	0	0.0	6	0	.000	0	0	.000	5	7	.714	0	0	0	0.0	0	0	0	0	0	0	17	1.7
Straloski, 1938-41	51	0	0	0.0	203	0	.000	0	0	.000	89	184	.484	0	0	0	0.0	124	0	0	0	0	0	495	9.7
Strickland, Pete, 1975-79	104	0	658	6.3	151	364	.415	0	0	.000	127	158	.804	0	127	127	1.2	173	7	363	73	5	14	429	4.1
Sulkowski, Bill, 1971-73	44	0	0	0.0	105	242	.434	0	0	.000	29	42	.690	0	123	123	2.8	78	3	16	0	0	0	239	5.4
Sutyak, Nick, 1958-59	12	0	0	0.0	12	40	.300	0	0	.000	9	11	.818	0	27	27	2.3	13	0	0	0	0	0	33	2.8
Swacus, John, 1940-41	40	0	0	0.0	25	0	.000	0	0	.000	22	35	.629	0	0	0	0.0	46	0	0	0	0	0	72	1.8
Szykowny, Larry, 1963-66	67	0	0	0.0	312	781	.399	0	0	.000	186	252	.738	0	274	274	4.1	179	0	0	0	0	0	810	12.1
Taft, Chris, 2003-04	65	53	1692	26.0	321	564	.569	0	0	.000	136	241	.564	200	288	488	7.5	100	0	69	92	110	23	778	12.0
Tait, Sutton, 1953-55	33	0	0	0.0	31	109	.284	0	0	.000	39	57	.684	0	92	92	2.8	63	0	0	0	0	0	101	3.1
Talbott, Wayne, 1973-78	56	0	0	0.0	20	55	.364	0	0	.000	17	25	.680	0	54	54	1.0	51	1	7	0	0	0	57	1.0
Taylor, Kellii, 1996-00	79	44	2142	27.1	235	643	.365	88	297	.296	103	163	.632	77	195	272	3.4	197	8	167	198	21	202	661	8.4
Thomas, Garrick, 1992-96	102	21	1403	13.8	208	497	.419	108	294	.367	68	101	.673	105	104	209	2.0	202	10	89	123	16	63	592	5.8
Thompson, Bob, 1965-67	31	0	0	0.0	17	62	.274	0	0	.000	6	19	.316	0	69	69	2.2	53	0	0	0	0	0	40	1.3
Thompson, Chas, 1981-85	54	1	388	7.2	62	125	.496	0	0	.000	49	67	.731	0	44	44	0.8	50	0	53	49	3	22	173	3.2
Troutman, Chevon, 2001-05	124	70	2991	24.1	486	778	.625	13	44	.295	289	457	.632	288	423	711	5.7	299	9	155	197	86	134	1274	10.3
Tweardy, Jim, 1969-71	15	0	0	0.0	10	27	.370	0	0	.000	4	6	.667	0	21	21	1.4	15	0	0	0	0	0	24	1.6
Varga, Chad, 1994-97	63	56	1669	26.5	255	556	.459	18	51	.353	135	201	.672	174	180	354	5.6	190	9	41	119	29	42	663	10.5
Vaughan, Clyde, 1980-84	120	0	3741	31.2	770	1599	.482	0	0	.000	493	696	.708	0	922	922	7.7	217	2	90	184	20	64	2033	16.9
Virostek, Don, 1950-53	69	0	0	0.0	232	635	.365	0	0	.000	173	275	.629	0	614	614	8.9	246	21	31	0	0	0	637	9.2
Vujnovic, Daniel, 1938-39	21	0	0	0.0	19	0	.000	0	0	.000	10	29	.345	0	0	0	0.0	18	0	0	0	0	0	48	2.3
Wagoner, Ken, 1971-74	75	0	0	0.0	39	83	.470	0	0	.000	20	35	.571	0	96	96	1.3	92	2	166	0	0	0	98	1.3
Wallace, Dwayne, 1978-82	101	0	2836	28.1	360	842	.428	0	0	.000	224	313	.716	0	197	197	2.0	262	3	436	296	26	169	944	9.3
Wallace, Ed, 1978-81	20	0	61	3.1	7	27	.259	0	0	.000	6	12	.500	0	24	24	1.2	8	0	2	5	1	0	20	1.0
Washington, David, 1976-77	26	0	0	0.0	25	55	.455	0	0	.000	10	14	.714	0	12	12	0.5	50	1	64	0	0	0	60	2.3
Watkins, Chip, 1981-85	115	17	1745	15.2	167	374	.447	0	0	.000	153	217	.705	0	407	407	3.5	269	17	46	153	38	75	487	4.2
Willard, Kevin, 1995-97	60	6	1023	17.1	58	184	.315	24	106	.226	36	51	.706	14	54	68	1.1	124	2	143	92	4	44	176	2.9
Williams, Andre, 1981-85	114	8	2522	22.1	287	572	.502	0	0	.000	164	213	.770	0	473	473	4.1	331	22	79	170	32	49	738	6.5
Williams, Charles, 1980-82	11	0	41	3.7	3	6	.500	0	0	.000	7	16	.438	0	4	4	0.4	6	1	1	5	0	0	13	1.2
Williams, Wayne, 1975-79	108	0	906	8.4	346	786	.440	0	0	.000	192	294	.653	0	398	398	3.7	358	21	284	87	41	49	884	8.2
Withers, Tom, 1968-70	20	0	0	0.0	14	42	.333	0	0	.000	12	22	.545	0	31	31	1.6	13	0	0	0	0	0	40	2.0
Worrell, Derrick, 1999-00	10	1	111	11.1	15	38	.395	0	0	.000	7	13	.538	6	16	22	2.2	4	0	3	6	4	1	37	3.7
Woznicki, Dick, 1956-58	32	0	0	0.0	32	106	.302	0	0	.000	24	38	.632	0	33	33	1.0	40	1	0	0	0	0	88	2.8
Yurko, Robert, 1948-51	60	0	0	0.0	139	443	.314	0	0	.000	70	120	.583	0	0	0	0.0	0	0	0	0	0	0	348	5.8
Zavackas, Donatas, 1999-03	118	106	3191	27.0	325	727	.447	147	363	.405	302	374	.807	209	310	519	4.4	321	12	186	199	18	47	1099	9.3
Zeleznik, Miles, 1937-38	21	0	0	0.0	61	0	.000	0	0	.000	24	36	.667	0	0	0	0.0	35	0	0	0	0	0	146	7.0
Zeller, Hank, 1944-46	26	0	0	0.0	106	0	.000	0	0	.000	88	134	.657	0	0	0	0.0	85	0	0	0	0	0	300	11.5
Zernich, Michael, 1950-53	71	0	0	0.0	280	806	.347	0	0	.000	285	438	.651	0	328	328	4.6	268	23	63	0	0	0	845	11.9
Zernich, Steve, 1941-43	20	0	0	0.0	30	0	.000	0	0	.000	9	18	.500	0	0	0	0.0	30	0	0	0	0	0	69	3.5
Zernich, Wally, 1943-47	31	0	0	0.0	66	0	.000	0	0	.000	53	102	.520	0	0	0	0.0	117	0	0	0	0	0	185	6.0
Ziegler, Travis, 1989-93	17	0	33	1.9	4	13	.308	0	7	.000	5	10	.500	2	3	5	0.3	5	0	3	2	0	3	13	0.8
Zimmovan, Frank, 1953-56	64	0	0	0.0	148	446	.332	0	0	.000	82	160	.513	0	364	364	5.7	191	17	0	0	0	0	378	5.9
Ziolkowski, Ed, 1940-42	33	0	0	0.0	73	0	.000	0	0	.000	40	77	.519	0	0	0	0.0	49	0	0	0	0	0	186	5.6